COMEDY
IS A MAN IN TROUBLE

The publication of this book was assisted by a bequest from Josiah H. Chase to honor his parents, Ellen Rankin Chase and Josiah Hook Chase, Minnesota territorial pioneers.

COMEDY
IS A MAN IN TROUBLE

Slapstick in American Movies

Alan Dale

University of Minnesota Press / Minneapolis   London

Published by the University of Minnesota Press
111 Third Avenue South, Suite 290
Minneapolis, MN 55401-2520
http://www.upress.umn.edu

Library of Congress Cataloging-in-Publication Data

Dale, Alan S., 1960–
    Comedy is a man in trouble : slapstick in American movies / Alan Dale.
      p.   cm.
    Includes bibliographical references (p.   ) and index.
    ISBN 0-8166-3657-5 (alk. paper)
    — ISBN 0-8166-3658-3 (pbk. : alk. paper)
    1. Comedy films—United States—History and criticism. I. Title.
    PN1995.9.C55 D35 2000
    791.43'617—dc21

                                                    00-009080

Printed in the United States of America on acid-free paper

The University of Minnesota is an equal-opportunity educator and employer.

11 10 09 08 07 06 05 04 03 02 01 00   10 9 8 7 6 5 4 3 2 1

For

Arnold Rampersad,
whose big idea this was,

and

Maria DiBattista,
for believing I exist

I do not know that I have a carefully thought-out theory on exactly what makes people laugh, but the premise of all comedy is a man in trouble.

—Jerry Lewis

Contents

Preface

This book is about slapstick in American movies in the fifty years following the earliest classics of the 1910s. The quality of the movies has risen and fallen and risen again according to changing conditions in the entertainment industry, but the taste for slapstick persists. So this book is more contemporary, less elegiac than the most important previous American book on the subject, Walter Kerr's indispensable *Silent Clowns*, published in 1975, which focuses on the lost age of silent comedy. I wrote this to give fans a body of criticism that doesn't see slapstick preserved in soundless amber, but rather as an always vital, universally enjoyable mode that we should take gladly where we find it.

The past decade or so has provided enjoyable proof of the permanent viability of slapstick. The current boom includes such heartening evidence as *Raising Arizona, Evil Dead II, Beetlejuice,* the Robin Williams and Amanda Plummer scenes in *The Fisher King, Groundhog Day,* the drag sequences in *Mrs. Doubtfire, The Mask, Friday,* the remake of *The Nutty Professor, Kingpin,* the action sequences in *Grosse Pointe Blank* and *A Life Less Ordinary,* and the postwedding scenes in *I Think I Do,* all of which indicate that something is consistently going right—a lot of people know what they're doing.

I think the explanation lies in the fact that certain of the aspects that made silent slapstick moviemaking so good still obtain. For instance, improvisational stand-up and TV sketch comedy have served in the stead of the old live theater routes as a training ground in physical comedy for a raft of exceptionally talented performers (whose appearance, like that of writers and directors, is one of the imponderables). In addition, although finished scripts continue to be far more important, all scripts are retailored to suit the star if the star has any stature, and it's expected that the lead comedian will continue to come up with ideas during shooting. (Some pictures make audiences aware of the spontaneity on the set by including outtakes during the closing credits.) Adam Sandler, for example, has called his stint on *Saturday Night Live* "a boot camp for movies." He said that when a performer on the show had come up with a character, he would produce those segments, working with the director to coach the other actors and set up the shots in order to get what he wanted.

Comedians, unlike the silent slapstick stars, don't have their own units anymore, but all stars are more likely to have their own production companies, and many comedians work with writers and producers, not to mention managers, from picture to picture, thus building up a team whose goal is to transmit their signature style to the screen. So stars still receive special treatment—a hand in the script, the right to ad lib, expensive top talent to support them—that can improve the movies. A significant number of these pictures were also made by star directors who have the same latitude. In fact, the comic moviemaking style of the Coen brothers, Sam Raimi, Tim Burton, Terry Gilliam, the Farrelly brothers, and Danny Boyle is a major selling point of their movies.

At the same time, these comedians, both those in front of and those behind the camera, draw on the American talkie tradition of verbal slapstick, which is important to this book, and have profited from the postcounterculture eclipse of the codes of family entertainment, in place since the invention of vaudeville in the 1880s, to produce some of the most memorable comic mayhem, outside cartoons, since the era of the silent shorts, and some of the most memorable raunch since the Renaissance. Thus this book traces a tradition of slapstick moviemaking forward from the silent era to the present, when actors, writers, and directors have to function in a more industrially rationalized system but still, to the extent that they can, seek out and refine spontaneous inspiration.

Current slapstick moviemaking added to my enthusiasm, but at the same time, the very appeal of the project posed a problem: slapstick movies provide such blatant pleasure that it seemed almost unnatural to write a book about them. The trick has been to talk about slapstick without putting off any more than is avoidable the very moviegoers who ought to be most interested. For me the flags to slalom between stood out most starkly in a disagreement I arbitrated between a guy who saw Freudian significance in the fact that Bugs Bunny is always whipping a carrot out of his "pocket" and a guy who, suspecting that this typically academic interpretation made plain the irrelevance of *all* interpretation, countered in disgust, "He's a *bunny,* man!" The moral: don't overdo it, but don't underdo it, whatever "it" may turn out to be. Such disagreements are possible because slapstick elicits reactions that are automatic but that differ widely depending on who's performing the tricks. Our reactions may be automatic, but they're also complex; a friend asked me why I laugh so hard at slapstick movies and I couldn't stop short of a book in reply.

Of course, the process was more difficult and protracted than that makes it sound and depended on an army of people for various forms of aid that I would like to acknowledge. First of all, thanks to Marvina White, director of the Princeton University Writing Program, whose faith in my teaching enabled me to feed myself while writing this book; Sean Wilentz, for twice letting me teach a seminar on the topic in the American Studies Program at Princeton and for his keen advice about revisions; and Judith Ferszt for helping ensure that the seminar actually took place. Thanks also to Ron Magliozzi, Eddie D'Inzillo, and especially Charles Silver, the benignant house god of the Film Study Center at the Museum of Modern Art in New York, for patient and active help, well beyond my expectations. The scope of my work would have been much narrower without their efforts. Thanks also to Madeline Matz of the Library of Congress's Motion Picture Division; to Mary Corliss of the Museum of Modern Art's Film Stills Archive; to Faye Thompson of the Academy of Motion Picture Arts and Sciences' Margaret Herrick Library; to the New York Public Library for the Performing Arts at Lincoln Center; and to the Oral History Collection of Columbia University. On a less personal note, I would also like to acknowledge how much I've gained from the public programming of the Museum of Modern Art and Film Forum in New York, the Pacific Film Archive in Berkeley, American Movie Classics and Turner Classic Movies on cable, and the huge selection of movies available at Le Video in San Francisco and at Movie Madness in Portland, Oregon.

This project would have been much more difficult, if not impossible, without the many biographies and autobiographies I read, all of which yielded something useful, at the least. Hollywood biographies now tend to be far more meticulously researched than they were as recently as fifteen years ago; even when I disagreed with them critically (and if I hadn't there wouldn't have been much need for my writing on the same topics), they provided reliable data and sources for my own work.

On a personal note, I owe a long-standing debt of gratitude to my parents for more than I can list here, and to my sister Emily Dale and my cousin Vicki Norgord for their interest in the progress of my work. Special thanks to my sister Jennifer Simpson, who rented and watched many Jerry Lewis movies in a row with me, a show of support no one else was willing to make. (Though I was led onto this path by my college friend Heather Stanton, who laughed uninhibitedly when we caught *The Disorderly Orderly* on TV once.) Also, thanks to Hilda Daniel for the loan of the first book and to Gina Vanlue and Andy Marvick for unfailing friendship (and technical support).

I would especially like to mention my indebtedness to Diane and Terry Rafferty for inspiration, encouragement, advice, and friendship, with respect to this book and things in general. To Christopher Hughes, without whose tireless editorial assistance this project would not have appeared in any form, let me just say: "Un Nume, un fato / di te più forte / ci vuole uniti," in this book, anyway.

Once the book was written, Mary Murrell at Princeton University Press offered invaluable advice about editing, and Lindsay Waters at Harvard University Press and Mark Edmundson were key to placing the book at Minnesota. Thanks also to my editors there, William Murphy, Pieter Martin, and Doug Armato, and also to Gretchen Asmussen, Laura Westlund, Mike Stoffel, and Bill Henry for their enthusiastic support and shrewd guidance very much in the spirit of the project.

CHAPTER ONE

Comedy Is a Man in Trouble

I should have been a clown; it would have afforded me the widest range of expression.

—Henry Miller

Since the beginning of the twentieth century, "slapstick" has been our name for popular, rather than literary, low physical comedy. The word derives from an implement—"the double paddles formerly used by circus clowns to beat each other. The loud crack of the two paddle blades as they crashed together could always be depended upon to produce the laughter and applause." The term is now often used by itself as a pejorative, meaning "merely" low physical comedy, but in part because popular comedy and literary comedy are thought of as belonging to distinct audiences, separate occasions. This was not always the case. Aristophanes, for instance, combines slapstick with literary comedy, as does Shakespeare. And if you think that the slapstick of Greek Old Comedy must have been more tasteful than what we get in the movies, read *Ecclesiazusae,* in which Pheidolos attempts to take a shit front and center, and you'll find that the Farrelly brothers, admirable as they are, did not invent this scene for *Dumb & Dumber.* The footnote may have been invisible, but it was there.

In the course of analyzing character type and story structure in Old Comedy, Kenneth McLeish, in his *Theatre of Aristophanes,* mentions every major male film clown I write about, and you want to keep that sense of continuity in mind when thinking about the topic. However, this book focuses on the first fifty years of slapstick in American movies, thus leaving out Aristophanes, but taking us well into the talkies. People tend to think of slapstick as something from our silent era, when it did reach a peak. Not just a heap—though men like Mack Sennett, Hal Roach, and Al Christie, who had studios specializing in short films of this genre, produced by one rough estimate forty thousand reels of comedy in the silent era—but a summit.

However, the silent era is not a *lone* peak. The silent comedians developed not only a style of physical clowning, which has largely disappeared, but also a means of achieving it, which has proved more adaptable. They came out of a national network of live popular theater, in existence for fifty-odd years, which included itinerant medicine shows, minstrel shows, Wild West shows, and circuses, up through the more urban modes of burlesque and vaudeville. That the theater was live was extremely important for their development because having to perform several times a day, in town after town, week after week, gave physical comedians the chance to perfect a repertoire of basic routines. It also required them at times to develop bits on the spot, in response to a new audience, other acts on the bill, or an unforeseen situation.

Experience improvising was especially important because of the other condition for the high quality of slapstick in the silent era, which was that the movie teams worked at first without scripts and then later from loose outlines, even when making features. The silent stars worked in units with their own gagmen and techies; production involved a nonstop pitch of ideas about everything from the basic setting or premise, through the details of action and accident, to the final shape of the picture. This process continued while the cameras turned, which must have been what Harold Lloyd had in mind when he said that visual comedy was more expensive than verbal. (He also cited the high salaries of the indispensable "idea-men.") Even the end of shooting didn't end the fine-tuning—Arbuckle and Lloyd are credited with instituting prerelease sneak previews after which the team would compare notes and then recut and often enough reshoot.

The movies developed out of gag committee effort and were reshaped according to preview audiences' responses, which raises the question of credit. The answer lies in the fact that the star presided over the committee; all ideas were pitched *to* him for his approval. Thus all material was filtered through the star's sensibility, since he had to perform nearly every bit. Keaton was clear as to who was in charge: "We [i.e., the stars] directed our own pictures, making up our own gags as we went along, saw the rushes, supervised the cutting, went to the sneak previews."

The historical irony of silent comedy is that the clowns' theatrical experience trained them for the movies, which then, of course, destroyed the network they sprang from by stealing the audience. And so purely physical, essentially silent slapstick hit a trough in the talkie era for this reason, but also because even when the silent clowns were still around, audiences quickly preferred the novelty of any sound to silence, the studio executives realized that they could exert more control over their stars and directors by concentrating on the scripts, and slapstick fell out of fashion in favor of romantic screwball comedies (which did, all the same, incorporate physical knockabout). There were still slapstick careers in the talkies, but Buster Keaton's pictures at MGM, Joe E. Brown's at Warner Brothers, Wheeler and Woolsey's pictures and Leon Errol and Lupe Velez's hit-and-miss teamings at RKO, the Three Stooges' shorts and Arthur Lake's *Blondie* feature series at Columbia, the Hope and Crosby *Road* series and the Martin and Lewis pictures Hal Wallis released through Paramount, and Donald O'Connor's *Francis* series at Universal were all profitable relative to *low* costs, and as Lloyd pointed out, visual comedy is the most expensive kind when done with care. Eddie Cantor's and Danny Kaye's extravaganzas for Goldwyn and some of Red Skelton's MGM musicals had big budgets, but the investment didn't go for improvisational shooting to make the comedy fresher. Only the insanely fertile MGM and Warner Brothers cartoon units were able to manufacture first-rate slapstick on next to no money. Yet even the low-budget live-action comedies were genuinely popular—it's clear that the appetite for slapstick remains robust regardless of the quality of what's available to satisfy it.

With this history sketched out, you still want to know what slapstick *is*. To start, you can look for coherence in the kinds of gags. M. Willson Disher claimed that there are only six kinds of jokes—falls, blows, surprise, knavery, mimicry, stupidity. They all play a part, but for comedy to register as slapstick, you need only the fall and its flip side, the blow. (The importance of the blow is evident in the adoption of the term "slapstick," since that's what a slapstick was for.) In their iconic form, the fall is caused by a banana peel, and the blow is translated into a pie in the face. Thus the essence of a slapstick gag is a physical assault on, or collapse of, the hero's dignity; as a corollary, the loss of dignity by itself can result in our identifying with the victim. The mishap can be heightened by the plot—it's worse if the hero's late for his wedding than if he's just out strolling—but that's a difference of degree, not of kind.

However, many of the most intriguing gags have more complex perceptual or emotional resonance. There is, for instance, the disproportion of Buster Keaton in a rowboat trying to tow an ocean liner in the 1924 feature *The Navigator,* a superexaggeration of the hero's obliviousness and ineffectuality, and neither fall nor blow. But a fall itself may point to something else; for instance, the hero's unawareness of a standing circumstance, as in the 1936 talkie *The Milky Way* when Harold Lloyd, arms spread as if embracing life, springs toward the camera over a hedge at the bottom of the frame. As he arcs up and then down, the camera reveals a pond just this side of the hedge (the framing makes us share his inattention, so that we really feel that it's something we might do). Or a blow may indicate the hero's unawareness of a changed circumstance. In the 1915 Keystone one-reeler *Mabel and Fatty's Wash Day*, for instance, a neighbor snaps his soapy fingers under Fatty's nose; Fatty turns away as he sneezes and then turns back to fling a wet rag at the man, who has in the meantime walked off. The rag hits Fatty's wife, who's now standing where the neighbor stood.

All these gags depend on a rupture in the expected link between physical effort and result, which the actor may exploit nonsensically, treating one object as if it were another, for instance, when Buster chalks the end of his violin bow as if it were a pool cue and bites the end off his clarinet as if it were a cigar, both in his 1921 two-reeler *The Playhouse*. Or it can make sense in the circumstances, as in Chaplin's 1936 feature *Modern Times* when Chester Conklin is pinned on his back in the machinery with only his head protruding, and Charlie, trying to feed Chester his lunch, uses a roasted chicken to funnel coffee into his mouth.

The most elaborate double-take gags are those that create false assumptions by careful camera placement, for instance in *The Playhouse* when we see Buster asleep on a rickety bed in a bare room and a big angry man comes in and tells him to get out. We assume we're watching an eviction melodrama until stagehands whisk the three walls away and we find Buster is a theater employee being told to get off his duff.

Such gags are elaborate yet conceptually simple compared to those that play off the conventions of narrative film syntax. The most celebrated example is undoubtedly the sequence in Keaton's 1924 feature *Sherlock Jr.,* in which the hero's dream self walks up to a movie screen and enters the action. But every time he makes a move appropriate to the setting, the film-within-the-film jump-cuts to another setting in which the follow-through of that move is no longer appropriate and has unfortunate consequences. It's a very tricky sequence, and murder to describe, though any child would get it in a single viewing. (The only problem with it is that the jump cuts make the internal film incoherent.) My current favorite is the little scene establishing what a sleepy island Paradiso is in Harold Lloyd's 1923 feature *Why Worry?* A man pulls a donkey cart up in front of a building, gets out, and goes inside. In a straight-on shot, the donkey turns his head to the right, and we cut to a point-of-view shot of a man asleep; back to the straight-on shot, and the donkey turns his head to the left followed by another point-of-view shot of another man asleep. Back again to the straight-on shot of the donkey, who, corrupted by the laziness of humanity, lies down for a nap. The punchline of the donkey collapsing for some shut-eye, and the quietly logical way conventional narrative movie editing works in general, disguise the momentary substitution of donkey consciousness for human consciousness as the default mode of the movie's perception. However, once you become aware of it, it is, in its way, as effective a burlesque substitution as Chaplin's chicken-for-funnel.

Because slapstick plays on our fears of physical and social mal-adjustment, many of the typical gags slide into nightmare territory. Dis-proportion itself can be eerie, but often the hero acts out classic night-mares; for example, being caught onstage unprepared (Harry Langdon in the 1926 feature *The Strong Man)* or losing your pants at a party (Harold Lloyd in the 1925 feature *The Freshman*). Fatty's accidentally hitting his wife in the face with the rag is also bad-dream-like, and the movies are full of futile efforts that are gag versions of running without getting anywhere: for instance, in the 1924 feature *Girl Shy* when Harold Lloyd is rushing to stop the girl's wedding and he sneaks a ride on a moving car that half a block later pulls into a driveway.

There's also verbal slapstick to take into account. The term is an analogy, which generally refers to dialogue performed at a breakneck clip. As Alva Johnston said in 1941 of writer-director Preston Sturges's headlong 1940 talkie *The Great McGinty,* "The picture has a speed which has seldom been equaled since Mack Sennett used to achieve ve-locity by loosing herds of lions at the actors." Overall, Sturges has been the greatest exponent of verbal slapstick in American movies. He might have developed his style from any number of contemporary sources: the 1928 Broadway stage production of *The Front Page,* in which Ben Hecht and Charles MacArthur specified throughout in the stage directions at which point in the *middle* of another character's dia-logue a performer was to begin talking; the rocketing early talkies fea-turing such motormouth comedians as John Barrymore, Lee Tracy (star of *Broadway* and *The Front Page*'s original Hildy Johnson), Robert Williams, Adolphe Menjou (Walter Burns in the original 1931 movie version of *The Front Page,* one of Lloyd's hired jaws in *The Milky Way,* and perpetrator of a rascally Barrymore parody in the 1936 Fox musical *Sing, Baby, Sing*—he gulps Bordeaux glasses of bay rum, and when his agent asks if he'd like a little water, he roars in scorn, "Are you suggesting that I *bathe?*"), and Cary Grant (Walter Burns in the 1940 romantic comedy remake of *The Front Page, His Girl Friday*);

the Marx Brothers' Broadway shows of the twenties and movies of the thirties, in which the jokes come so thick you wish you had a court reporter making a transcript for you (as Groucho himself did, to preserve ad-libs for future use); Frank Capra's direction of dialogue in *Platinum Blonde* (1931) and *It Happened One Night* (1934) and Howard Hawks's in *Twentieth Century* (1934), *Bringing Up Baby* (1938), and *His Girl Friday*.

Sturges claimed, "Dialogue consists of the bright things you would like to have said except that you didn't think of them in time"; verbal slapstick adopts the pace we'd converse at if we all thought of our brightest remarks in time. Thus it helps if the characters are witty or wised-up. They don't absolutely have to be urban, but we tend to think of it as the right speed of dialogue for people able—just—to maintain the mph demanded by big-city life, where everything is always happening at once. Finally, it can be achieved just by having them trample each other's lines—they don't have to be listening to each other, or even to be intelligible, for us to respond to the humor. Perhaps the quintessential moment of verbal slapstick is Aunt Elizabeth's arrival in *Bringing Up Baby,* when we laugh not because of the dialogue but because everyone is talking at once, including George the terrier. In fact, we laugh largely *because* we can't follow what anyone is saying.

Verbal slapstick also has characteristic gags, such as the sarcastic aside, the comeback that turns the first speaker's words around (Jean Harlow in *Platinum Blonde:* "Don't mind mother," Robert Williams: "I don't mind her if you don't"), insipid verbosity that turns the speaker's own words against himself, orotundity (a W. C. Fields specialty, and thus not necessarily a speedy one, though Raymond Walburn did it faster than Fields), one-liners, puns, vivid slang, outrageous metaphors, double entendres, nonsequiturs, malapropisms, mispronunciations, getting names wrong, and foreign accents, all of which predate the movies and none of which waited for talking pictures to reach the screen. The silent title writers had gone in for wisecracks since Anita Loos started the game in 1916, and they frequently imitated vocal tricks typographically: in *The Strong Man,* when strapping Gertrude Astor tries to convince Harry Langdon that she's the demure young thing he's been searching for, the title reads, "Well, I'm Little Mary!" It's the firing-on-all-cylinders speed that was new to the talkies, made possible by the removal of title cards, which disrupted the pace they tried to set with wisecracks. And when the studios transfused vaudeville and stage performers into the movies, you could finally hear the verbal jokes, as well as certain voices that were entertaining in themselves.

But what really ties verbal slapstick to physical slapstick is that the comedians used them in similar ways. For instance, in the 1938 Lucille Ball vehicle *Annabel Takes a Tour,* Jack Oakie has a running gag mispronouncing the name of the manager of the hotel they're staying in: for "Pitcairn," he'll say something like "Spitcurl" instead. The joke is planted at regular intervals and then given a capper when Oakie calls him Pitcairn and the addled man violently corrects him, "It's Spitcurl!" In the talkies, the moviemakers instinctively developed verbal jokes in the manner of visual routines.

Thinking of the more complicated visual and verbal gags brings up the issue of structure, and by far the most common structural device in slapstick movies is the chase. It's the ultimate kinetic expression of the hero's being out of step: his wishes can't be borne, his idiosyncrasy can't be resolved; he simply has to hotfoot it out of the range of the authority or society he's run up against (cops, typically, but not exclusively) if not out of the world of the picture altogether. (As a variation, the hero will chase a man he suspects of coming on to his girl.) For the semi-improvisational Keystone units, a chase had the virtue of providing an ending whether or not they'd come up with a resolution for the vignette; that is, it was the narrative equivalent of a fade. If the cameraman could crank the camera, the clowns could provide laughs while seeming to be engaged in the story. It's still there in the top clowns' features, such as *Safety Last!* in which Harold's pal is chased by the cop from floor to floor on the inside of the building while Harold goes up the outside, and it's pretty much the entire plot of *The General.* It was also a foolproof way for animators like Tex Avery and Chuck Jones to develop their six-minute cartoons.

However, perhaps the single most useful type of humor to know is the kind that replays melodrama as camp. The impulse to parody melodrama is such a constant in slapstick that James Agee, in his landmark 1949 *Life* magazine appreciation of silent slapstick, "Comedy's Greatest Era," listed it as one of the two main branches of Keystone shorts—"parody laced with slapstick and plain slapstick"—further describing the parodies as "the unceremonious burial of a century of hamming, including the new hamming in serious movies." At Keystone, parody was so natural it could come into play automatically as the troupe, working on the street, spontaneously cooked up a plot to take advantage of an actual parade they could shoot for free. As Sennett recounted:

Mabel Normand could throw herself into any part instantly, even into a part that didn't exist.

"Who am I?" was all she asked when she saw we were under way.

"A mother," I said.

"I would be the last to know," Mabel commented.

"Now take this doll," I ordered. "It's your baby. Get going. Run up and down the line of march and embarrass those Shriners. Make out that—"

"—I'm a poor lorn working girl, betrayed in the big city, searching for the father of my chee-iuld." Mabel finished the sentence. "This characterization requires a shawl. Who ever heard of a poor, forlorn little mother without a shawl over her poor little head?"

Almost every major slapstick performer had experience in popular theater, and Sennett, Chaplin, Arbuckle, Lloyd, Keaton, and Laurel felt an irresistible impulse to parody the kind of low-grade theatrical they had either appeared in or shared bills with.

That cross-eyed ostrich Ben Turpin is usually cited as the silent specialist in this line, but the most thoroughgoing, and funniest, example I've come across is the 1914 Vitagraph two-reeler *Goodness Gracious* starring Sidney Drew and Clara Kimball Young. (The 1916 Triangle two-reeler *The Mystery of Leaping Fish,* starring Douglas Fairbanks as the glassy-eyed hophead detective Coke Ennyday busting a dope-smuggling ring, is a close second.) In *Goodness Gracious* Young plays a working-class girl who wants to live out the kind of romance she loves to read and weep over; to ensure she gets things just right, she doesn't put the book down while making her way through the world. First she takes to the streets, then becomes a rich man's secretary, typing with one hand so that she can hold her romance novel open with the other. Inevitably she falls in love with and marries her boss's son, only to have the father disown him; son and father are reconciled when the couple catches the father's attempted killer. There's no respite in the corniness of the plot or in the double-timed lampooning of it, and Young is spectacularly batty: mechanically fluttering her eyelids and flouncing in what could be a Balinese automaton's parody of coquetry; feeding pages from her novel to her starving children; trudging through a stage effects blizzard to her father-in-law's, and, when she enters his library, striking a statuesque pose and tossing one last handful of confetti snow on her own head. (It's a worthy forerunner of the *Carol Burnett Show* send-ups.)

Burlesques of melodrama announce a wised-up, rather than defensive, disreputability for slapstick comedies, from *Goodness Gracious* (which is just what sensible people might exclaim about the kind of melodrama that movie rips to shreds) to the *Naked Gun* series. However, though melodrama seemed ridiculous to the silent comedians, it also perversely provided them with a framework when they moved from the often freer-style shorts to features. Harold Lloyd's feature *Girl Shy* is much more sophisticated than Keystone shorts in terms of comic tone, performance, and photography, yet the romantic comedy plot ends up with Lloyd rescuing the girl from marriage to a sneering, villainous bigamist. And a full nine of Keaton's thirteen silent features involve melodramatic challenges to his manhood.

Chaplin alone used melodrama in his features without seeming to realize that he wasn't spinning his story lines from sheer inspiration and so doesn't benefit from the flippancy that makes comic melodrama preferable to serious melodrama. The combination of slapstick and melodrama, when slapstick had so often parodied melodrama, doesn't seem so odd when you know that the Keatons' parody of a one-act melodrama *The Yellow Jacket* was so popular that vaudeville theaters would book both acts on the same bill as often as possible. In his wonderful 1922 novel *Merton of the Movies*, Harry Leon Wilson conceives of all slapstick shorts as melodrama broadened for laughs. A self-serious director of features, worrying about the effect of these slapstick parodies on the general audience, asks another filmmaker, "What'll we do then for drama—after they've learned to laugh at the old stuff?" The other man calms him down by saying, "Don't worry; that reliable field marshal, old General Hokum, leads an unbeatable army." Slapstick romantic comedy features of the silent era enabled the audience to laugh at, and to get into, the hokey plot at the same time, and they set a pattern of storytelling that still goes over, as in all three of Jim Carrey's 1994 hits: *Ace Ventura: Pet Detective*, *The Mask*, and *Dumb & Dumber*.

People who love slapstick usually can't resist inventorying the gags and plot devices and humor. It's a useful exercise but finally must give way to a larger question, since the gags and plot devices all come after the initial impulse to play a story for slapstick. You inevitably want a more involved abstract statement, a definition. *Webster's* calls slapstick "comedy that depends for its effect on fast, boisterous, and zany physical activity and horseplay (as the throwing of pies, the whacking of posteriors with a slapstick, chases, mugging) often accompanied by broad obvious rowdy verbal humor." But this is a definition in the form of an inventory; it doesn't get you nearer the motivation behind slapstick. My own attempt—that slapstick occurs anytime things go wrong physically for the hero in such a way that we know the movie-makers are inviting us to laugh—likewise takes you only so far, but it does indicate there's somewhere beyond to get to.

We need to gather more expansive ideas to get there. For instance, in her introduction to Buster Keaton's autobiography, Dilys Powell wrote of a sequence in Keaton's feature *The General* that "one laughs because the behaviour is an intensified reflection of universal impulses and moods: bewilderment, determination, exasperation." These three moods cover the material for almost all pure physical comedy sequences. Bewilderment and exasperation are two key emotions the hero feels when he comes up against what Frank Capra, a graduate of Mack Sennett two-reelers and Harry Langdon's feature production team, called the "intransigence of inanimate objects." (This echoes what the Dutch historian Johan Huizinga wrote, "Which of us has not repeatedly caught himself addressing some lifeless object, say a recalcitrant collar-stud, in deadly earnest, attributing to it a perverse will, reproaching it and abusing it for its demoniacal obstinacy?" as an example of personification, which he cited as a fundamental habit of mind.) In response, the hero's determination propels him through the story, by the end of which he often enough triumphs by means of the very objects and forces that bewildered and exasperated him at the outset.

But there's more. If you think about slapstick in terms of the standard props of the silents—banana peels and pies, of course, Limburger cheese, buckets and mops, ladders, fences, revolving doors, electric fans—it can seem like a peculiar and not necessarily relevant sidestream of comedy. But the way Faulkner describes the hazards that attend human mobility in *Light in August* opens our eyes to a fuller, broadly applicable context:

> He watches quietly the puny, unhorsed figure moving with that precarious and meretricious cleverness of animals balanced on their hinder legs; that cleverness of which the man animal is so fatuously proud and which constantly betrays him by means of natural laws like gravity and ice, and by the very extraneous objects which he has himself invented, like motor cars and furniture in the dark, and the very refuse of his own eating left upon floor or pavement.

Faulkner doesn't stage a slapstick episode; he describes slapstick as an elemental aspect of existence. He even overwrites a description of the most rudimentary comic prop, the banana peel, which becomes "the very refuse of his own eating left upon floor or pavement," to give slapstick the lurking grandeur of an existential condition. His instinct is just right—it isn't too much to say that slapstick is a fundamental, universal, and eternal response to the fact that life is physical. Of the two components, body and soul, we have empirical proof of the first alone. It's the body that we can *see* interacting with physical forces and objects, and our intense exasperation that this interaction doesn't run smoother—hence Faulkner's sense of betrayal—stimulates the urge to tell a story in a slapstick mode.

The word "existential" sounds too tony for slapstick but indicates its prevalence in our experience. The fact is that slapstick feels too familiar for a philosophical term *because* it happens to us all the time. My grandmother loved to recount how she and my aunt got wedged hip-to-hip in the closing doors of a department store elevator and started laughing so hard they couldn't pop themselves free. Likewise, and with superb fitness, on the first evening of screenings for the first slapstick seminar I taught, as I was mounting the steps to the theater with a can of film, a laser disc box, and a videotape in my arms, I raised my head to greet a student, missed the last step, and fell forward at full length on top of the slapstick treasure I was clutching.

The grotesque but demotic silent slapstick comedians, both more and less like us than any other movie stars of the era (they look less like us but are utterly unidealized), all had stories about real-life mishaps as well (which, because of my own experiences, seem believable, though the stars would have had professional reasons for inventing them). Roscoe Arbuckle's wife Minta Durfee remembered him in his vaudeville days throwing himself on a Murphy bed, his weight forcing the mattress through the bed boards, and ending up with "his hips and buttocks pinned in the bed frame, and his head under the headboard." He had to be pulled out by a passel of belly-laughing Arizona miners. You don't have to be fat to feel that this kind of thing is always happening to you. That's the appeal of the slapstick outlook, even in life— we have to laugh at the loss of our dignity, which is what makes the constant recurrence of such losses bearable. Insofar as such mishaps provide us with anecdotes, we *like* them to happen, in retrospect, if not while they're happening.

Slapstick clowns have the added advantage of using them as material. Buster Keaton described a train wreck he and his itinerant vaudevillian family were in:

> What a pileup in that compartment! Mom and Louise on the floor, Jingles and me out of the upper berth on top of them, and then, on top

of all of us, grips, boxes, valises, saxophone, typewriter. And Joe standing razor in hand and lather all over his face where he got shoved into
the mirror when the freight engine bumped our Pullman.

Buster recalled for his interviewer the train company's adjuster giving
his father Joe a check for damages and then added, "A hundred and
fifty bucks and a new routine for free." When the comedians then act
these mischances out on-screen, we are in a perfect situation: we can
laugh at the kind of fiasco we know from experience but that's happening to somebody else for once, and in a more extreme form than we
could perhaps survive. (Even the solicitous are morally free to laugh
because nobody got hurt.) Keaton was fully aware of this transference
when he said, "An audience will laugh at things happening to you, and
they certainly wouldn't laugh if it happened to them."

But just *how* we're laughing—at the hero, with the hero, at our-
selves—is an intricate matter. To enjoy slapstick, the audience has to
make a basic projection. As Bert Williams said in 1918:

> One of the funniest sights in the world is a man whose hat has been
> knocked in or ruined by being blown off—provided, of course, it be the
> other fellow's hat! . . . This is human nature. If you will observe your
> own conduct whenever you see a friend falling down on the street, you
> will find that nine times out of ten your first impulse is to laugh and
> your second is to run and help him get up. . . . The man with the real
> sense of humor is the man who can put himself in the spectator's place
> and laugh at his own misfortunes.

Williams takes Keaton's statement a little further, acknowledging the
schadenfreude in seeing the other fellow's hat squashed (one of the
most common incidents in all slapstick movies through the 1960s), but
also understanding the wonderful possibility of identifying with the
other fellow in his trouble as well. This explains Williams's last sentence, in which he encourages a fusion of actor and spectator: the
"other fellow" becomes the actor we identify with, "us" in the movie.

The immediacy of slapstick makes this fusion possible. It's often
considered the most outrageous of comic styles, and yet, relying as
much as it does on such ineluctable forces as gravity, momentum, and
bodily functions, it's the most necessarily rooted in physical actuality.
As Sennett's biographer Gene Fowler wrote, Keystone comedies "cari-
catured earth's hourly problems, injustices and defeats in a manner
that seemed peculiarly real in the midst of the unreality of the action."
Even gag sessions found the writers quibbling over the literal plausi-

bility of each other's ideas, as in Lloyd's transcription of a typical session in which a gagman carped: "And while we are on the subject of relentless realism, a model T Ford fires on a magneto, not a battery as you innocently suppose. What becomes of your battery gag now?" In the silent era, when movies were made for the masses who couldn't afford to attend the theater and opera regularly if at all, this also meant that slapstick comedies showed working- and middle-class America with naturalistic detail. Chaplin's grimy, run-down slum settings are the most obvious examples, but it's also true of the rooming houses, young marrieds' bungalows, lumber camps, firehouses, saloons, restaurant kitchens, and backstage scenes you see in all the silent comedians' pictures.

The social dimension of slapstick draws on less extreme forms of comedy—romantic comedy, for example—which I discuss at greater length in this book because critics have slighted them. But I wouldn't want to underestimate the importance of our exasperation with the natural laws that govern existence, exasperation so great it comprises responses as diverse as slapstick and Christianity. They are as different as the following legend of St. Ambrose, bishop of Milan, shows:

> Once when the bishop was walking in the city, it happened that a man accidentally fell and lay prostrate on the ground. Seeing this, a passerby began to laugh at him. To this man Ambrose said: "You're standing now, but be careful you don't fall!" The words were hardly spoken when down the man went and lamented his own fall as he had laughed at the other's.

Next to Bert Williams's easygoing, secular, modern analysis of the same situation, the severity of this hieratic version stands out in hard-edged relief. A Christian text couldn't tell this anecdote as a slapstick joke because slapstick sees falling as an amusing inevitability we have to live with as we can. By contrast, in Christian theology, falling has the worst possible connotations, of course. The Christian fear of falling, with the pits of hell always imagined down below, indicates a ceaseless resistance to physical existence, with our enslavement to gravity a symbol for all the animal lapses to which we're given.

Another central source of trouble for Christian thought is the body itself—the necessary precondition, for experience in general as for slapstick, that spoils everything. I don't mean to suggest that Christians, either individually or institutionally, have had no sense of humor. The medieval burlesque Feast of Fools, "when the solemn decorum of cathedral services would be suddenly turned upside down as the inferior clergy heard the glad tidings that 'He hath put down the mighty from their seats, and exalted them of low degree,'" and Chaucer and Rabelais demonstrate otherwise. My point is just that one of the central elements of the theology—the debasing effect of the body on the soul—enables Christians to overcome this discord only by denying and finally getting rid of the body, whereas slapstick achieves accord here on earth by a comic concession to the body at its most traitorous. Both of these stand in contrast to the pagan approach of the Olympic Games, in which athletes attempt to achieve a perfect union of body and will. These three ritualistic approaches form a gamut: Christianity seeks eternal triumph over physicality after life; Olympians seek by means of the body a temporal triumph that will be remembered long after the athlete's prowess has faded; slapstick seeks a temporal acceptance of physicality by a cathartic exaggeration of its very limitations. The first two have heroism in common, the second two athleticism; all three have produced figures who are revered and memorialized. But slapstick is the only one you can engage in without trying.

In addition, slapstick has its own secular sense of the soul enclosed in the body that only holds it back, symbolized most clearly by the yearning hero who's such a hapless pipsqueak he can't impress on the world (especially the girl) how much he deserves what he wants. His littleness itself often stands for how much he deserves what he can't get. The body that can't win the girl, overcome the villain, or even reliably stay right end up, is indeed a burden to him. Christian hope resides in finally shedding the body altogether in an ecstatic transport into the spiritual realm, which is what the body-centered desires threaten to deprive you of for all eternity. In slapstick the central irony is that the hero's body itself comes between him and the satisfaction of his *physical* desires. "Desires" is overstated for the simplest of slapstick goals, say, tying your shoe, but is right for the most developed slapstick stories, which are romantic comedies. Slapstick offers a stylized exaggeration of our frustration with the physical but turns it into high-spirited, affirmative entertainment.

The slapstick hero's skill at deploying his paradoxically acrobatic clumsiness is central to his status as an Everyman. He generally doesn't have enough definition beyond his physical characteristics for a full dramatic persona but is instead a comic martyr, suffering the compromises of dignity that we're spared for the duration of our sit in the theater (provided we don't spill our popcorn). The clown suffers in our stead everything from delay, frustration, and discomfort to humiliation and even on a few occasions death. *All* of which we laugh at—the worse it gets, the harder we may laugh. (And it stays with us: when I drop something, I'm equally likely to swear or to laugh, sometimes both. If I'm lucky enough to laugh, I'm usually thinking of some similar incident in a slapstick movie I've seen. And sometimes if I'm in a bad mood and swear, I remind myself of Oliver Hardy, and then I laugh.) But whereas the Messiah's martyrdom is a tragedy with a comic outcome, that is, salvation (see Dante), the slapstick clown's martyrdom is comic-as-in-funny (and often has a romantic happy ending besides). Slapstick enables the beleaguered audience to stay here on earth and have the best good time; with a perfect sense of completeness, the clown's martyrdom becomes the good time the audience is having.

This sense of martyrdom, which may sound overwrought, explains why movies about "real" people's troubles, like King Vidor's *The Crowd* and Preston Sturges's *Sullivan's Travels,* can use as a resolution and a climax, respectively, scenes of audiences laughing their worries away at vaudeville acrobats and a cartoon short. Also, you can hear in an audience's expectant "Oh nooooo!" when they spot the "plant" of a slapstick joke that though they know what's coming, they don't mind knowing (as they do when they can guess whodunit). As William Dean Howells wrote in 1903 in the character of a magazine contributor chatting with him about vaudeville: "For my part there are stunts I could see endlessly over again, and not weary of them. Can you say as much of any play?" Thus predictability doesn't necessarily lessen the effect, which points to the element of ritual in slapstick. It's one of our comic rituals because it's common—it happens to everyone, it's available to everyone for the price of a movie or vaudeville entrance, and everyone can readily grasp it.

Furthermore, because slapstick accidents are mainly survivable (even in cartoons, where they're as lethal as being blasted in the face with a shotgun or falling off a cliff, Daffy Duck and Wile E. Coyote always return whole), slapstick can train the comic outlook on events as grand as historical and natural calamities. This is what we mean by "comic" in the widest sense. Harpo Marx said of his impoverished childhood, and presumably the European Jewish experience behind it, "You could laugh about the Past, because you'd been lucky enough to survive it." There's something about the way we save our skins and bring forth another generation that in turn saves theirs that is deeply comic, but also funny. (We're so damned resilient—we really have some nerve despising rats and cockroaches.) As C. L. Barber wrote about Falstaff, "Whereas, in the tragedy, the reduction is to a body which can only die, here reduction is to a body which typifies our power to eat and drink our way through a shambles of intellectual and moral contradictions." Flying too low for tragedy isn't felt as a disadvantage in the resolutely middle-class world of American pop culture. Slapstick marks the death of you as a person of dignity and honor, who has to live his life just so and suffer tragically when the gods, other men, or his own drives make that impossible, and your rebirth as one of the happy, comfortable crowd not expected to uphold any impossible, vaguely aristocratic standards.

If this interpretation—which is emphatically an interpretation of the movies as experiences rather than as statements about their ostensible subjects—seems overdone, it's in part because it bestows on slapstick a kind of cultural authority it obviously doesn't require to reach its audience. Jerry Lewis wrote, "I appeal to children who know I get paid for doing what they get slapped for. . . . I flout dignity and authority, and there's nobody alive who doesn't want to do the same thing." Mack Sennett expounded even more fully about why he relished the flouting of dignity and authority he saw in burlesque in the early 1900s:

> The round, fat girls in nothing much doing their bumps and grinds, the German-dialect comedians, and especially the cops and tramps with their bed slats and bladders appealed to me as being funny people. Their approach to life was earthy and understandable. They whaled the daylights out of pretension. They made fun of themselves and the human race. They reduced convention, dogma, stuffed shirts, and Authority to nonsense, and then blossomed into pandemonium.

This is as unpretentious and straightforward a statement about this aspect of slapstick that I know of; the standards that make slapstick unseemly to people who believe in a certain kind of social decorum don't faze Sennett at all. When he worked with D. W. Griffith at Biograph in Manhattan (1908–1912), he repeatedly tried to sell comedy scripts about policemen to the august director, to no avail. When he finally made one of them himself, with the actors in frowzy costumes because Griffith's company had all the genuine police uniforms, he knew it was a good picture not only because of the profit it made for Biograph but because of the complaints: "The Chicago police raised their hands in pious horror about that little film and let on they were insulted something awful. Well! Authority had been ridiculed! That was exactly the artistic effect I was after. I decided to make more cop pictures."

But the flouting of authority itself can be overemphasized in another respect. Chaplin (borrowing from Dickens) thinks that "authority" means *unjust* authority, that slapstick is necessarily on the side of the oppressed. Hugh Kenner fixed on this as the reason for

> the over-estimation of Chaplin, solicited by his all-too-human *persona* and reinforced by the sort-of-Marxist coloration of so many Anglo-American film historians; Chaplin's encounters with the power structure—greedy monopolists and their kept cops—suggest to the man who is interested in film as a means of propaganda that a positive (i.e., revolutionary) solution to the tramp's difficulties is in sight.

But Harold Lloyd and Buster Keaton don't initiate assaults on dignity and authority from a locked-out position as Chaplin does; they're much more minding-their-own-business types, trying to take their place in the ranks of society as it is. And Chaplin's later work, in which the authority *is* unjust, dominates summaries of his overall output, which ignore the amorality of the early Tramp, who would kick anybody and everybody's backside. (Iris Barry wrote of silent comedy, "A hero may not push a boot into anyone's face sportively, but a comedian may.") Sennett sides with the "little guy" without the political whisker licking, and even Chaplin's and Lewis's ambition and egotism get in the way of their supposed meekness. Slapstick stars right up to the present are a hard-driving bunch who take their preeminence in their movies for granted (when they aren't fighting costars to assert it), even when they're playing virtuous and pitiable.

And there are other problems that arise when people try to take a work of slapstick seriously: they usually attempt to "elevate" it by praising it either as satire, which often seems overstated or wrong, or for its pathos, which is often enough right but which is to praise a comedy for the moments when it ceases to be comic. Chaplin, the Marx Brothers, and Preston Sturges are the most common losers by the claim, usually intended as an anointment, that they are satirists. Even in a picture as obviously intended as satire as *The Great Dictator,* Chaplin can't really stay on this beam; it's not how he works. The Marx Brothers, among the least sententious comedians ever, are far too anarchic to be satirists, much like the Chaplin of the peerless Mutual shorts. And Sturges focuses on the twinned themes of a man's material and sexual success. He can be called a satirist only in the most general sense of someone attuned to human foibles, which he exploits as much as he satirizes. (The exception is *Sullivan's Travels,* which satirizes the studios' ethos—before capitulating to and justifying it.)

The fact that slapstick comedians don't really make pointed satires is related to the fact that they take their place in the comic tradition only minimally by literary transmission. Gilbert Seldes said in praise of silent slapstick that "it uses still everything commonest and simplest and nearest to hand; in terror of gentility, it has refrained from using the broad farces of literature—Aristophanes and Rabelais and Molière—as material." And M. Willson Disher insisted with respect to styles of clowning that the persistent types "are manifestly not borrowed but spontaneously created afresh." Although nearly every familiar style of low-comedy routine will be mentioned in a study of Aristophanes (indicating something eternal in this form of comic address), slapstick movie clowns have always re-created them from more proximate sources—in their theatrical experience and personal lives, and in response to ongoing conditions of existence. They're not educated men, and their comedy is probably the livelier for it—their ignorance is our bliss.

However, praising slapstick for pathos is the more disturbing way in which people try to explain its greatness. Of course, the hero's haplessness can make him seem pitiful, which makes him something less than a hero—Chaplin's flaw and Jerry Lewis's even more so after him. Jerry Lewis's statement "I do not know that I have a carefully thought-out theory on exactly what makes people laugh, but the premise of all comedy is a man in trouble, the little guy against the big guy," is more revealing perhaps than careful thinking could have made it. The idea that comedy is about getting a man into and out of trouble could be the haiku version of this whole book. The problem with what Lewis says is that he voices the common perception that the comic hero has to be a little guy—either in the sense of height and build, or in the sense of a meek, gentle, common man (what Chaplin meant when he regrettably began referring to the Tramp as "the little fellow"). Roscoe Arbuckle and the six-foot-tall Lewis himself prove that a comic hero doesn't have to be little, and Chaplin could be just as funny when he was abusive or a gent in evening dress or both.

Nevertheless, because the slapstick hero is a martyr yet the comedian is untrained in literary discipline, it does make sense that these heroes would slide toward pathos, an easier but also enduringly popular theatrical form. So it isn't a shock that many people take as their model Chaplin from his 1921 feature *The Kid* onward (with a few exceptions, *Pay Day*, his 1922 two-reeler, and *Modern Times* being the best). In 1929 Gilbert Seldes wrote, "The particular type of fun [slapstick shorts] made was not popular with intelligent people at the time; it was unrefined; it was vulgar; and only the multitude applauded—and rocked and roared with laughter—until the supreme genius of

Chaplin proved itself by effecting a revolution in critical judgment."
To get at the quality of this "supreme genius," Seldes, when describing
The Pawn Shop, arguably the ripest of Chaplin's Mutual two-reelers,
writes, "All of this is tremendously funny; behind it there is the flicker
of a tear; it has the irony and pity, the piety and wit, of all the great
Chaplin pictures." Seldes says all this even though he's just accurately
described two of the moments in this thoroughly unsentimental picture
when Chaplin has made fun of teariness: Charlie's "tragic appeal to be
reinstated" when fired, indicating that "he has eleven children, so high,
and so high, and so high—until the fourth one is about a foot taller
than himself," and when "Charlie is taken in by a sob-story about a
wedding ring," after which he clobbers himself on the head with a
gavel. Seldes's summary of the short is smart and precise; he cops the
buzz. But when he wants to expand on what makes it *great,* he starts
hallowing his tears, as if they were *the* sign by which art is known.

I'm not suggesting that there's no pleasure in pathos—that's objectively wrong. The problem in Chaplin is that when he gets weepy, he
seems to be inviting the audience to join in a session of mutual self-
congratulation for identifying with his unappreciated soulfulness, encouraging us to whimper, We're too good for this world, too, Charlie!
It's baffling to read such praise for the Chaplin movie that not only
avoids pathos but ridicules it, just as it's baffling to read Otis Ferguson's complaint that *Modern Times* "is a feature picture made up of
several one- or two-reel shorts, proposed titles being *The Shop, The
Jailbird, The Watchman, The Singing Waiter,*" when that seems to be
just what enables Chaplin to work in his most expert form at feature
length without relying on sentimentality to link everything up.

However, it was Chaplin himself who propagandized for prestige
on the strength of his sentimentality, and by 1931 Frederick Lewis
Allen could define "highbrows" as people "who looked down on the
movies but revered Charlie Chaplin as a great artist." Idolizing Chaplin
can blur the clearest vision. James Agee, in "Comedy's Greatest Era,"
praises the simultaneously narcissistic and masochistic ending of *City
Lights* not only as the best thing Chaplin ever did but as "the greatest
piece of acting and the highest moment in movies." And it's not just
that Agee disagrees with me about its not being a comic moment,
since he claims, "It is enough to shrivel the heart to see." The disagreement plunges to bedrock: why praise a comedy for its heart-
shriveling moment?

Among these very best critics of slapstick, Walter Kerr comes closest
to satisfactorily appreciating the serious bent of Chaplin's work:

Chaplin wasn't after tragedy as such, obviously, though the character he had already fashioned for himself embraced, by accident and instinct, certain of the tragic hero's qualities. He was an outcast by temperament, and he had aspirations of a sort. What Chaplin wanted to do was to dig for the seriousness of comedy's origins, knowing perfectly well that such seriousness was there and was intimately related to the prankish nose-thumbing it had provoked.

When the hungry, homeless Tramp steals a hot dog and then eludes the cop who spots him in *A Dog's Life,* Chaplin could be said to be thumbing his nose at a serious situation, but not in the self-regarding, earnest ending of *City Lights.* What it comes to is that Kerr's saying Chaplin "wasn't after tragedy as such" is simply saying as generously as possible that Chaplin didn't really understand what tragedy was. O'Neill blended comedy and authentic tragedy in *Long Day's Journey into Night* when he had the compulsive skinflint Tyrone turn off the extra lights after he's made a big deal about letting them burn. And in Sidney Lumet's 1962 movie version of the play, Katharine Hepburn came up with a great bit of business: when Mary hollers, "I hate doctors!" Hepburn brings her hand down on the table and flips the silverware into the air, giving us sick giggles over the theatrically phony gestures of a manipulative, emotionally remote matriarch. What Chaplin blended with his slapstick wasn't tragedy at all but pathos, a debased form of tragedy that he was familiar with from his childhood in touring theater troupes.

C. L. Barber's discussion of pathos-based storytelling gets at the problem with it:

> When, through a failure of irony, the dramatist presents ritual as magically valid, the result is sentimental, since drama lacks the kind of control which in ritual comes from the auditors' being participants. Sentimental "drama," that which succeeds in being neither comedy nor tragedy, can be regarded from this vantage as theater used as a substitute for ritual, without the commitment to participation and discipline proper to ritual nor the commitment to the fullest understanding proper to comedy or tragedy.

The levelheaded Seldes also knew what was wrong with pathos in the movies; he criticizes early moviemakers because they "began by importing the whole baggage of the romantic and sentimental novel and theatre." He even praises slapstick burlesques of the perennial sentimental modes—"Our whole tradition of love is destroyed and out-

raged in these careless comedies; so also our tradition of heroism"—
and yet goes on to praise Chaplin in blood-clotting terms for his "piety
and wit," his "indescribable poignancy," his "wisdom" and "loveliness." Praising Chaplin, Seldes comes across as fraudulently as Jerry
Lewis did when in promotional material for the 1951 Martin and
Lewis picture *That's My Boy,* he praised Chaplin and himself by claiming, "I really belong to the old school which believed that screen comedy is essentially a combination of situation, sadness and gracious humility." I prefer Seldes when he generalizes that because "the genteel
tradition does not operate" in slapstick, "fantasy is liberated" and
"imagination is still riotous and healthy," which indicates that there
must be something comedy can do as comedy and still be great.

Additionally, pathos does nothing for Chaplin even when it's central to a sequence. People have always rightly marveled at Chaplin's
sticking forks into dinner rolls and making them do a little table dance
in *The Gold Rush* (1925); he perches his head over his hands to make
himself into a Mardi Gras figure with a giant head, tiny fork legs, and
relatively big bread feet. What's amazing about this interlude is that
Chaplin moves his head and the forks as if they were indeed members
of a single body. It isn't the pathos of the situation, the fact that he's
fallen asleep while waiting for New Year's Eve guests who don't show,
that moves you (as Seldes claimed). As pathos, this scene overall isn't
as good as the nerve-racking no-show birthday party in *Stella Dallas.*
And it isn't the "cuteness" of the idea that gets to you. This was
Colleen Moore's mistake when she tried a similar kind of hand dance
in *Ella Cinders* (1926). Lacking the physical skill to effect the illusion,
she overrelied on the characters' darlingness in entertaining three
moppets.

More surprisingly, it isn't even the originality of the concept that
makes it stand out; Arbuckle had earlier performed this bit on film, as
Chaplin acknowledged. Originality in terms of the gags themselves is
almost never the correct answer in slapstick. For example, Buster
Keaton's suicide attempts in the 1921 two-reeler *Hard Luck* seemed
particularly redolent of his style to me until I began researching this
book, when archival viewing revealed that Keaton didn't originate the
sequence, not in the movies, anyway. Similar sequences occur in
Harold Lloyd's 1920 two-reeler *Haunted Spooks;* Bobby Vernon's
1920 two-reeler *All Jazzed Up,* made by Al Christie; and Colleen
Moore's 1919 Christie two-reeler *Her Bridal Night-mare.* Keaton's sequence is the best in itself and works especially well for a stone-faced
comedian; however, it didn't sprout from Keaton's artistry but from

the conventions of this group of moviemakers. You need some other handle to describe what makes a slapstick artist's work distinctive, and in the case of the dinner roll number, it's Chaplin's performance of the dance that's astounding. He moves with the eerie precision of a half-animate creature in a fairy tale while bearing the finicky and nonchalant expression of a trouper who's done the exquisite dance so many times he's *achieved* the look of effortlessness. We're magnetized by this inordinate and idiosyncratic physical grace that doesn't reduce easily to words or to the kinds of feelings, like satire and pathos, that so often promote complacency.

Chaplin's dance is a great moment of pantomime by any standards, but that still leaves the question of what makes the movies overall great, which leads to a bigger problem. I wouldn't hesitate to say that such recent movies as *Raising Arizona, Beetlejuice, The Mask,* and *Kingpin* contain great slapstick, and *everyone* agrees that the silent slapsticks are "great," but do we know what we mean by that when applied to slapstick movies? Are they great in the same way or to the same degree that Shakespeare's comedies are great? Are even the best of them, *The Pawn Shop, The General,* and *The Kid Brother,* comparable to such masterpieces as Carl Dreyer's *The Passion of Joan of Arc* (1928) or G. W. Pabst's *Pandora's Box* (1929), which of all silents require the least adjustment for outdated conventions? Do they even represent achievements on the order of such European movies with extended use of slapstick as Kote Mikaberidze's Soviet silent *My Grandmother* (1929), Luis Buñuel and Salvador Dalí's *Un chien andalou* (1929) and *L'Age d'or* (1930), René Clair's *The Italian Straw Hat* (1927) and *Le Million* (1931), Vittorio De Sica's *Miracle in Milan* (1950), Louis Malle's *Zazie dans le métro* (1960), Bertrand Blier's *Going Places* (1974), or Pedro Almodóvar's *Women on the Verge of a Nervous Breakdown* (1988)? Though Europeans, particularly Max Linder and to a lesser extent Jacques Tati, have made slapstick movies of the same kind and quality as the American silents, we have little in our canon comparable to these European movies, which, with their close ties to contemporary visual art and literary movements, have graphic, narrative, and moviemaking power unmistakably more sophisticated than you find in the American movies. In his 1925 feature *The Salvation Hunters,* Josef von Sternberg made a muted reduction of slapstick archetypes, and in such later pictures as *Monsieur Verdoux* (1947) and *Limelight* (1952), Chaplin attempted more literary kinds of irony and introspection. But none of these is up to the European pictures artistically, nor are they as funny as either the European pictures or the American slapstick classics. In fact, I can see that even Ingmar Bergman's laboriously unfunny slapstick farce *All These Women* (1964) is more consciously, literarily ambitious than even the best American silent slapstick.

Likewise, our best slapstick movies altogether lack the amplitude of the physical comedy in literary masterworks, for instance, this farcical moment during the battle of Borodinó in *War and Peace*:

> Instinctively guarding against the shock—for they had been running together at full speed before they saw one another—Pierre put out his hands and seized the man (a French officer) by the shoulder with one hand and by the throat with the other. The officer, dropping his sword, seized Pierre by his collar.
>
> For some seconds they gazed with frightened eyes at one another's unfamiliar faces and both were perplexed at what they had done and what they were to do next. "Am I taken prisoner or have I taken him prisoner?" each was thinking. . . . The Frenchman was about to say something, when just above their heads, terrible and low, a cannon ball whistled, and it seemed to Pierre that the French officer's head had been torn off, so swiftly had he ducked it.
>
> Pierre too bent his head and let his hands fall. Without further thought as to who had taken whom prisoner, the Frenchman ran back to the battery and Pierre ran down the slope stumbling over the dead and wounded who, it seemed to him, caught at his feet.

This kind of antic collision is familiar from countless silent shorts and cartoons. As Joe Rock described the two-reelers he made with Earl Montgomery: "We always finished our comedies with a shot of us running away from a cop, a schoolteacher, or a principal, and then running smack into them again. If we'd run away from cops, we'd run back into cops." Despite the lethally chaotic setting, Pierre's running smack into the enemy officer can't help but make him buffoonish, as he is in much of the novel, because of the nonchalant way he's sauntered into a situation beyond his comprehension. But at Borodinó, unlike most of the slapstick battle scenes that were profuse in the silent era, men are maimed and killed. They *suffer* physically, which enables the work to arc higher.

Black physical humor found its way into slapstick fairly early on in the shorts that Roscoe Arbuckle made for Joe Schenck. In the 1918 two-reeler *Good Night, Nurse!* for instance, Arbuckle walks by a hospital operating room out of which comes flying first an amputated leg and then a crosscut saw. In *War and Peace* Tolstoy writes with grotesque humor when Anatole Kurágin's leg is amputated, because of wounds suffered at Borodinó, and then held aloft with the boot still on it for its former owner to see. But Tolstoy does so specifically to show Prince Andrew, also wounded and lying nearby in the same operating tent, overcoming his feelings of melodramatic vengeance against Kurágin for the planned abduction of Andrew's fiancée, Natásha. What's unsettling about Anatole's begging to be shown his own leg somehow prepares you for Andrew's rapture. The grotesque comedy brought on by the massacre tells you that the settled world, in which the romantic rivalry plot makes sense, is lurching beneath you; transcendence isn't such a reach when you've lost stability anyway. M. Willson Disher wrote, "Satisfy people's desire for the ridiculous and they will accept your idea of the sublime," and it's truer of Tolstoy than of Chaplin.

By contrast, the appearance of Buster Keaton in *Good Night, Nurse!* as a surgeon in a bloody apron is funny because shockingly out of place. We can't take the gore seriously as a fact of medicine, or we'd no longer recognize the movie as slapstick. It could only gain in terms of a complication that these clowns weren't seeking. Whereas Pierre's buffoonery as he floats through the phases of his life with almost no satisfaction and certainly no enviable reputation has to be seen in comparison to Prince Andrew and Anatole Kurágin: all three men have important romantic relations with Natásha. (Eventually Pierre marries her and fathers her children.) Pierre is at times laughable, but allegorically speaking, he's the character who in the end can respect himself and who survives. Prince Andrew is clearer-sighted than Pierre, but also stiffer. He has to be fatally wounded before he can transcend melodrama; Pierre does not.

Consider also the verbal slapstick of Flaubert's agricultural fair episode in *Madame Bovary*, which begins by alternating entire passages of civic speechifying with entire passages of Rodolphe's seduction of Emma. At the awarding of the prizes, Flaubert speeds up this device to line-by-line alternation between Rodolphe and M. Derozerays, the chairman of the jury, producing this matchless joke:

> "A hundred times I was on the point of leaving, and yet I followed you and stayed with you . . ."
> "For the best manures."
> ". . . as I'd stay with you tonight, tomorrow, every day, all my life!"
> "To Monsieur Caron, of Argueil, a gold medal!"

Flaubert's double entendre achieved by overlapping dialogue is a standard verbal slapstick device of the early talkies, with words like "applesauce" taking the place of "manure." Laurel and Hardy's 1931 four-reeler talkie *Beau Hunks* is unabashed, however, opening with Ollie thinking of his fiancée and singing, "I love you, I love you, I love you, I love you / You are the ideal of my dreams," while Stan cuts a fertilizer ad from a newspaper. Within moments Ollie's sweetheart will dump him by telegram. Technically the opening gag in the 1941 W. C. Fields feature *Never Give a Sucker an Even Break* is even closer to Flaubert's joke. There, Fields stands in front of a billboard advertising his previous picture *The Bank Dick* when a truck farmer rolls by calling out his wares: "Raspberries!"

In *Madame Bovary* you get the joke that Rodolphe's sweet talk is manure, though it smells like frankincense to Emma, but you become absorbed by Flaubert's reticence in recasting what is in essence a witty direct statement on the part of the narrator as a low-down dung joke occasioned by an "accident" of construction. Both the joke and the author's reticence contribute to our ambient sense that Emma's downfall isn't as tragic as it might be in a more conventional treatment. That is, because Flaubert won't *tell* us to experience it as tragedy, we hesitate and stare at hackneyed material (which, Baudelaire guessed, Flaubert chose *because* it was hackneyed) suddenly become unfamiliar. Emma's tragedy seems to be that she is, as a type, too shallow for tragedy. Slapstick also denies the possibility of tragedy, but with no unease. All failings come out comic; in *Never Give a Sucker an Even Break* Fields's character, listed in the credits as "The Great Man," knocks a bottle of booze over the railing of an airplane's open-air sundeck and leaps after it, landing in a garden on top of a thousand-foot butte where he plays a kissing game with the pretty blonde girl who lives there. Slapstick is a mode of affirmation, and slapstick movies are not reticent, not even Buster Keaton's (though they are mysterious).

Educated people can appreciate the comic aspects of *War and Peace* or *Madame Bovary* but tend not to know how to let comedy be comedy when it's not as broadly ambitious as these works. To my mind, they look too hard and latch onto works such as *City Lights* that abandon slapstick for a less satisfying hybrid effect. But if Arthur Miller and Toni Morrison are any indication, it isn't by straining for significance that an artist of any genre is most likely to achieve it. This works against the view of Chaplin as the greatest slapstick artist because he began to strain so early and then, in his later career, so hard. I prefer to all of Chaplin's "heart-shriveling" peaks a bit of unadulterated slapstick in Keaton's feature *Steamboat Bill, Jr.* when Keaton's character, with his slightly fatalistic calmness and absentmindedness, is sneaking across his father's boat at night to visit his girl on *her* father's boat. At one point he falls about ten feet to the deck, landing on his ear, and then, upon getting up, sees a rope across his path, which he lifts to stoop under. Afterward he pauses and looks back at the rope, registering that this action was somehow inessential. Then cut and he's off. The ten-foot fall justifies this nearly subliminal gaglet—he's dazed—yet it can also be taken as an emblem of the syncopation of the body's and the mind's impulses, or of the way a man may be most distracted when he thinks he's concentrating hardest. There's always another perspective on your actions, which you don't necessarily want to be clued in to; just hurry on with what you're doing and hope the percentage of superfluous actions won't be too great. However, you *can* rely on others to see you as you can never see yourself, and you definitely can't ensure that you won't appear ridiculous to them. I wouldn't say these ideas I've pinched out of this momentary bit are the only or even the central ideas of slapstick. But they do suggest the unassuming concision with which slapstick can represent a cluster of notions about how we actually get through our days.

Pure physical slapstick is harder to talk about than literary uses of it precisely because it's pure, because there aren't other styles of narrative and character for it to resonate with in an overall scheme. (To enjoy talking about it, you have to enjoy struggling with the difficulty of paraphrase.) Slapstick is a genre that Tolstoy considered one tool in a vast workshop; when it becomes the main stylistic mode of a movie, you have to figure out what it means in and of itself. It is not going to be a *discursive* meaning, something that can be read as a theme or a statement. Among the movie genres, slapstick is probably the least literary, and the slapstick entertainers in general are not attempting to express an otherwise paraphrasable thesis in slapstick. When one of them has, as Chaplin did most obviously in his later phase from *The Great Dictator* through *A King in New York,* he got increasingly far from his best. Of course, novelists do more than merely dramatize preconceived ideas, but it's not inappropriate to say that they do suggest themes in the course of telling their stories. In *War and Peace* Pierre, stunned after the battle of Borodinó, dreams of a voice saying to him, "To endure war is the most difficult subordination of man's freedom to the law of God." You don't necessarily have to accept this as the novel's statement about war, but it does serve as a focal point for thinking about the meaning of the experiences the novelist has set forth.

By contrast, an all-slapstick war movie like *The General,* one of the rare silent slapstick pictures with a wartime setting in which men actually die, doesn't say anything about war. The war does serve as an animated historical backdrop but functions in comic terms merely as a physical obstacle to the hero's desires that by the end helps him satisfy his desires. And that it's the Civil War is a relatively arbitrary decision, free of political implications. Keaton's source book was pro-Union; he made the hero a Southerner I would guess because in this episode of the war, the Northerners lost, and Keaton felt you couldn't end a comedy with a military execution. Likewise, slapstick doesn't *say* anything about our condition as physical beings, though that is its one great subject. It simply nudges our feelings about this condition, with an uncloying, anxious cheerfulness that doesn't force a resolution to those feelings.

Slapstick doesn't feel profound but rather feels true to our experience very much as we live it. It's a popular phenomenon that predates modern pop culture but that in movies shares pop culture's immediate access to the audience. Agee noted the class slant of slapstick's popularity in the early silent era: "'Nice' people, who shunned all movies in the early days, condemned the Sennett comedies as vulgar and naive. But millions of less pretentious people loved their sincerity and sweetness, their wild-animal innocence and glorious vitality. They could not put these feelings into words, but they flocked to the silents." He recalled "the laughter of unrespectable people having a hell of a fine time, laughter as violent and steady and deafening as standing under a waterfall." Slapstick itself evokes these comparisons to natural phenomena; Gilbert Seldes wrote that the laughter "shook us because it was really the earth trembling beneath our feet," in defense of the commonness of the comedy that spoke to its mass audience by offending their "sense of security in dull and business-like lives." Slapstick also suggests metaphors that bring out its democratic appeal: Gene Fowler called Sennett a "dependable barometer" of public taste because he "himself had the average man's amusement tastes," further explaining his success by calling him "the Abraham Lincoln of comedy, by, for and of the people."

The result of this culture commonly arrived at by people who could not put these feelings into words is that slapstick, like popular culture in general, is more taken up with conveying attitudes, emotions, and experiences than ideas. This is often true even of the most prodigious movies—*Intolerance* is masterful for many reasons, none of which has anything to do with the abstraction expressed in the title. Slapstick movies are artistically whole in an almost wholly intuitive sense. They seem repetitive to some people because slapstick *is* mechanical, but in a good way, I think, that gives you the satisfaction of seeing experts put together marvelous contraptions with the given pieces. The only way to appreciate slapstick as much as it deserves without paradoxically devaluing it by overrating it in inappropriate ways (the academic curse) is to understand that when a routine is more resonant than the basic slipping on a banana peel, it's not in overtly literary ways. It resonates because the makers have shaped the material according to their own experiences, and that experiential modeling makes us laugh harder or in unusual ways. Chaplin is funnier and *greater* as a wordless but physically eloquent slum kid in *The Pawn Shop* than as a grandiloquent Shaw manqué in *Monsieur Verdoux*.

Slapstick may always mean the same thing—a response to the frustration of physical existence—but it has been blended with other tones even in popular American movies. Robert Altman's *M*A*S*H* (1970), arguably the most aesthetically satisfying American movie with major slapstick forays, displays intriguingly off-center attitudes, is surprisingly naturalistically performed, especially well designed and shot, and nervily put together. However, as sophisticated as *M*A*S*H* is, especially for a service comedy, its meanings aren't discursively literary, though this doesn't stop them from getting far beyond satire of the army. *M*A*S*H* is certainly not about war or mortality, as much as it features very bloody scenes of surgery.

For all the naturalism of Altman's semi-improvised comic style, and of the sexual and surgical content, it's not very realistic. Rather, it's an allegory of the battle between the sane, adaptable draftees and, in a phrase taken from Richard Hooker's novel, the Regular Army Clowns. It brings to mind the contest between Sir Toby Belch and Malvolio in *Twelfth Night,* and the scene in which "our" side carries Elliott Gould's Trapper John in a chair while drunkenly singing "Hail to the Chief" in honor of his appointment as chief surgeon indicates that the "good" chief is indeed the movie's Lord of Misrule. *M*A*S*H emanates* its encouragement to swing with the flexible people who take the mind-preserving hip attitudes toward sex, drugs, race, religion, sportsmanship, and patriotism. Flexibility is always at some level the gist of comedy, enabling as it does, for instance, the marriage of pride to prejudice once each bends toward the other. And in a slapstick picture like *M*A*S*H* it's nearly the entire meaning, which is why it doesn't matter that the Korean War is treated as if it were historically synonymous with the then-current Vietnam War. Altman knows how to use the sight of battle casualties to give the picture weight without ever cheaply exploiting them. But *M*A*S*H* says nothing about war per se except to show that the best way to conduct yourself in any situation, even the direst, and maybe especially the direst, is to know your job without taking yourself or the rules of conduct too seriously.

All this has to do with the fact that slapstick doesn't feel profound because that word ties in to the kinds of cultural prestige that slapstick is not interested in and often openly mocks. Effortlessly, slapstick makes the audience feel in with the in crowd, part of a world full of adaptable, and often enough optimistic, Everybodies. If you think of *M*A*S*H* as a realistic drama, it can seem smug because Hawkeye and Trapper John's values are never tested. But as a slapstick comedy, it's irresistible—unless you're a Frank Burns. Frank has to be turned out, as Malvolio does, because in the abstract, he represents opposition to the heroes' urges to be human in the comic sense that allows everyone to come together, in pairs, but also as a larger community. Finally, the meaning of slapstick as we've had it in pure form in our movies resides not in the handling of specific topics but in its conventional nature as ritual. It isn't a dramatized statement about a topic; its significance lies in the experience of the movie itself, the comic catharsis, on the part of the individual viewer within the group.

I won't have anything further to say about *M*A*S*H* in this book, but I think that with its football game recalling a whole line of slapstick movies, including *The Freshman* (1925), *Horse Feathers* (1932), and the Martin and Lewis picture *That's My Boy* (1951), it's a good example of how the tradition has remained unbroken. In this book, I've chosen to write about artists who I think show both the *very* wide range of expression that slapstick affords its most inspired clowns and the ongoing movie tradition over roughly fifty years. In short: Chaplin offers the purest example of the performing impulse behind slapstick. Harold Lloyd and Buster Keaton developed their longer pictures as romantic comedies and in so doing reveal a nest of universal conflicts expressed by both slapstick and romantic comedy. Looking at the limited success female stars have had in slapstick tells us about the sexual slant in our responses to physical comedy. The Marx Brothers bring social material as close to the surface as it can get in slapstick without turning it into something else. They express immigrants' total skepticism of the dominant culture as a means of assimilating into it in its most frivolous mode. Preston Sturges has a literary comic sensibility but works out of deep pockets of impulse with the physical freedom and intensity of the silent comedians, offering the most sophisticated combination of high and low comedy until the movies of Paul Mazursky. And Jerry Lewis renewed slapstick clowning for the talkies. His appearance on-screen in 1949 is the Big Bang for contemporary slapstick performers; in the next fifteen years, he reformulated the tradition so indelibly that his model is still dominant.

I could also have written with pleasure at greater length about Roscoe Arbuckle, Sydney Chaplin, Douglas Fairbanks, Harry Langdon, Raymond Griffith, Lupino Lane, Laurel and Hardy, W. C. Fields, Tex Avery, and Chuck Jones. However, this is not an encyclopedia but rather a personal critical response to those artists who have stirred me the most, written to evoke what slapstick fans come to care about most: the qualities that distinguish one artist from another. I chose subjects for my chapters to give a sense of historical coverage, but at the same time I wanted to employ a method of analysis that readers could use themselves in any case (if they had the information at hand and could clap their eyes on the movies). In addition to describing each artist's inspiration in terms of movement and subject matter and affect, which are sui generis, I develop my analysis from three major components in every case: the artist's biography, to see how personality and background informed his work; the artist's theatrical experience, with an eye for how he inflected the shared conventions; and the artist's position in the filmmaking industry, to determine how much artistic control he exerted on a given project. Above theoretical definition and historical survey I favor capturing the astonishing variety this simultaneously predictable genre offers its practitioners. To do that and make sense, you always have to know where the artists came from and under what conditions they worked.

To some people, it may seem that I'm ruining slapstick by analyzing it to this extent, or in this way. And people have a hard time talking about comedy in general because they think that once you start analyzing it, you've missed the point. I respect this hesitation because slapstick is meant to be openly enjoyed in mass company. You certainly don't need to think about it to enjoy it, and so I've tried to provide an example of how to describe the personal, nondiscursive expressiveness of slapstick as slapstick in a way that's compatible with laughing your ass off.

CHAPTER TWO

Chaplin as Proteus, Low-Down and High Up

During Adenoid Hynkel's harangue to a mass rally in the 1940 burlesque of Nazism, *The Great Dictator,* Charles Chaplin, as the charismatic leader of Tomainia, leans into a radio microphone, which bends away, holds its new position, and then snaps back toward him. It's a single sight gag in two modes: when the mike arches away, that's political satire; when it recoils, that's slapstick. The impossible back bend is an editorial live-action cartoon in response to the Nuremberg rallies staged by Leni Riefenstahl for *Triumph of the Will* that cues us to loathe the Dictator. It *shows* us that Hynkel is such a jackal even inanimate objects would flee if they could. The recoil that follows is in part just a way to exit the satirical gag but also represents the triumph of the *thing* and so mitigates the satirical response. For that moment when he's out of sync with the physical world, in the way we fear we will be when we have to speak in public, Hynkel becomes a slapstick protagonist.

Physical gags heighten our self-consciousness about our own clumsiness and miscalculations and then dissipate it immediately in laughter. The significance of this bit with the mike lies in the fact that it's fleeting—it shows that Chaplin's instinct for slapstick is so deeply embedded that he resorts to it even when he doesn't mean to. Mack Sennett, who plucked Chaplin out of vaudeville and put him in movies, wrote: "I know a man who claims that all inanimate objects are perverse. He says things deliberately hide from him. I believe this man has discovered an important new natural law." It isn't clear that Chaplin anticipated all the implications of Sennett's natural law when he made his maniacal Führer a clod. Slapstick binds the clown to his audience: we identify with anyone who gets it in the face when he's just trying to carry on—even if he is a fascist despot.

In *The Great Dictator* Chaplin polarizes his responses throughout; he plays a double role, not only Hynkel but also a Jewish Tomainian barber who looks just like the anti-Semitic Dictator. Chaplin conceived of the double role as a happy solution to the difficulty brought on by his decision to make a talkie at long last. He figured that Hynkel could speak in jargon while the Barber, in essence the Tramp of the 1918 three-reeler *Shoulder Arms* twenty years later, could remain for the most part silent, thereby showing his own talent for both burlesque and pantomime. But the double edge of the bit with the mike shows that the polarization is more intimate than the melodramatic division of evil Dictator and harmless Barber.

That is, Chaplin is divided in his feeling toward Hynkel himself. He may have concocted Hynkel in a satiric vein, but to animate him, he had to identify with him, incorporate him into his own artistic realm where he thinks and feels in terms of slapstick. Chaplin is able to bring the satire and slapstick together only once, at the end of Hynkel's legendary balletic transport with the balloon-globe when it ka-pows in his face: a prediction of the world conflagration that his megalomania will lead to, and another example of the physical world spiting him, with sharp comic punctuation. But in many ways the Dictator is as upfront a self-representation as the Tramp had been when the young Cockney first mismatched too-big and too-small components from the Keystone wardrobe in 1914.

Shooting in 1939 and 1940, Chaplin was taking a risk in parodying the style and program of Hitler's Germany. During production the Hays Office warned United Artists, the distribution company Chaplin cofounded and co-owned, of censorship problems, and the English office of UA "doubted whether it could be shown in [the then nonbelligerent] Britain." By time the picture opened, on 15 October 1940, France had fallen. Chaplin had taken a similar chance when he made *Shoulder Arms* toward the end of World War I. Although in that short he travesties the Germans as bullying buffoons (it's diet cherry propaganda), he also plays the miseries of the American trenches for laughs. (For instance, at bedtime in his rain-filled bunker, the Tramp has to fish up his pillow to plump it; when he finds he can't lie down and keep his head above water, he uses a phonograph horn for a sleeping snorkel.) Hitler requires a more complex response, of course, and *The Great Dictator* is almost four times as long. Doughboys are said to have loved *Shoulder Arms,* but you can't be entirely sure who Chaplin is making *The Great Dictator* for besides himself, though it's far from a star vanity project in the usual sense.

It *is* clear that he's no longer just the newly famous comedian worried about fulfilling his first million-dollar-plus contract that he had been in 1918. In 1939, having saved his fortune by converting it to liquid assets before the 1929 crash, he shot his movies in his own studio and released them himself through UA. Starting in 1916, he was often called a great artist in the press as well; by 1939 he had directed not only *The Gold Rush* (1925) and *City Lights* (1931), held by most critics to be the classics of his Tramp features, but also *A Woman of Paris* (1923), which proved that his pictures could succeed artistically even when he didn't star in them. The ambitions behind *The Great Dictator* are greater than they had been when he made *Shoulder Arms,* but though they're definite, they're also skittish.

Chaplin begins *The Great Dictator* by returning to the setting of *Shoulder Arms*—returning to the safety of successful material, but only to lead us out from it to new ground (a pointed, topical political attack, new for him and new in the sense of news). Thus *The Great Dictator,* in line with the standard history of fascism and World War II, begins with World War I. Here we see the Jewish Barber as a private entrusted with pulling the string on Big Bertha, the gargantuan piece of artillery with a hundred-mile range that could, in Henry Miller's words, "destroy what the eye could not see." Chaplin gives us a good establishing look at the weapon, which looms even more colossal than the machinery in *Modern Times* because it's outdoors and so we can see that it's big enough to bully *nature,* to eat up the space its missile travels over. We slowly glide closer to the gun as Chaplin sets us up for the slapstick undercutting: aimed at Reims cathedral on the horizon, the gun blows up an outhouse about two hundred yards away. The second firing barely sends the projectile free of the gun's opening—it plops onto the ground at the base. An order to check the fuse passes down the chain of command to the Barber, but he can never get close enough to the shell because as he tries to tiptoe around it, it starts to rotate, whichever direction he moves in and however fast.

The shell explodes, and then enemy planes start circling overhead, and the Barber is ordered onto an enormous antiaircraft gun, which he sits on while looking through a scope and changing his position with two cranks. The Barber's inevitable ineptitude with the antiaircraft gun doesn't lead anywhere, really; he gets himself upside down and falls out of the seat. There are new orders to attack, and the Barber drops a grenade up his sleeve while trying to hurl it. Then, on an infantry prowl, he gets lost in the battle smoke and finds himself behind enemy lines, and so on. Though it's still early in the film, you have to admit you're giving the benefit of the doubt a mite too generously to a veteran who shouldn't need it. Chaplin scaled the war scenes to what he felt was the enormity of the historical disaster of the Great War but didn't have an intricate enough plan for what should happen on his extensive outdoor sets. You glimpse too many extras standing around. Like all directors who attempt epic stories, Chaplin is a general on the set, but he's not a general on the battlefield. He was concerned about politics more than slapstick, but not enough about politics to galvanize, or to compensate for, the one-thing-after-another slapstick construction.

This section of the movie is too loosely put together; there's no mortar between the bricks, and there's nothing as inspiredly silly as the Tramp camouflaged as a tree in *Shoulder Arms*. (In the one shot of him hiding in the forest in which we don't initially spot him in the center of the frame, Chaplin came as close as he ever did to Keaton's sublime trompe l'oeil.) If you don't entirely reject the opening of *The Great Dictator*, it might be because Reginald Gardiner shows up as Schultz, a German officer who later proves to be aristocratically above the petty prejudices of a Hynkel. Gardiner has a deranged, lordly insouciance: when he's on the lam from the SS for opposing Hynkel's attacks on Jews, he takes his golf clubs and a hatbox. As a caricature of the grand style of Prussian nobility, Gardiner manages to seem both gaga and pompously correct, and yet resourceful for all that.

The Barber and Schultz have a scene flying a plane upside down that includes a superb snatch of curt comic patter, and then they crash just as the Tomainian defeat is announced. The crash leaves the Barber with amnesia and causes him to languish in a hospital until the early thirties, when Hynkel's party takes power. The Barber comes to himself just in time to face storm troopers bullying their way through the ghetto with nightsticks and buckets of paint, slapping "Jew" on storefronts. Despite the Great Director's initial political motivation, the Barber's run-ins with the storm troopers show how much Chaplin has adapted the political setting to slapstick conventions rather than the reverse. After all, the Barber resists not out of partisan conviction but because he's been away so long that he doesn't know how the political situation stands. Innocent of politics, he's just protecting his property and reacting to the gross brutality of the SS.

Furthermore, the storm troopers are all tall, muscly-but-seedy, older men who look like veteran adversaries to little-guy slapstick heroes. They don't conjure a vision of the Aryan future but rather look like ex-boxers, stogy chompers, beer-swilling free-lunch-counter loafers—the kind of men from whose clutches Chaplin had decades of practice extricating himself. They know how to react to being hit over the head with a frying pan, when Paulette Goddard as Hannah, a feisty Jewish orphan, gives us an example of what the Nazis deserve. It's touch and go—when you think of the storm troopers as slapstick bullies, you can't think of them as SS men, and when you think of them as SS men, you can't laugh. The problem arises from the fact that in slapstick routines, the slaps look walloping but land light in your mind. And you're usually glad when the bullies show up because it means there's going to be a fight, some action. But you can't be glad when the SS shows up; perhaps it's just as well, even if it's to the movie's detriment.

It's also hard to talk about Goddard's role because the subsequent revelations about Nazism, and our thinking about the psychology of it, make her declarations that we all oughta fight back, which she would do if she were a man—and which she does anyway—seem inadequate as a response to the enforcement machinery of a totalitarian regime. Goddard's role is a Capraesque concept of individual gumption as the basic form of political activity that Preston Sturges probably doomed to obsolescence that very year in *The Great McGinty*—and *McGinty* takes place in a normally functioning democracy. (Of course, political sentimentality has never become obsolete in Hollywood—witness *Dave, The American President, Bulworth,* and Kathy Bates as the soul of *Primary Colors.*)

The Barber and the Dictator are, naturally, dead ringers, but their identities don't get confused until late in the picture. The dual role doesn't produce a comedy of errors as in the 1921 two-reeler *The Idle Class,* where the Tramp shows up at the society costume ball and is taken for Edna's rich husband, who is caught in a suit of armor with the visor stuck down. Nor is it a geological layering of social strata as in the 1915 two-reeler *A Night in the Show,* where Chaplin disrupts a stage show both as a man in evening dress in the orchestra and as a worker in the balcony. But in a sense, the Dictator and Barber *are* juxtaposed because the Dictator's voice booms into the ghetto over the radio. And Chaplin introduces us to Hynkel head-on in his aspect as media phenomenon, broadcasting his vision of the Tomainian millennium.

Chaplin didn't speak German but had such a keen ear that he was able to imitate Hitler by sound. In the rally speech already mentioned, he repeats certain low-register words like *Wiener schnitzel* too much, and the way Hynkel's bark turns into a cough is good for one indulgent laugh, but not two. However, it isn't the linguistic jokes themselves, or the use of sound to show that Hynkel's hold on the masses enables him to shut off applause with flip-switch precision, that make you laugh anew at Chaplin. It's the gusto of the egomaniac up there bellowing his lunatic expansions of corny political ideas. There's some way in which the actor has let himself go—for instance, snorting like a hog as he broaches the Jewish question—that really catches you, more than the satire of Hitler. And when you realize how loud this silent comedian is yelling, you understand that Chaplin isn't merely engaged at the level of political outrage; he's pushing his own art further, amplifying the old, coarse, blandly self-interested Tramp of the silent one- and two-reelers.

This reversion in Chaplin's performing style points up the difficulty of characterizing the Tramp. Pauline Kael wrote in her 1982 review of *Richard Pryor Live on the Sunset Strip,* "When Chaplin began to talk onscreen, he used a cultivated voice and high-flown words, and became a deeply unfunny man; if he had found the street language to match his lowlife, tramp movements, he might have been something like Richard Pryor, who's all of a piece—a master of lyrical obscenity." (Chaplin's fussy voice and speeches remind me of what Irving Howe wrote about the more-than-occasional pointed pinkie in Theodore Dreiser's prose: "And worst of all, he had a weakness, all too common among the semi-educated, for 'elegant' diction and antique rhetoric.") Kael objects to the disparity between Chaplin's movements and voice, but there was a deeper way in which the silent Tramp was never all of a piece, a way that worked.

Chaplin claimed to have explained the Tramp to Sennett as soon as he assembled the outfit:

> You know this fellow is many-sided, a tramp, a gentleman, a poet, a dreamer, a lonely fellow, always hopeful of romance and adventure. He would have you believe he is a scientist, a musician, a duke, a polo player. However, he is not above picking up cigarette butts or robbing a baby of its candy. And, of course, if the occasion warrants it, he will kick a lady in the rear—but only in extreme anger!

This is improbable as a recollection of an actual conversation because it brings together traits of the Tramp that we find spread among movies made over a fifteen- to twenty-year span. And the gentleman-poet-dreamer aspects tend to dominate later.

It *is* true that the Tramp would have you believe he is a gentleman—that's the story line of *The Count* and an element of *The Rink,* both 1916 Mutual two-reelers. However, these movies present his imposture not as a heroic attribute but as a form of low cunning onto which we can project our fantasies. And when the Tramp kicks Mrs. Stout in the rear end in *The Rink,* she hasn't provoked his anger at all. The kick completes the mayhem—Mrs. Stout topples a line of men leaning on a refreshment table. More importantly, some of the aspects that might mark the Tramp as a poet or a dreamer—kissing the pawnshop ball after bouncing it off his coworker's head, or coyly presenting a lily to the construction site foreman as compensation for having turned up late on payday—don't really connect with anything else we see of the character. I'm pointing this unconnectedness out not as a flaw but as a founding characteristic of Chaplin's performing at its greatest.

Chaplin's changeability means that although the Tramp registers strongly, you couldn't guess what he'll do next or even come up with a comprehensive taxonomy of what he's done. Thomas Burke, a London chronicler who wrote a profile of his friend in 1932, spoke of the man in the same terms: "At no stage can one make a firm sketch and say: 'This is Charles Chaplin'; for by the time it is done the model has moved. One can only say: 'This is Charles Chaplin, wasn't it?'" The Tramp may emerge from the London of Dickens but doesn't obey realism's demands for predictability. He's always ready to grab any opportunity that arises in these early, hastily thrown together commercial comedies no matter how it alters his character.

Chaplin's biographer David Robinson provides useful terms for discussing this protean quality:

> A music hall act had to seize and hold its audience and to make its mark within a very limited time—between six and sixteen minutes. The audience was not indulgent, and the competition was relentless. The performer in the music hall could not rely on a sympathetic context or build-up: Sarah Bernhardt might find herself following Lockhart's Elephants on the bill. So every performer had to learn the secrets of attack and structure, the need to give the act a crescendo—a beginning, a middle and a smashing exit—to grab the applause.

The unmotivated violence of slapstick that Walter Kerr writes about ("At Keystone, no kick ever needed to be justified. The invitation of an available backside was motivation enough. If one man had a pitchfork in his hand and another man, entirely unoffending, was observed bending over, there was just one thing to do: use the pitchfork") is only the most obvious form of "attack." But when Chaplin whips the lily out from behind his back for his foreman and smiles cloyingly at him, that's also attack. Attack can be any momentary gesture or act that brings the performer forward, regardless of what it does to our sense of the story or character overall (story and character being kinds of "structure").

You can generalize about why Chaplin would be so changeable, but when you generalize about the nature of the changeability, you tend to run together bits from different movies that weren't conceived with aesthetic unity uppermost in mind. Watching the movies one at a time, as they unspool one gag at a time, you see that what Chaplin called many-sided is actually incoherent, unresolvable, but in a productive way. This managed incoherence produces a readily recognizable comic character who always exists in tension with the spontaneity of the working methods of a man turning out comedy shorts by the day, week, or month.

So we recognize the Tramp at whichever end of the social xylophone Chaplin is plonking: lumpen prole, laborer, waiter, clerk, yeoman, or drunken toff. Yet this character is always threatening to disappear in a puff of comic invention, in moments of ad hoc inspiration that don't lead to anything and never recur—most famously, perhaps, in the 1917 Mutual two-reeler *The Cure,* when the successive partings of a changing booth curtain reveal Chaplin in an inexplicable suite of poses, which are different from his more clearly *motivated* impersonations of gentlemen or women. But at times *all* of Chaplin's changes seem opportunistic (which may be why he never played a stable middle-class guy of the kind Lloyd's shy characters would clearly grow up to be after the end of the picture). This unaccountable Chaplin is a young entertainer flipping through the possibilities of character that his mind and body have the skill to make visible.

Thus in the early shorts the Tramp is defined only by transient desires and aversions, and he shares his liberation with Chaplin the actor. Every kind of tie can be cut for anarchic freedom: freedom from responsibility for the character within the screen story, and freedom from consistent character and drama for the actor. Harold Lloyd wrote in 1928, "A one-reel film runs only ten minutes; even in two reels there is little room both for establishing character and being funny; and confronted with that choice, it is character that must be sacrificed." In his short movies, Lloyd *sacrifices* character; it was Chaplin's great early inspiration to throw it away with both hands and a flourish.

This rejection perhaps derives from a certain distance that Chaplin was referring to when he wrote, "I realized I was not a vaudeville comedian, I had not that intimate, come-hither faculty with an audience," a distance his coperformers certainly noticed in him offstage. (Thomas Burke depicted him as a "hard, bright, icy creature" who was "not much interested in people, either individually or as humanity.") Chaplin then said, "I consoled myself with being a character comedian," which, I think, is how he'd describe the fact that his performing style focuses on attack, in Robinson's usage. It does not, however, mean being a coherent character in a realistic sense, as Lloyd was in his best features. In movies, character comedians can either play multiple characters, like Jerry Lewis in *The Family Jewels* appearing as "himself" as a sympathetic chauffeur and in makeup as the candidate uncles (a yarn-spinning sea salt, a cynical circus clown, an absentminded photographer, an inept airplane pilot, a British gentleman sleuth, a splaytoothed Brooklyn mobster); or play one character disguised as many, like Lewis pretending to be by turns the doctors from Paris, Vienna, and Hong Kong in *Living It Up* so that he can foil the real doctors' examination; or pinwheel through voices, expressions, postures, and levels of knowledge and awareness and maturity without concern for realism, which is what Lewis does most of the time in his movies (a natural style for a spontaneous nightclub comedian). Except for a handful of dual roles, Chaplin as the Tramp, like Lewis after him, takes the last road, displaying divergent characteristics as they come handy to the work of stringing gags together.

But more than one road leads to Rome: Gilbert Seldes said that Al Jolson, the ultimate come-hither vaudevillian, had the art of hokum, which to Seldes was "to make each second count for itself, to save any moment from dulness by the happy intervention of a slap on the back, or by jumping out of character and back again, or any other trick. For there is no question of legitimacy here—everything is right if it makes 'em laugh." When Chaplin jumps out of character, it doesn't feel like hokum. It feels freshly impudent, a commentary on hokum, in part, and he creates a peculiarly detached but vital character who is instantly recognizable in any dress or setting. Which is true even though you could say that whereas Jolson is always "himself," Chaplin *never* is. Thus, in this early style, Chaplin always defers his ultimate definition of the figure by adding something out of the blue that doesn't add up but is unforgettable—*because* it doesn't compute.

In this way, the Tramp is antisocial because consistency of character is a social thing, in that it permits the audience to anticipate in unison the roll of the incoming waves. Ordinarily we want some emotional stability while we're sitting among strangers in the dark, where personal responses, like laughing and crying, become public acts, declarations even (especially if you laugh when other people are crying). But Chaplin, like Aristophanes before him and the Marx Brothers after, knew how to make inconsistency reach a large audience, and we find, while all together facing the screen, that a lot of us in the audience are antisocial, too. K. J. Dover, describing Aristophanes' all-around insolence, sees the antisocial impulse as central to comedy:

Devaluation of gods, politicians, generals and intellectuals may be taken together with ready recourse to violence, uninhibited sexuality, frequent reference to excretion and unrestricted vulgarity of language, as different forms of the self-assertion of man against the unseen world, of the average man against superior authority, and of the individual against society.

But it's a delicate balance: when Chaplin made this aspect of his work too deliberate and too verbal in *Monsieur Verdoux,* the American mass audience rejected it, and him, really, as well.

The fact that when any other motivation fails the Tramp will kick his costar in the pants to get things going ties in to Chaplin's past both at home and onstage. Like his working-class audience, he had witnessed any number of brawls, drunken and otherwise. Mack Sennett brought straight into his comedy the roughhousing of big rural Canadian bear-men and the fighting and practical joking of ironmongers with whom he'd grown up and worked. When Jerry Lewis met Chaplin, they discussed Sennett, and Chaplin said, "There were only two things he required from the actors—put on makeup and get going with the rough-and-tumble." Chaplin may have found the "'he-man' atmosphere" at Keystone "almost intolerable," but he had rough memories of his own to draw from; for instance, a drunken attack he witnessed in a kitchen on baking day when he was touring the provinces as a child, which led to his having to testify in court. Although the 1914 Keystone two-reeler *Dough and Dynamite,* set in a bakery, would have needed violence to meet Sennett's requirements, it has another source in this incident in Chaplin's childhood.

However, what's peculiar about *Dough and Dynamite* is that without provocation, Chaplin is always pummeling his coworker rather than the terroristic strikers whose jobs they've both taken. The young Chaplin had been shocked by the "crazy violence" of a pair of brothers whose act as "comedy trapeze clowns" involved kicking "each other in the face with large padded shoes" "as they both swung from the trapeze." But when he first achieved success as an adult supporting Harry Weldon in a Karno company sketch, Chaplin got into some split-level knockabout:

In the show he [Weldon] had to slap and knock me [Chaplin] about quite a bit. This was called "taking the nap," that is, he would pretend to hit me in the face, but someone would slap his hands in the wings to give it a realistic effect. Sometimes he really slapped me, and unnecessarily hard, provoked, I think, by jealousy.

In Belfast the situation came to a head. The critics had given Weldon a dreadful panning but had praised my performance. This was intolerable to Weldon, so that night on the stage he let me have a good one which took all the comedy out of me and made my nose bleed. Afterwards I told him that if he did it again I would brain him with one of the dumbbells on the stage.

To put himself over on-screen, Chaplin resorted to a fund of violent experience out of desperation, in a sense, though in his early movies he often resorts to it *first*—he's not taking chances with Sennett or his audience.

Kerr thinks that Chaplin's performing improved as he learned to motivate the Tramp's responses, specifically violence. To Kerr, the Tramp's kicking the visitors' bratty little boy in the 1923 First National four-reeler *The Pilgrim* is the turning point. What Kerr doesn't see is that critics care more about motivation than audiences do, and that in the case of slapstick, the audience may be better critics. If you look at the two most extended stretches of homosexual flirtation in Chaplin, you can see that the degree of motivation makes little difference to your enjoyment. In *The Cure* the drunken Charlie thinks that Eric Campbell's gouty villain is making eyes at him and starts making them back. We know that Campbell is working on Edna, seated behind Charlie, but Chaplin the director cuts from the three-shot to an all-male two-shot as if to force us to share his delusion as he, for the only time in the entire movie, kittenishly expresses an interest in another man. When in *City Lights,* fourteen years later, the Tramp coyly smiles at Hank Mann before their boxing match, so lingeringly and expectantly that Mann steps behind a curtain before taking his trousers off, the scene is backed up by exposition: the Tramp took the bout only because it was fixed that the other guy would go easy on him and they'd split the purse fifty-fifty. But that guy had to cheese it fast, and Mann has taken his place, but not with the same understanding; to Mann it's winner take all. Thus the Tramp has a reason to want to soften Mann. But though his ineffective effort is amusing, it's not very probable, which matters once you've introduced the question of motivation. Most importantly, the exposition itself, a standard slapstick switch of context, adds little to our response to the flirtation. I laughed harder at *The Cure.*

Motivations are, after all, an improvement only if they're on a par with the actions they spur. But Chaplin's idea of motivation, in all the features from *The Kid* on, is far too often sentimental. In *The Pilgrim,* the Tramp, an escaped convict, reforms when he has the chance to save the pretty girl and her aged mother's mortgage money, and of course in *City Lights* he wants to get money for the blind girl's eye operation, God help us all. Unlike Chaplin's volatile performing style, sentimentality *isn't* antisocial. It glues the audience together with values that they already share, and which are fraudulently tested in the course of the movie. It sets the smiley-face seal on complacency, which siding with the callously self-interested waiter-bum on roller skates in *The Rink* never could. (The waiter doesn't even try to make an egg cream properly—the shell goes in with the egg and is followed by a carnation.) Of course, you can't tell an entertainer what he may and may not do, but you can suggest which effects seem more potent. I can't get unaddicted to Chaplin's early evasion of character and opportunism as a performer.

The Great Dictator matters to me mainly because the Barber/Dictator is the last time we see Chaplin's former incoherence, and it's chiseled large. However, for the most part, the contradictory traits are parceled out between the characters; they don't coexist within them. True, when Hynkel does a *Sieg heil!* salute and with his other hand scratches the conveniently exposed armpit, Chaplin is drawing a connection between himself as the Tramp and as the Dictator that doesn't fit thematically but that makes you more alert to what's going on up there. But for the most part, Hynkel remains a more unsettled character than the Barber, who is insistently likable. Not only does the Barber's voice lack the mercurial quality of the Tramp's physical expressiveness, as Kael said, but the physical expressiveness itself is muted in the Barber by his status as a political victim. This calls up a less alert response from us than the early Tramp did, when he kaleidoscopically dished it out and took it.

Of course, giving the Tramp a voice was tricky. Chaplin couldn't just ignore what the character had come to mean to his audience. He knew his decision wasn't altogether satisfactory, to judge from his confession to Groucho Marx, "I wish I could talk like you." Probably Chaplin didn't give the Tramp the lower-class London accent he himself had had when he first basted the character together because that would have seemed too particular for a figure who had long been considered a universal type. (He might also have feared it would restrict his American audience to people who could make out lines delivered in Cockney.) We do know that although Stan Laurel had confided to his mother that he was afraid he couldn't be an actor because he couldn't "talk right," when he entered talkies, he didn't tart up his Northern accent. But Chaplin was in a tighter spot than Laurel because he had more to lose. However, seeing the Tramp as a universal humble soul itself reflects a questionable progression in Chaplin's thinking that occurred between the invention of the Tramp and the talkie era.

Chaplin had been taking his art very seriously for almost twenty years before he spoke on-screen. For instance, while shooting *The Kid,* he told Gouverneur Morris about "the form it was taking, keying slapstick with sentiment." Morris replied: "It won't work. The form must be pure, either slapstick or drama; you cannot mix them, otherwise one element of your story will fail." But Chaplin insisted that the mixture was an innovation that would be convincing because of the sincerity with which he intuitively created his picture-world. What's significant, and unfortunate, is that Chaplin would claim that "with each succeeding comedy the tramp was growing more complex. Sentiment was beginning to percolate through the character," in essence equating complexity with sentiment. You have to remember that although the slapstick in *The Kid* is top-notch, the mixture of slapstick and sentiment is not different in kind from the style of any number of Mary Pickford movies that predate it.

Chaplin had already mixed "raw slapstick and sentiment, the premise of *The Kid*" (in his words), as early as the two-reeler *The Bank,* made for Essanay in 1915, but the first high mark of his sentimental streak was *A Dog's Life.* I recently watched it for the first time in fifteen years and was stunned that so much of what I remembered as "Chaplin," the scenes I think of as the essence of his work as the Tramp spread throughout his short films, were all in this one movie. There he is stealing a hot dog through a hole in a fence; rolling back and forth under the fence to escape the cop who's seen him; devouring muffins from a plate whenever the food stand owner turns his back, even for a millisecond; always eating dust in the race from the bench to the employment office windows as openings are posted first at one then the other. I saw *A Dog's Life* when I was about ten, and this last sequence, with its exasperating dreamlike inevitability, spoke to a basic anxiety in me. I think of the sequence whenever I stand in lines, at the grocery store, the airport, wherever, because it enables me to nurse my low expectations with better grace.

A Dog's Life is probably Chaplin's best argument for combining slapstick and pathos. His instinct was certainly borne out financially, so he had no incentive to realize or care that for many of us, slapstick indignity can be much more, not less, reverberant for being a somewhat impersonal kind of comedy. Without being bums, we undergo things like the race to the employment office windows all the time. And stealing the hot dog and rolling under the fence to escape the cop are magnificent fantasies of renouncing all debts, no matter how just. (The cop as symbol of authority is one thing, but no one would personify social inequity in a peripatetic hot dog vendor.) The Tramp as frank-furter thief illustrates how completely a slum boy can slough the mea-gerest scraps of social order. And the thing is, the higher in class you go, the more you feel the pressures of social forms and ties, so that there isn't a level of society from tramps on up whose members couldn't project into the perfect agility of Chaplin's trickster anarchy.

The sentimentality of *A Dog's Life* is something else altogether. Having the Tramp save a dog from a dogfight is a bit off because the dogs' ganging up on another dog only registers with us if we translate it out of its context—the dog pack—into ours. Translation out of con-text is one of Chaplin's richest veins; for instance, in the justly famous scene in the 1916 Mutual two-reeler *The Pawn Shop* when he listens to a broken alarm clock with a stethoscope, opens the back with a can opener and sniffs the contents for spoilage, and on from there. But the incongruity of treating a dog who's losing a dogfight as an *under*dog doesn't really occur to Chaplin. He takes your approval of the emotion for granted, but it doesn't reach your imagination the way less purely affective incongruity does; for instance, when he feeds the dog milk from a nearly empty bottle by dipping the dog's tail in it and using it as a pacifier.

Chaplin next brings Edna Purviance on as an abused dance hall singer and gets a big laugh out of the storm of tears she rouses with a sad song. But then, because she's too shy to seduce the rough customers into buying drinks, she's fired and cheated of her pay. So the Tramp rescues her just as he had the dog. The three of them form a cute little family, but there's something diminished about this kind of response; your mind is not racing to keep up as it does when he takes that clock apart. And the Tramp's interest in Edna is just too darned innocent. It's one thing for Harold Lloyd playing some boy living with his grand-mother or fresh out of his parents' house to be shy around girls. When he courts his future wife Mildred Davis in *Grandma's Boy*, he doesn't show any great virility, but that's the point of the movie. He becomes a man and a conventional hero by learning to be physically assertive, to stand up for himself. In *A Dog's Life* the Tramp starts out with physi-cal aggression as one of his resources, and there's no question of it making a man of him—he's a dog. But dogs are notorious for their urges, whereas you wouldn't necessarily guess from their films together that Chaplin and Purviance had been lovers in actuality. Really he's

neither man nor dog when he helps the dog and the girl out. He's starting to worry about his reputation; he's becoming the keeper of his own
flame.

Pay Day, a 1922 two-reeler (his last), was made at the far end of the
First National contract from A Dog's Life, when Chaplin was eager to
start releasing through the recently formed UA. It's a later movie that
Chaplin slapped together in a hurry, but it doesn't suffer from its econo-
my. Pay Day is also about leading a dog's life; however, Chaplin didn't
try to gain consistency from feeling, and it's altogether more interesting
to me now. Here the Tramp isn't really a tramp but a lowly construction laborer. His first task requires pickaxing in a trench almost deeper
than he is tall to loosen dirt that he then shovels out. The amount of effort in his visible upper body translates into a merely inconvenient
saucerful of dirt in the shovel, until the foreman is standing directly in
his path; then he tosses out a whopping mound. Having hit the foreman in the face, Chaplin ducks down into the trough, just before Edna
(playing the foreman's daughter) arrives. Looking for her father, she
gracefully skips over the trench, immediately after which Chaplin's
head pops up, as if out of a toaster, his eyes round as English muffins.
His expression isn't randy, and in fact later he moons over her from behind, as if she were untouchable (he dries the potential moistness with
a stinky cheese joke). But you know that his vision of her now includes
a glance up her skirts. It isn't downright raunchy, but it's not the joke
of a gentleman-poet-dreamer, either.

The Tramp then has to stack bricks on a second-story platform as
they're tossed up to him by workers below. It's an amusingly buggy sequence, which Chaplin announces with a stage artiste's prance and a
fanny waggle before he begins catching bricks, as fast as they can be
hurled, on his insteps, behind his knees, on the shelf of his rump, behind
his back without looking, tight and high between his legs. It was filmed
in reverse, of course, which gives it its fantastic quality and a deranged
emphasis on the physicality of labor. By removing the possibility of
mishap, Chaplin gives manual labor a weightless momentousness. It's a
light-spirited defiance of the law of gravity (and one of the few times
that like Keaton, Chaplin thought in terms of laws more ineluctable
than man's; the snowstorm in The Gold Rush is another).

In Pay Day Chaplin also avoids the idealization of women that
makes their roles so pastel-smudgy in many of his pictures. In addition
to Edna's minor role here, there's Phyllis Allen as the laborer's enormous, mean wife, who paces outside the construction yard on payday
to shake him down. She sees him secreting bills in his hat lining and so

follows him, only to watch him pass a flirtatious lovely on the street and, calculating how much money he'll need to entertain a girl like her that night, transfer some more money from pocket to hat. He then turns and bumps into this wall of a wife, one look at whom tells us why he stays out carousing as late as possible.

We then cut to the end of his hard night boozing with the boys, which includes prime bits involving overcoats and umbrellas, and, even better, the crush of passengers boarding a streetcar. First Charlie can't run straight enough to beat the crowd; then an auto cuts him off; the third time, fired with determination, he just climbs over the other people in line, putting his boot on a man's hatted head. He's the first on board, but the crowd behind him jams him all the way through the car to the front, like forcemeat. When a fat man hoists himself on at the back, Charlie is excreted out the front. Next he manages to get a grip on a car that passengers are clustered on like insects, but the pants he's holding onto give way, and he's on the street again while the man on the streetcar is left to ride home in his boxers. Finally, he spots a late-night wienie wagon, leaps on board, and picks up a paper to read while straphanging from a salami. The ogling, the drunkenness, the al-most crawly swarm of riders, the de-pantsing, the salami: Chaplin is marvelously unfazed by baseness here.

It seems appropriate to call Chaplin the Tramp in *Pay Day* because he has the same low-down resourcefulness as a character and the same opportunistic incoherence as an entertainer keeping an eye on the main chance in every setup. The look in Chaplin's eyes is different in this pic-ture from the more directly appealing look of *A Dog's Life* (both be-fore and after the employment office worker refuses to give him a handout, for instance). He's not heaving sighs in our laps, even when he longs for Edna. And he frankly isn't bothered that the husband-wife relationship is grisly, because he doesn't expect any sympathy for being mismated. When he wanted to, Chaplin knew how to mime the solidi-ty of our self-centeredness—self-centeredness not as a vice but as a fact, like a territorial border, that surrounds, in fact, defines, all personality—and then play it against his prerogative as a performer to defy any defi-nition of personality.

Pay Day doesn't have any special payoff. The last sequence shows the laborer straggling home just in time to get up for work, and his wife catching him trying to get some sleep, in the tub if the bed's off-limits. It just ends, with a close-up of the wife *schimpf*ing and a shot of his dripping-wet legs. But its combination of low humor and high in-ventiveness, lack of illusion about its subject, and unfailing faith in comedy make it fitting as Chaplin's last short, a more lived-in return to the glories he had achieved at Mutual. The Victorian-reformist *A Dog's Life* is a great movie for kids. It indicates that if things are rotten for you, there's some abiding spirit that cares. *Pay Day* says that you and your carcass are on your own; it *should* have been Henry Miller's favorite Chaplin.

If there was a battle, as well as collaboration, between sentimentality and slapstick in Chaplin's pictures, eventually a kind of soulful nobility came to dominate as he smoothed out his creative incoherence as a lead performer. (He increasingly reached for the kind of unity he had earlier ripped, in *The Pawn Shop,* for instance, when he undercut the hearts-and-flowers happy ending with an applause-prompting end-of-the-act stage jig.) Thus the voice we hear from the Jewish Barber in *The Great Dictator* isn't the voice of the raucous *Pay Day* bricklayer, and it isn't even the voice of a comic stage Jew, in contrast to the Yiddish inflections of the other Jewish characters (except for Goddard) who live in the movie's ghetto. But the incongruity of his featureless voice is sanctimonious—it's the voice not of the Tramp in *A Dog's Life* but of the film's director, telling us that the predicament of "the little fellow" isn't a British thing, a German or a Jewish thing, or a working-class thing, since the Barber is petit bourgeois, a shop owner. It's a human thing, the same everywhere. (It's a small world, after all.) The Barber embodies a concept of insignificance that Chaplin associates with all kinds of moral worthiness—honesty, hard work, courtesy, gallantry, the whole load. At one early point, Schultz says he'll get the Barber the Tomainian cross for his heroic efforts, and the Barber demurs: "That's all right, sir, I'm only too willing to oblige." But though the Barber goes through the bewildering rituals of battle slapstick with that meekly uncomplaining voice, there is an undertone of complaint—how can the Germans think of Jews as aliens when they served their country in the conflict? (as if resistance to racial discrimination needed to be justified at that level)—as well as the implicit claim that the little man doesn't know why he's fighting, that he's not responsible for the state of the world.

Although his star rose unimaginably fast, Chaplin's use of squalid settings for his movies never carries the implication of social protest over his own experience of poverty (not even the 1917 Mutual two-reeler *The Immigrant,* with its herded steerage passengers). A new, lush life offered itself within a few years of his debut in pictures, and Chaplin wanted to be "worthy" of it. So although he drew his comedy from memories of his childhood in a more literal sense than any other screen comedian, he had a complicated reaction to how those sources pegged him socially. In 1912, back in London between tours of the United States, he attended a party on Fred Karno's sumptuous houseboat. Suddenly a man in a rowboat "dressed in white flannels, with a lady reclining in the back seat" shouted derisively across the water at Karno and his guests:

> "Oh, look at my lovely boat, everyone! Look at my lovely boat!" . . . Karno leaned over the rail and gave him a very loud razzberry, but nothing deterred his hysterical laughter. "There is only one thing to do," I said: "to be as vulgar as he thinks we are." So I let out a violent flow of Rabelaisian invective, which was so embarrassing for his lady that he quickly rowed away.

The "Rabelaisian invective," though Chaplin would not have called it that at the time he needed it, surely, is the more likely voice of the Tramp, but it was probably too painfully revealing for Chaplin to use on-screen. As Constance Collier, who David Robinson guesses may have coached Chaplin in elocution, said of him in the 1910s, "It was impossible to go to the big restaurants . . . [because] he couldn't bear the masses of knives and forks on the table, and the magnificence of the head waiters gave him a feeling of inferiority."

Once Chaplin was a beloved international star, wealthy and courted by celebrities, he knew that the sources of his art—stealing food, for example, which is a staple of the biographies of boys who grew up in slums—were increasingly far away. When he followed Lady Astor in speaking to fishermen in her constituency, he said, "It's all very well for us millionaires to tell you how to vote, but our circumstances are quite different from yours." So he must have known that it isn't the Jewish Barber, to whom he piously condescends, who is close to the Chaplin of 1939 and 1940, but Hynkel, the autocrat who runs things his way and becomes enraged over *inconveniences,* don't mention opposition. (Chaplin had worked for fourteen years up through 1936 on a project to star himself as Napoleon, and it's conceivable that this aborted project fed his performance as Hynkel, though it appears his view of Napoleon wasn't as negative as his view of Hitler.)

As all testimony reveals, Chaplin was the autocratic head of his own studio and enjoyed all the prerogatives that brought. Already in 1917 Carlyle Robinson, hired as Chaplin's publicist, had noted the "comedy" of Chaplin's imperial daily arrival at his studio: "Instantly everyone stopped whatever they were doing. Actors, stagehands, electricians, everybody stood in line, at attention. Then Chaplin entered the studio gates. . . . They might just as well have blown a trumpet or fired a cannon." A studio typist told Robinson, "the whole gang does that [every day] for a gag. Charlie has no illusions, but he adores it!" The typist tried to make it sound innocuous, but this comic pomp was darkly revealing. Twenty-some years later, while watching footage of Hitler in preparation for the role of Hynkel, Chaplin called out, "Oh, you bastard, you son-of-a-bitch, you swine. I know what's in your mind," which we can take as both an accusation and a confession. For instance, footage of Hitler can be matched for grotesqueness by a snippet from the unused footage of *The Immigrant* shot in 1917 that David Robinson describes: "One of the out-takes for this last shot contains an unrehearsed moment: the extras are clearly not acting to order, and Charlie the Tramp is suddenly transformed into Chaplin the director, turning on them in sudden rage." "Son-of-a-bitch" is exactly the term Eddie Sutherland used to describe Chaplin when warning Harry Crocker what his worst days as Chaplin's new assistant would be like, and Henri d'Abbadie d'Arrast chipped in that the star had "a sadistic streak." And Jim Tully, another assistant, wrote in 1927, "Never did a despot dominate a country as Chaplin rules his studio."

All of which works for *The Great Dictator.* After all, we are a mass audience, with, partially, a mass psychology; so when after Hynkel's first speech, Chaplin pulls his old stunt of pouring water in his ear and spitting it out of his mouth, it has a new spiral as the act of a self-mythologizing emperor. One part of us grants self-proclaimed demigods enough credence to think they might have the powers they claim, and the water-squirting trick fits neatly with the kind of shamanism all honchos go in for. When we see the medicine show quack behind the curtain in *The Wizard of Oz,* it suits the part of us that's skeptical, but the image of the great and powerful Oz, booming at us from the flames and fumes, burrows deeper than skepticism.

Chaplin *is* torn by his political ideas, however, and so he explicitly approves of the Barber, who has no vices, as the Tramp did often enough, and certainly as Chaplin's rich soaks did. The Barber is by this stroke diminished, an ideal of harmlessness for us to identify with. But why should we? Chaplin, perhaps not entirely aware of the blazing egotism of it, doesn't fully identify with the Jewish Barber—he commissions for himself the plaster colossus Hynkel. We may not be dictators, but we all have our own realms where we are lords—at home if not at work, or *some*where. I identify more with Hynkel than with the Jewish Barber as well because Chaplin has not only made Hynkel more comically inventive (the Barber's routines—shaving a man in time to

radio music, staggering blind with too much luggage out on a project-
ing beam—feel standard, whereas Hynkel's feel newly conceived for
his "glorious" standing) but also put more of what he knows and feels,
more of actual observed behavior, into the fascist demon. In movies,
fascist demons and asexual no-name saints both emerge from the tradition of melodrama; in life, most people would probably say they'd met
far more of the former.

Still, most comedy, not just slapstick, gets us to like the hero by
showing him as a dreamer, a misfit, even a loser. This is why Keaton
and Lloyd are able to merge slapstick and romantic comedy so smooth-
ly. However, there's a rarer kind of comedy that lands on our beaches
like a tsunami, the kind in which the protagonist is a winner and just
keeps outwitting his opponents to the triumphant, if maddening, end.
Walter Burns in *The Front Page* is this kind of comic hero. In the 1931
version, Adolphe Menjou is utterly believable as a man used to getting
his way in business, and as a result you can see how his aura of power
makes him sexually attractive (as you could again with Ian Richard-
son's Prime Minister Francis Urquhart in the BBC series *House of
Cards, To Play the King,* and *The Final Cut.*) With Cary Grant in the
role, we're helpless. We're drawn to power and success, and Chaplin's
Hynkel in the early part of the movie has that kind of charisma. And
he develops it: at one point, Hynkel grabs a blonde secretary and
snorts in the same way he had when speaking of the Jews at the rally.
Here Chaplin is getting at some weird combination of libido and aggression, divulging a dirty little secret that only people with the force
to get to the top are in on. However, Chaplin is leery of showing himself *securely* roosting atop the world. Hynkel doesn't keep winning to
the end.

To energize the picture in the last third, Chaplin brings on Jack
Oakie as Benzino Napaloni, dictator of Bacteria. The silly, insulting
names throughout (punning on adenoids, herring, garbage, bacteria,
and ptomaine, a stew of bodily functions, disease, and decay) don't really tell you how good Chaplin's and Oakie's scenes together are.
Oakie's entrance is inauspicious, largely because Chaplin had grown so
careless as a director that the process shots of Napaloni's train arriving
at the Bahnhof don't match. But as soon as Oakie debarks, he gives the
movie an unexpected heartiness. The business of the two dictators not
knowing whether to salute or shake hands (a routine Max Linder performed with hats and handshakes, even faster) isn't fresh, but you
quickly realize that, as with Chaplin's Hynkel, it isn't really the physical stunts that are getting to you; it's the comedy of the force of person-

ality. Oakie's Napaloni is a man without nerves and an out-and-out vulgarian who constantly does and says things (in Italian-immigrant English) that should destroy his image as a big shot, like calling Hynkel, "Hynkie, my dictator frien'." But in another way, this makes him believable as a politico—a porcine Tammany machinist puffing himself up to the size of a parade balloon. Napaloni has the common touch, and you're drawn to his buffoonish health.

Oakie's arrival also brings on a strange transition to a broader contest between satire and slapstick that we saw with the radio microphone. Whether Chaplin intended it or not, the satire gives way to the slapstick in a structural sense when Napaloni's rivalry with Hynkel makes you feel for Hynkel. Though I find the actors' performances hilarious, I can imagine not finding the Hynkel-Napaloni routines funny. However, you're put in the position of pulling for Hynkel if you're going to go along with the movie at all. The rivalry we see was real—Chaplin and Oakie reportedly played to the crew, trying to outdo each other for laughs, and Chaplin was a sore loser: "Finishing a scene in which he felt that Oakie had scored the biggest laughs from the bystanders, he could hardly conceal his irritation."

But Chaplin's script gives Napaloni an edge. Hynkel raves with total confidence on the podium but is persnickety and worried in his office alone with his propaganda minister Garbitsch (Henry Daniell). (Hynkel speaks English, again violating Chaplin's original intention of making a talkie without talking very much.) This is yet another indication that the topical political satire is only the catalyst, but not the central element of the movie, because you can feel Chaplin putting Hynkel in the role of the underdog. When Napaloni catches on to Garbitsch's trick of seating visitors to Hynkel's office in a low chair facing a portrait head of the Dictator, Napaloni perches his hams on Hynkel's desktop, stubs out one cigarette on the bust, and strikes a match off it to light another. Or when Napaloni, absently tossing peanut shells in Hynkel's face at a military review, claims credit for Bacteria for the show of air power, you want him to be wrong; when the planes crash, you're disappointed to find out he was. Even in the bratty competition of the two tyrants raising their barber chairs in order to be seated higher than the other, you pull for Hynkel, but Hynkel is the one who hits his head on the ceiling and slidewhistles all the way back down. Wanting Hynkel to win out over Napaloni lowers you to sandbox level, but with spirit and force.

Discussing the "two real points of human nature involved" in the gag of dropping ice cream from the balcony where he's seated onto the dowager below in the 1917 two-reeler *The Adventurer,* Chaplin wrote:

> One was the delight the average person takes in seeing wealth and luxury in trouble. The other was the tendency of the human being to experience within himself the emotions he sees on the stage or screen. . . .
>
> If I had dropped the ice cream, for example, on a scrubwoman's neck, instead of getting laughs sympathy would have been aroused for the woman. Also, because a scrubwoman has no dignity to lose, that point would not have been funny. Dropping ice cream down a rich woman's neck, however, is, in the minds of the audience, just giving the rich what they deserve.

It's interesting that though Chaplin speaks from the perspective of underclass resentment, claiming that "nine tenths of the people in the world are poor, and secretly resent the wealth of the other tenth," which certainly included him, even in 1917, he thinks that a scrubwoman "has no dignity to lose." This implies that though he resents wealth, it represents dignity to him by itself. The Hynkel-Napaloni scenes turn *The Great Dictator* around in these terms: Hynkel has dignity to lose and so is fair game. But there's a slapstick response Chaplin didn't figure into his statement: when a *protagonist* consistently loses his dignity, even if he is rich and powerful, we start to root for him. Slapstick humanizes. The original objective of the satire was to strip Hitler of his dignity, but in the act, the two points of human nature came together for Chaplin and his audience—although we delight in seeing the powerful Dictator in trouble, we identify with the frustrations he undergoes in his contest with his rival.

With its dual leads, both of whom we can identify with (though in different ways and in spite of their creator's conscious intentions), *The Great Dictator* goes in for more writerly kinds of symmetry than Chaplin had ever attempted before. (Unfortunately he skipped the most important symmetry, between the Barber's and Hynkel's experiences in World War I, the one parallel that could have given the movie some historical depth.) However, the Barber's infamous final speech shows the problems of a scenarist who isn't a writer. (Remember, the silent slapstick comedies in which Chaplin was schooled were shot without scripts.)

But there are structural problems with the scripted ending of *The Great Dictator* that no amount of spontaneity or personality could cover. It's a problem that there's no transition from Hynkel's treaty banquet with Napaloni to the duck-hunting scene in which Hynkel is mistaken for the Barber who has escaped from a concentration camp. Chaplin just seems to be ready for the last act, and on it comes. This means that there's no culmination to Hynkel's rivalry with Napaloni as a slapstick story. The culmination is the attack on Osterlich, which is borrowed from headlines, and in 1940 scarcely had slapstick or satirical resonance. Chaplin took on the subject because it was big and urgent, but he didn't have the right skills to make it work. I would guess that the urgency enabled Chaplin to excuse himself for whatever was ramshackle in the construction. Getting the message out mattered most; the Barber's impassioned six-minute speech took over the movie from the tail end.

Chaplin *was* taking a big chance by seeking comedy in bad news, but he didn't drill through to the core. He comes close in one quick bit of the Barber in the prison camp—the prisoners are made to goose-step in tight ranks, and the Barber's place is unfortunately in front of a very tall man. (It isn't Chaplin's fault for not guessing what the camps would be used for.) Chaplin's ability to see comedy in proximity to the gruesome developed as early as his childhood when he laughed with the other onlookers as sheep slaughterers bumblingly chased an escapee from the abattoir next to his family's backstreet room. (When he realized what the sheep's fate would be, he ran "screaming and weeping to [his] Mother, 'They're going to kill it!'") But when the storm troopers return to the ghetto after the Jewish banker Epstein has refused to finance the Anschluss, we get straight melodrama. There's almost no sense of the slaughterhouse, in the literal or existential sense, in Chaplin. In a movie about Nazi Germany, even in 1940, that's not something to brag about, and there's none in *Shoulder Arms* or *Monsieur Verdoux*, either. (*Shoulder Arms* turns an infantry trench into a shooting gallery. This is one of the ways in which Céline's slapstick world of horror is more complete than Chaplin's.) In *The Great Dictator*'s version of Kristallnacht, an old Jewish man is made to scrub a sidewalk, and the SS shoots a young Jew who defends his father, the only death in the movie.

And then shortly we come to the speech given by the Barber, who, on the run in stolen military garb, is mistaken for Hynkel and so must make a broadcast to the now extended realm to preserve his disguise. Reluctant at first, the Barber quickly warms to the opportunity to address the atrocities (limited as they are) that we've witnessed. The speech is meant as an antidote to Hynkel's mad-dog foamings, and so Chaplin has chosen to make the Barber's vigor answer Hynkel's. But it misfires, because Chaplin's thinking is rambling, with a vacillating attitude toward progress, and such puzzling exclamations as "And so long as men die, liberty will never perish." It's especially unfortunate that the Barber blames the world situation on greed, speed, machinery, knowledge, and cleverness, because we haven't seen these "vices" in the movie. Hynkel isn't especially greedy—he's in love with power and with the drama of galvanizing his audience with prejudicial rant. He's theatrical, which is something Chaplin advocated: "An idea without theatrical sense is of little value. It is more important to be effective. With a theatrical sense one can be effective about nothing." Hynkel's is the most effective kind of theatricality about the most morally vicious (and politically disastrous) kinds of nothing. But the Barber's speech is also "effective"—when he talks about doing away with "grrrrrrrreed," you hear the rolling tones of an actor impressing himself with his high-mindedness. Furthermore, addressing the speech to Hynkel's soldiers doesn't resonate for us because we haven't met any in the picture; the Barber aims abstractions at abstractions. Chaplin as the Barber gets carried away with virtue, but unlike Hynkel, the Barber is not able to carry us with him.

Hard to believe, but we were spared an even worse ending, a redemptive dunking, in which fascist soldiers hearing the speech were to abjure militarism and anti-Semitism—for example, a Nazi was to save a little Jewish girl from an oncoming car. I would say that the only way to end it would have been for the Barber in disguise as the Dictator to take over and reorder the society. In other words, to step the political problem up to the kind of fantasy Aristophanes used to resolve what in his plays were also urgent political problems, the Peloponnesian War, for instance. This is how Vittorio De Sica and Cesare Zavattini handled the problem of urban squalor in *Miracle in Milan*, which is a comic masterpiece. It may well be that Chaplin thought the Barber's speech had to be serious to have some practical effect; his own later reading of the speech over the radio suggests as much. For whatever reason, he didn't have the comic authority to *raise* the political calamity of fascism to the level of nonsense.

This speech has always rubbed a lot of people the wrong way because it's intellectually sentimental. (It's also weirdly self-deprecating in that its ambitions trivialize the much better comedy that leads up to it.) The inadequacy of Chaplin's ideas in response to Nazism offends even more people than his usual sentimentality does, but the speech just forms a subset of his larger failure to trust slapstick. Such a scene is unthinkable in a Keaton picture, as are most of the mawkish bits in Chaplin's movies. You can try the cynical save that he knew mawkishness worked on his paying audience, but I think it's clear that it worked on him as well.

So you can't say that Chaplin's mawkishness is altogether calculated or inauthentic, even if it makes you cringe. When the Barber speaks over the wires to Paulette Goddard's Hannah, crushed to earth by Tomainian soldiers invading Osterlich, where she has immigrated to escape the Reich, he speaks stirringly, "Hannah, can you hear me? Wherever you are, look up!" and it shot home to me that Chaplin had given Goddard's character his mother's name. In other words, he cast himself as the mover of the forces that crush the woman named for his mother, who herself was crushed by life. As a child, he was troubled by Hannah Chaplin's disturbed accusation when he visited her in the asylum to which he had had to commit her, "If only you had given me a cup of tea that afternoon I would have been all right." In *The Great Dictator* he took on that primal guilt, travestying it, turning it into clowning, but at the same time exaggerating it to the dimensions of the present world conflict. In *The Kid* Chaplin stepped in as an adult to right his own childhood as a semiorphan. (If he can't form a sexual bond with Edna as the mother, it's because his emotions relating to the situation are those of a boy, not a man.) With the Barber's speech in *The Great Dictator,* he's trying to rescue his mother but is haunted by the impossibility of the effort. (She had died in 1928.) In 1939 and 1940, an appeal to fascists' better natures can't have seemed very likely to succeed.

You could say that Chaplin wanted to horrify himself as much as possible by playing the man responsible for Hannah's condition. It may also explain why the courtship between the Barber and Hannah is so sexless, even though Chaplin is playing opposite his own wife. It could be that Chaplin feels sexless as the Barber opposite Goddard because he'd called her character Hannah, or it could go the other way— that he finally put a name to how he feels about his heroines. After all, *Modern Times* is no different. Chaplin wrote that "every man, whether he be young or old, when meeting any woman, measures the potentiality of sex between them. Thus it has always been with me." Offscreen, but not always on. And he didn't think that the role of sex was that significant in his movies: "Unlike Freud, I do not believe sex is the most important element in the complexity of behavior. Cold, hunger and the shame of poverty are more likely to affect one's psychology." Which may be fine (though not as an understanding of Freud), but the unsexiness of his comedy is what limits it as a representation of the world, no matter what it tells us about him. His incidental flirtation with the cop's wife in *The Kid,* like the brief bit with the secretary in *The Great Dictator,* are redolently goatish. These hoof clickings extend his comedy, and it's disappointing that his range isn't even lower.

Below-the-waist comedy *had* been one of Chaplin's earliest instincts on the stage. In late 1900, when Chaplin was eleven, the Eight Lancashire Lads were hired to play cats and dogs in a Christmas pantomime. Though playing a cat, Chaplin sniffed another boy's rear end and then lifted his leg against the proscenium. As an adult in pictures during the enforced sanitization of popular culture that lasted from the early days of vaudeville until the 1970s, Chaplin had to avoid overly explicit messy jokes. Though nothing a family couldn't snicker over, some tainted matter still got in: the stuffed dog that the drunkard Charlie thinks has pissed in his hat in *The Cure,* wet babies in *The Kid* and *The Great Dictator,* the suggestion of piles of horse, mule, and elephant dung to be shoveled in *City Lights.* Moreover, Chaplin's very movements make us aware of his body, wriggling, itching, hungry, in a refined way that isn't *too* refined, thank God. In *The Great Dictator,* however, the Barber-Tramp *is* refined. Hynkel gets all the coarse humor—pouring a glass of water down the front of his own pants and flapping them as if to distribute it evenly; bumping the globe balloon off his rump—and with it a more volatile physical expressiveness. As a result, he's comic in a fuller sense.

The duality of Dictator and Barber, of egotism and universality, bodily humor and family humor, cruelty and sentimentality, show that in *The Great Dictator* Chaplin has made an allegory of some of his earliest, strongest impulses and their cancellation. At the same time that Chaplin is playing his largest-scale villain, literally a world-class bastard—acting on his childhood perception that villains "were more colorful than the hero" and therefore the most desirable parts when playing theater with chums—he's denying the basic cruelty behind his comic persona by giving us the nice-nice Jewish Barber. His biography shows, however, that there's a certain degree of sadism even in the Tramp's trademark waddle. As he told an interviewer in 1916, "he had based his characteristic shuffling walk on that of an old man called 'Rummy' Binks":

> When I saw Rummy shuffle his way across the pavement to hold a cabman's horse for a penny tip, I was fascinated. The walk was so funny to me that I imitated it. When I showed my mother how Rummy walked, she begged me to stop because it was cruel to imitate a misfortune like

that. But she pleaded while she had her apron stuffed into her mouth. Then she went into the pantry and giggled for ten minutes.

The cruel and sentimental sides *could* coexist in the Tramp character; it's Chaplin who set them against each other in *The Great Dictator,* but in conflicting ways.

However, the egotism, bodily humor, and cruelty make the choice an easy one for some of us; we're solidly on the Dictator's side, when it's a question of entertainment. *The Great Dictator* is fascinating because Chaplin seems to be admitting so much about himself, but without an out-and-out admission—he doesn't play a movie director or actor. He's led in by the desire to make a political statement, but the intention fractures in the articulation, which is perhaps more personally revealing than a more coherent political critique would have been (one that he was capable of writing, anyway). And though Chaplin probably wouldn't have wanted the public to realize how much of his parody of Hitler was a parody of his own personality, he might have been drawn to this unsparing self-inspection, because, as Thomas Burke recounted, Chaplin "liked being hurt, and I realised that his cold-blooded nature was interested in the throbbing of the neuralgia and the effects of the throbbing. He loves studying himself."

Chaplin's absorption in himself, such as he was, is cousin to the wonderful egotism with which he said of Hitler, "The face was obscenely comic—a bad imitation of me." Even political repulsion comes in the *artist*'s characteristic medium—"The salute with the hand thrown back over the shoulder, the palm upward, made me want to put a tray of dirty dishes on it." *The Great Dictator* preserves in monumental form Chaplin's refusal to fuse his various impulses as a performer. Here his impulses, toward selfishness and innocence, play tug-of-war with the actor's body. But though the two incarnations can be mistaken for each other, they never meet. At the same time, there's another scale along which the performance is measured—Chaplin playing out his grungy Tramp comedy from memories of his down-and-out childhood in London while enjoying the heights of fame, wealth, and social success that comedy had brought him to.

I think the Dictator gains more than the Barber from the crosscurrents. Hynkel is Chaplin's mirror image once the aggressive, antisocial Tramp had turned into the fabulously wealthy and powerful man who still saw the comedy and allure of raising hell with the people around him. I can't say that Chaplin as the Dictator or the Barber returned to the flowing changeability of the Tramp in his earliest triumphs.

Though divided, Chaplin's star persona is more than settled in *The Great Dictator*—it's petrified; the magma has cooled. But Hynkel is a more honest performance than the Barber and is the most complete and accurate record Chaplin gave in his movies of what it was like to be him once he had become him.

CHAPTER THREE

Junior: Harold Lloyd and Buster Keaton

The Sunset Inn in Los Angeles, an "ordinary" restaurant at the beach but with "the best dance band in town," hosted "regular Saturday night parties . . . where [Roscoe] Arbuckle, Buster Keaton, and other comedians entertained everyone well into the morning hours." When the owners decided to name a dish in honor of star cutup Buster Keaton, they made it a shrimp cocktail. As much as Chaplin, Harold Lloyd and Buster Keaton both keyed their comedy to their shrimpy builds. These three clowns, long ranked as the major silent slapstick stars, all had wiry, athletic frames on an unimposing scale, and we now assume a connection between their physical stature and how we feel about slapstick protagonists in general. This helps in part explain *why* they have been canonized as the top three.

But there's a major distinction among them: Chaplin's range as a performer is less restricted than Lloyd's or Keaton's. Neither of them ever played a character as stylistically volatile as the Tramp or as extreme as the ranting Great Dictator. Chaplin can go so far because he interprets his physique for us as implying that this wisp could never belong anywhere, to anyone, and so the common social restrictions on behavior don't apply to him. Chaplin originally used this freedom to be less, as well as more, delicate: he would play the less against the more. But from his Essanay shorts on, and ever increasingly, Chaplin's persona had a higher proportion of Pierrot to Harlequin than Lloyd's or Keaton's, and Chaplin came close to equating pathos with art. This meant he began using his build to certify his underdog pedigree, not only opposite big-guy adversaries like Eric Campbell and Mack Swain but even opposite the boy newsies who shoot peas at him in *City Lights*.

Lloyd and Keaton interpret their physiques as the outer form of an in-between stage in a boy's life, when his desperation to play a part in the society around him far outdistances his know-how. Lloyd described his autobiography as "pictures . . . of a boy growing into responsibilities," and that describes his and Keaton's features as well.

Their roles divide principally between eager working-class boys and passive or insouciant rich boys, but they're reassuringly consistent across the class spread. Especially in their feature films, which are almost all romantic comedies, Lloyd and Keaton associate their slightness with a young man's gamut of emotions and work out his dilemmas within the compact world he inhabits. It's a formula, but a satisfying one.

Romantic comedies with very young heroes are in part coming-of-age stories, and Lloyd and Keaton draw on universal feelings associated with growing up, fitting in, and winning a girl. But they express these feelings through specialized stunts, which is why their theatrical naïveté still doesn't cloy. Adolescent stories are generally comic because time takes care of the fundamental problem, immaturity. Still, the comedy doesn't have to be as funny as it is in Lloyd's and Keaton's pictures. There's an excess in their movies that intensifies the thematic emotions without pushing them. Chaplin went further in his performing style, but some directions are better than others. Keaton, when he had control of his pictures, and even the wistful-by-golly Lloyd, were never *too* delicate.

Lloyd and Keaton were both in their twenty-eighth years when they switched to full-length pictures in the early twenties. They're men who on-screen yearn like adolescents for the girl, or for glory, which will get them the girl. Yet neither seems driven by hormones. Of the big three, only Chaplin ever comes across as horny; both Lloyd and Keaton played characters named Lamb. And I group the two of them in my mind though they're opposites in some ways. Lloyd is most memorable as the eternal juvenile, the freshman who believes that the right attitude and enough effort guarantee results. With a cartoon inability to remain flattened, his discouragement is always a passing emotional mood. Keaton's boys also make valiant efforts, but with their propensity to be fascinatingly stymied, their discouragement opens onto a vision of the greater forces arrayed against them. Lloyd's discouragement always gives way to another burst of optimism, whereas Keaton's fatalism lingers even after a climactic break in his bad luck enables him to get what he wants. For instance, near the beginning of his 1928 feature *Speedy,* Harold and his girl, after a day of fun at Coney Island, imagine the future in a home of their own: their twin boys have Harold's round glasses drawn on their faces. Harold will keep meeting the melodramatic obstacles until the dream is set to become reality. By contrast, at the end of Keaton's 1927 feature *College,* after Buster has won the girl by means of a sporting victory and a physical assault on his rival, the movie projects forward to Buster's married life. However, it doesn't stop with kiddies: it dissolves to the couple as oldsters living alone, and then to his-and-hers gravestones. When Lloyd jumps ahead to the lovers' dotage at the end of his 1938 feature *Professor Beware* to show that his Egyptologist has escaped the fatal curse, the old man appears to think this means he needn't fear death now at all.

Chaplin, with his shabby clothes and twitchy face and walk, doesn't register as a romantic lead. Even when he ends up with the girl, as in *The Immigrant, The Gold Rush,* or *Modern Times,* the plot of the movie isn't synonymous with his courtship, because his character is founded on a lack of attachments. The Tramp isn't the marrying kind; even when he's married, as in *Pay Day,* he doesn't identify his pleasure or comfort with the wife. By contrast, Lloyd and Keaton pass for handsome juveniles (even though Keaton's sculptural mask is a bit special—it looks designed). They are not really grotesque, though they are exaggerated types, but not so exaggerated that they can't play love interests. Chaplin often pushes his image into the grotesque range, most memorably when he coquettes gruesomely, shrugging his shoulders and making sheep eyes. Sexually he's a bit too gamy for romantic comedy.

Lloyd reflects the average moviegoer, as everyone has always said. It's tempting to say the same of Keaton, which may sound odd, but the magnetic impassivity that makes him seem so special also makes him seem unactory. (For this reason, Keaton and Louise Brooks require less adjustment for today's viewers than such greater silent actors as Lars Hanson and Lillian Gish.) Lloyd looks ready for the street in his characteristic two-button suit, straw boater, and round glasses. (The glasses were nonprescription, and he didn't wear them off-screen.) The hat was standard gear in the twenties, and the horn-rimmed glasses were a novel-but-acceptable fashion item that he felt "allowed [Harold] to be the boy next door or anyone you could see." Keaton had his recognizable stage clown getup (which in the movies was less grotesque than his miniature adult getup had been in the family's vaudeville act), but he could abandon this outfit for period costumes, uniforms, rich boy's dress clothes, or a different kind of oddball effect appropriate to the story (e.g., the sissified ensemble he wears home from college in *Steamboat Bill, Jr.*).

According to Keaton, the silent clowns made the characters and plots in the longer-format films relatively normal as a matter of principle: "Once we started into features we had to stop doing impossible gags and ridiculous situations. We had to make an audience believe our story." Keaton gets by as an average guy in his short films largely because the format is so concise the audience has to assume a lot about the character anyway. So we take his remoteness in stride and even appreciate it because his muted responses don't get in the way of the fast-paced miniplots. But in his features, the mass audience expects not just possible gags but more emotional emphasis and doesn't get it—he may care for a cow *(Go West)* or his locomotive *(The General)* as much as for the girl. But the features do show Keaton acting out the male movie-goer's fantasy of proving himself and making good and involve him with boats and trains and gadgets. And then those muted responses draw us into a mesmerizingly unfamiliar range for slapstick, if we follow him. As Agee wrote, "There are people who never much cared for Keaton. Those who do cannot care mildly."

Lloyd seems to have been that normal guy he plays, but his character's seeming so had to be manufactured. When you see the shorts he made before coming up with the "glasses character," as he referred to him, you realize that he needed *some* kind of rigging to bring his face into focus. In the 1915 Keystone two-reeler *Court House Crooks,* Lloyd, as a young man framed for theft, seems peculiarly defenseless without the glasses. You understand why he had a rough start in the movies, working for several years as an extra. As he said of the persistence that was necessary at the start of his career, "The few directors I trapped gave me an indifferent glance and told me I wasn't a motion picture type. Everybody who spoke to me at all, told me that."

When Lloyd assembled a tramp costume (tight where Chaplin's was loose) to create the character of Lonesome Luke (for a series of one-, two-, and three-reelers made from 1915 to 1917) he wisely adopted a mustache, which he applied as two widely spread smudges in no known style. The mustache makes us look at him, but Luke's impassivity, unlike Keaton's, still doesn't provide enough of a show. As Luke, Lloyd doesn't exactly imitate Chaplin but searches for the ground the great precursor hasn't covered—yet clearly in Chaplin's mode of mangy isolation. You do remember Luke wambling like a speed walker, as if he could move in fast and slow motion at the same time. However, unlike the Tramp's movements, which Chaplin strung together in an array of tempos, Luke's movements are mechanically eccentric. He's deflectable but not stoppable, a cowardly, adaptable gyroscope.

Most important, Luke doesn't draw on Lloyd's enormous power to generate empathy. Lloyd himself wasn't happy as an imitator and so dropped the successful Luke character to develop the glasses character. A sound instinct, because the glasses make you concentrate on his face and make him seem both commonplace and yet sensitive, as if he were going to need a little extra help to achieve the happiness that normality supposedly ensures. They help him create a little drama before the story has started. But even with the glasses that enlarge his eyes, which are small by silent movie star standards, Lloyd's average handsomeness doesn't register until he starts playing an almost nerdily eager boy. Then his desperation pushes his scattering efforts into the realm of comedy, and his good looks make a happy ending seem inevitable.

Lloyd's comments about his screen persona to his 1959 interviewers suggest that he knew the contour of this persona well: "They must like you. They must feel sorry for you, they must work with you, and of course laugh at you, at your idiosyncrasies and your mistakes, but at the same time, they like you and they're with you and trying to help you." He accomplished this effect most pleasurably in his romantic comedy features. With his deftness at realistic pantomime, he comes across as touchingly foolish, but still a good date. We smile at his adolescent invincibility—he looks determinedly at the camera and pumps his fist down and snaps his head: he *won't* give up. And we laugh out loud when he mimes the flickering of opposite emotions in the middle of slapstick fiascos. His sickly smile when he keeps chewing a mothball or a dog biscuit or a powder pad because spitting it out would hurt him with the girl is classic. Still, as funny as his act is, it relies on a few tender moments to hold the story together, and Lloyd is surprisingly effective in scenes of direct emoting. He had the perfect light talent to match the requirements he theorized.

Keaton went in the opposite direction, never directly seeking sympathy, as he said in the late fifties:

> In our early successes, we had to get sympathy, to make any story stand up. But the one thing that I made sure of was that I didn't ask for it. If the audience wanted to feel sorry for me, that was up to them, I didn't ask for it in action. Certainly Chaplin has done that, asked for it—I've seen him do it—he gets sorry for himself.

A Lloyd character will feel the self-pity typical of a young man, and he's actually moving, in a prettified, movieish way, when he throws himself back against a tree trunk and laughs through his tears in the 1924 feature *Girl Shy* because he can't afford to marry Jobyna Ralston. Keaton's adolescent persona has a deep-seated self-protecting wariness and sometimes approaches the blinky babyishness of Harry Langdon and Stan Laurel. But Buster doesn't play the kid to win our sentimental indulgence. When things go wrong for him, he often sits down and cheerlessly accepts his fate, almost as if the audience weren't there, which may explain why in the twenties they weren't, at least in the same numbers as at Chaplin's and Lloyd's pictures.

Luis Buñuel approved of Keaton as "the great specialist against all sentimental infection," but his underplaying is often overstated. It had a practical genesis. Keaton appeared regularly in his parents' vaudeville act from the age of four until he was twenty-two. Biographer Tom Dardis has summed up the father-son part of the act, which came to dominate it, as "a unique kind of improvised physical exchange between Buster and his father, a roughhouse dialogue involving a breathtaking series of violent encounters in which Buster either hit his father or was hit by him." Keaton's stone face followed his father's empirical observation that in their "strictly male roughhousing," "the laughs came when the child was serious and stopped whenever he smiled." As Buster said later, "If we got a laugh the blank pan or the puzzled puss would double it. [Joe] kept after me, never let up, and in a few years it was automatic."

However, as Agee pointed out, "Much of the charm and edge of Keaton's comedy . . . lay in the subtle leverages of expression he could work against his nominal dead pan." In other words, his pan isn't really dead; he simply doesn't use his mouth and cheek muscles to express feelings. (He does laugh and cry in Arbuckle's 1917 two-reeler *Coney Island*—he was capable of it; he just didn't like it for his own projects, not least because he remembered that the 1917 "preview audience hated it and hooted the scene.") He uses his eyes plenty, however: in his 1928 feature *The Cameraman*, for instance, we see just his eyes peeping up over a display card of tintypes at Marceline Day to convey that he's in love with her. In addition, his gestures are as eloquent as his eyes, even when they're so hesitant as to be self-canceling, such as his way of reaching out with his hands and moving them slightly in no effective direction, as if futility had overcome the impetus to gesture before the muscular effort were completed. And he has a way of nodding his head slowly at the person he's talking to—like the souvenir dogs we used to put in the back window of cars—that tells us he more than half suspects he isn't getting his point across. At times his gestures have a stop-and-start rhythm as if they were produced by pixilation shot in slow motion—he has a great, loose-jointed, rocking shamble when he's acting nonchalant right before hightailing it. And by means of carefully timed counterpoint to the action, we're never uncertain about Buster's feelings behind the stone face. (Though, of course, at times the stone face itself is what he's feeling.)

In the 1925 feature *The Freshman,* Harold cries when his feelings are hurt, and moves on. Though Keaton's persona has a somewhat lower emotional age range than Lloyd's, Keaton doesn't cry, because he's attentive to subnarrative layers of mechanical, perceptual, and even existential oddity in his situation. This is the greatest bonus of his not playing for emotion, but also the one that may put most people off just because it's so unusual, certainly for slapstick. Keaton never articulated what he was after in his movies in abstract language; he worked them out sheerly in terms of slapstick story construction, how to keep the laughs coming. He once said to his father, "A good comedy story can be written on a penny postcard." This leaves no room for the conscious, writerly development of subtext.

Though Keaton's movies work on more levels than Lloyd's, it took Lloyd a long time to find his style (after which he never varied it), whereas Keaton showed mature control from his first solo short (after several years supporting Roscoe Arbuckle in his casually artful Comique shorts). Because Keaton doesn't explicitly emote, his curiosity about larger physical forces blends with his conventional romantic comedies in an unprecedented and inimitable way. Keaton created a distinct character: a boyish man who knows it's time for him to impress his will on the world, but whose bones haven't yet learned the method. Moreover, he's prone to doubts that the big contraption of a universe is susceptible to human will. This is the underlying logic of Keaton's romantic comedies: Buster has to make an impression (on the girl, her father, the world) in the face of his own doubts about the way things go. To get what he wants, he has to overcome a skepticism rooted in physical experience.

What both Lloyd and Keaton settled on was the kind of predictable distinctiveness that makes a character comic. Henri Bergson wrote, "It is comic to fall into a ready-made category. And what is most comic of all is to become a category oneself into which others will fall, as into a ready-made frame; it is to crystallise into a stock character." This is what the comic actors of the silent era were trying to do; it's what makes the Tramp outfit, or Buster's porkpie hat and stony expression (which he referred to as "a valuable trade-mark"), or Harold's glasses so important. Along with his stock outfit, the clown has to marshal stylized movements, gestures, and expressions and have a nose for material and gags that will make the movie feel as if no one else could have starred in it. (This is the ideal; we love plenty of movies that fall somewhat short of it in one way or another.)

There's a further twist here: Lloyd sought and sought for the right costume and character because he wanted to crystallize as a readily recognizable type of fool, yet the boys he plays in his feature films need most of all to break their comic rigidity and become grown men, the constant source of tension in all of Lloyd's, and Keaton's, features. Bergson says that "what is essentially laughable is what is done automatically. In a vice, even in a virtue, the comic is that element by which the person unwittingly betrays himself." The classic example of this is the jig, handshake, and speech that Lloyd's character Harold Lamb has copied from the movies to introduce himself to his fellow undergrads in *The Freshman*. He says, "I'm just a regular fellow—step right up and call me Speedy," the irony residing in the fact that this little routine itself marks him as anything but a regular fellow. He's so naive and eager he doesn't realize that life isn't like the movies, though naturally *The Freshman* isn't like life but embroiders the adjustments all middle-class adolescents have to make when they go out on their own.

Bergson reasons that comedy has above all a social function: "Any individual is comic who automatically goes his own way without troubling himself about getting into touch with the rest of his fellow-beings. It is the part of laughter to reprove his absentmindedness and wake him out of his dream." Thus Keaton's gestures and minimal reactions are unmistakably his own, but because he's playing romantic comedy, the very qualities that make him identifiable as a star are the ones he must outgrow to win the girl.

However, there's plenty of wiggle room for comics to emphasize one aspect of this maladjustment over others. For example, with the exception of his virtuosic one-man two-reeler *One A.M.*, Chaplin's clashes are social to some degree—whether run-ins with coworkers, customers, bosses, rivals for employment or a streetcar, or cops, in general or as the impersonal enforcers of an unjust society. Even when you could say this of sequences in Lloyd's features, most obviously those involving the Latin American brigands in the 1923 feature *Why Worry?* or the conniving transportation company officers in *Speedy*, Harold's main enemy is himself. (It's precisely the absence of emotional motivation that makes many of the short glasses comedies unmemorable—they lack focus because without that rudderless innocence, Lloyd comes across as *too* ordinary a guy for us to identify with.) What's unusual for romantic comedy is that there's only one feature in which Harold has to overcome the objections of the girl's father (his first, *A Sailor-Made Man*, from 1921). In his features, Lloyd has to overcome cowardice, hypochondria, an untenable situation caused by his having written letters home to his country girlfriend about his success in the city, pathological shyness that causes him to stutter in the presence of girls, overeagerness, scrawniness, impracticality, and, of course, bad luck. Lloyd also discovered the importance family could play in comedy. He went from gently dubious parents in *The Freshman* to the dismissive and even threatening burly father and brothers in *The Kid Brother* two years later, and in some ways he gained in potency. Increasing the role of family strife externalized the hero's internal struggle as primal melodrama and by that stroke heightened it.

Keaton sees social forces at work in his comedy but has his own approach to them. On the one hand, when Buster is running from the entire municipal police force in his 1922 two-reeler *Cops,* he mainly cares about how his public disgrace affects him with the girl. But if you look at it another way, it appears that the standard young hero's efforts to impress his girl lead him into a fatal conflict with not just one cop but every cop in the city. Keaton crowns Chaplin's social-conflict checker piece by linking the basic emotional conflicts to much larger mechanical, historical, and natural forces.

To effect this, Keaton uses jaw-droppingly large and extensive life-size props, settings, and special effects: a house in *One Week,* an entire town of collapsing buildings in *Steamboat Bill, Jr.,* an ocean liner in *The Navigator,* twelve-foot-tall targets blown apart during naval gunning practice on the open sea in *The Love Nest,* a locomotive in *The General,* a full-stage Cyclorama machine in the talkie *Speak Easily,* Civil War battles in *The General,* a waterfall in *Our Hospitality,* a tornado in *Steamboat Bill, Jr.* Keaton enlarges the dimensions of his props as he plays with them from movie to movie: the toy train set in the 1922 two-reeler *The Electric House* and the absurdly little cannon on the deck of the 1924 feature *The Navigator* become the comic jaws-of-death cannon on the full-size railroad car speeding down the tracks in the 1927 feature *The General;* the flimsy stage flat housefront falling on top of Roscoe Arbuckle in the 1919 Comique two-reeler *Back Stage* becomes the more than full-weight housefront falling on Buster in the 1928 feature *Steamboat Bill, Jr.* You can *see* his ideas expand.

Lloyd and Keaton were conscious of the effects they wanted, but their movies don't feel calculated to death. You can laugh at routines you've seen ten times, in large part because of the sheer ingenuity of the gags, but also because it feels as if the stars have invested something of themselves in these essentially light stories, though they both thought of their work more as a craft than an art (unlike Chaplin). This feeling of investment comes in part from the method of shooting silent slapstick features, with all the gagmen pitching to the director-star, who chose among their ideas and improvised on them while shooting. Retrospectively Lloyd and Keaton could restate theories by which they developed their pictures, but on a day-to-day basis, they more likely worked intuitively, suiting everything in the final picture to their experienced measure of themselves as performers. Thus the hero's conflicts reflect the actor's, in part; Lloyd and Keaton certainly knew how to make movies feel personal even if they weren't autobiographical, though sometimes they were. Starring in romantic comedies about adolescents trying to become men, the vividly ordinary Lloyd and the extra(but also)ordinary Keaton get to us more than we might guess slapstick clowns could.

Harold Lloyd is the only silent comedian remembered entirely for feature films rather than shorts. In these features, Lloyd has genuine conventional charm of a kind that the more inventive Chaplin and the more mysterious Keaton lack. This charm arose when the advantages of the glasses character as a young man who could hold together a more nuanced romantic comedy plot were given room to develop by the longer-format film. Lloyd spent a lot of time getting this formula right, and when he does get it right, it feels fully deliberate, perhaps because he has by far the surest sense of structure of all the silent comedians. (He probably owed his structural sense to the fact that he trained in the legitimate theater rather than vaudeville, with its blackout sketch opportunism.) For instance, in *Girl Shy* the way he meets Jobyna by helping her sneak her dog on the train establishes a common motif for all the slapstick stunts in the sequence, even when they slide into stranger psychological territory. Lloyd ends this strangers-on-a-train sequence with the love-fuddled Harold sitting in a city intersection and nibbling a dog biscuit, without the distaste he could barely hide when he ate one earlier to shield the entrancing girl and her smuggled pooch from the conductor. And the biscuit box keeps coming back as a comically romantic-melancholic refrain throughout the entire picture. Lloyd knows that foolishness can burnish rather than tarnish silvery romantic pathos (also the effect of a top-drawer thirties comedy like *The Awful Truth*), and further that a capper can make funny-romantic sequences seem truly wonderful, gift wrapped.

Lloyd knew how to shape stories, but his deserved popularity also owes a lot to his specializing in regular-guy-interest slapstick—the daredevil human fly climax of *Safety Last!*, the one-conveyance-after-another chase at the end of *Girl Shy*, the football game climax of *The Freshman*, the knock-down-drag-out fistfight climax of *The Kid Brother*, the street fight and streetcar race in *Speedy.* Keaton said of himself, "Like so many other American boys I was 'mechanically inclined.' I spent a lot of my time tinkering, grinding the valves, taking apart and putting together again the motors of our car and the 25-foot cruiser boat Pop bought." But in his pictures, the equipment gets so large that you become aware of the grandeur of the forces driving them, and of the star-director as a jester-god in a mechanical world. With Harold, the actor's effort and athleticism (as distinct from acrobatics because his is the kind of physical skill the average boy is much more likely to have developed—taking up amateur boxing at age sixteen like Lloyd rather than learning all the stunt falls in the vaudeville repertory like Keaton) merge more completely with the character's.

Some of this is forecast in Lloyd's shorts; for instance, his 1920 two-reeler *Get Out and Get Under,* in which Harold is racing to the theater in his car with his costume in a suitcase on the backseat. He hits a bump that sends the suitcase flying into the road. In a hurry, he can't eat up time stopping the car, so he just hops out, runs back for the suitcase, catches up with the still-rolling car, tosses the suitcase in, and leaps back behind the wheel. But in fact he's thrown the suitcase all the way over the car, leaving it in the road again, so he has to repeat the sequence, again without stopping the car. Similarly, in the 1917 two-reeler *Lonesome Luke on Tin Can Alley,* he rides a bicycle through a restaurant kitchen, rolling over a counter on his back without unseating himself or taking his feet off the pedals. In these sequences, Lloyd invents strange new Olympic events; he certainly makes his characters' mishap-filled adventures as fun to watch as sports. The first glasses short, *Over the Fence* (1918), is in essence a condensed slapstick baseball game: to impress the girl, Harold becomes a pitcher and home run slugger for the Yankees. Thus the Lynds, in their massive 1929 sociological data bank *Middletown,* could say of the "amusement hungry" townsfolk they were studying, "Harold Lloyd comedies draw the largest crowds." He just knew what his audience wanted to watch.

Even when Harold is less sporty and more anxious, he's playing out scenes that men will readily identify with. In his 1924 feature *Hot Water,* Harold loves his new car the way a suburban dad loves a car. Buster loves the *General* almost in place of the girl, and so, although boys love trains, Buster atop the *General* seems singular compared to Harold behind the wheel of his Butterfly Six. He shows this new car to his neighbors and in-laws as one of the standard means by which to make his wife appreciate him more as a provider-hubby. But then he's forced to take the in-laws for a spin, and everything goes wrong; the vehicle is destroyed, a disaster Harold feels like a man with car payments to make. Lloyd's resonant ordinariness is the windfall from his making comedies "where people would see themselves and their neighbors"; it's a form of tribute that he wasn't recognized on the street as a movie star.

Usually there's a naturalistic basis to the way Harold worries about things. When a man at Coney Island throws a greasy hamburger paper in his direction in *Speedy*, we feel the danger to the suit not as an abstract object in a slapstick routine but as something that this boy couldn't really afford to buy. As in any slapstick, the suit must be ruined, but your response is conditioned by an awareness that Harold has had to hustle to earn it. In these ways, he's the most believable of the big slapstick stars, and I don't mean that as a consolation prize. Lloyd conveys with true comic feeling how boys actually become men, and what's sexually inchoate about him is intriguing without coming across as fey (as Chaplin could be so piquantly, responding to Eric Campbell's flirtation in *The Cure*) or abstract (as Keaton could be so memorably, hugging Marion Mack through the night without changing position in *The General*).

The question of Lloyd's sexual immaturity on-screen has a notable background in his relationship to the actor who introduced him to the theater, John Lane Connor. Hal Roach claimed that "Connor was extremely effeminate and probably homosexual," and indeed, Connor's meeting with the twelve-year-old Lloyd, as he later recounted it, sounds like a homosexual pickup. Lloyd was gazing at a favorite storefront astronomy display: "Suddenly, I became aware of someone beside me and looked up into the amused eyes of a very smartly attired young man, who seemed to me the handsomest person I had ever seen. He began to talk to me, smiling a little, and told me he had seen me there every night for weeks as he went by on his way to the theater." Lloyd, who said earlier in this autobiography, "I was possessed from my earliest youth with a definite, violent desire to act that in no wise conformed with the rest of my character," discovered that the stranger was an actor, and,

> All in one breath, I asked this immaculate and handsome young juvenile if he'd like to come and live at our house.
>
> He came the next morning, moved in that afternoon, and, in the process, acquired a young slave to do his bidding. From then on, I lived in his dressing room. I sat and watched him make up, I brushed his clothes, I kept his dressing room and table clean, I ran his errands,

heard him recite his parts, and I am sure would gladly have died for him. I have never met anyone since who seemed to me as wonderful as he did at that time.

This boy crush, which didn't necessarily involve sex, even when Lloyd joined Connor's repertory company in 1911, at age eighteen, nevertheless gives an idea of the demonstrative sexual naïveté that is recognizable, minus the sexual ambiguity, in Lloyd's romantic comedy features. As does the sixteen-year-old Lloyd's voice in his letters to his father, who was wandering the Great Plains states in search of better business luck: "There is a peach of a girl at school, I am pretty much stuck on her, I think she likes me pretty well too, as she talks to me all the time in school"; and "I would like to see you awfully swell papa and if you want me to come up and visit you Christmas vacation I will. . . . I wouldn't mind beating you a couple games of pitch now. Well papa as I guess I have told you all the news, I will close for this time, with lots of love and kisses." These letters of Lloyd's are unusually sweet and breathless for a sixteen-year-old boy; Brendan Gill's 1962 *New Yorker* item assures us that Lloyd never lost this tone: "Though he is a grandfather several times over, his 'Say!' and 'Gosh!' are those of an impressionable youngster on his first visit to a big town"; "When Lloyd leaned toward me and said confidentially, 'A fellow can have lots of fun in Paris,' I got the impression that he was thinking of a trip to the top of the Eiffel Tower." We know what Lloyd must have meant by "fun in Paris," but he can't help conveying something more innocent sounding—fun for the whole family.

Lloyd's callowness makes his movies come across as sincere, though as the premier silent craftsman, he structures them impersonally enough to be enduring. (He doesn't rely on our indulgence.) It's amazing to watch how lightly Lloyd wears the pathos he builds up around his heroes' dejection. In what other movies has an actor repeatedly played the eager, lovesick boy so plainly and yet rousingly? What's silly about these movies is that we begin to feel that these young men's romantic fates must be settled at such an early age. We do feel the urgency, but we also register that Lloyd isn't just playing himself; he's crafting his juvenility in an adult-artisanal way.

Hal Roach, the producer and often director of Lloyd's early shorts and features through *Safety Last!* and *Why Worry?* in 1923, claimed that "Lloyd was a 'made' comedian" rather than a natural. He continued, "In Harold Lloyd's whole life with me, he never once said, 'What do *I* do?' He said, 'What does *he* do?' It was always 'that fellow I'm portraying on the screen,' never 'what I do myself.'" Lloyd worked this way on principle, saying of himself as a teenager in the theater, "I did mostly character stuff. I was never a successful juvenile. I have never liked to play my own personality." He didn't start playing a juvenile until he no longer qualified as one himself and thus had to *play* it, paying attention to external considerations of how the story would naturally build up from the character's feelings. Though Roach often disparaged Lloyd's work after their professional split, his description of Lloyd's self-consciousness jibes with our experience of Lloyd's features, which, in quality and tone, just like his character, are the most consistent silent slapstick productions.

It's this sense of craft that enables Lloyd to blend tones so successfully, more so than Chaplin, I'd say. For instance, although we remember *The Freshman* as a cheering college comedy, there is running through it a sophisticatedly troubling murmur, which breaks into a bellow at the Fall Frolic, a big party that the underfinanced college freshman Harold Lamb has paid for because he wants to be the most popular boy on campus. At the height of the carousing, Harold passes by the hotel lobby where the villain is molesting Jobyna Ralston, playing Harold's landlady's radiantly sympathetic daughter, who loves Harold as a shy-but-eager boy regardless of his campus standing. Harold slugs the cad, showing for the first time the kind of masculine assertion that would make him a success without all the ridiculous effort. The villain, angry at being shown up by Harold, tells him, though Jobyna begs him not to, that Harold isn't really popular but just the campuswide joke, good for a free party. The ridicule of Harold climaxes at this moment in the ballroom, where a student standing on a table leads the rest of the partygoers in singing "For He's a Jolly Good Fellow" in his "honor." Harold tries to be brave, telling Jobyna that a fellow has to expect that kind of thing, and then collapses, crying facedown in her lap. Thus at the one moment in the movie so far when Harold has come across as manly, this very act of aggression leads to his greatest humiliation, in any of his movies. (Lloyd was so uncomfortable with the scene of his crying that he later cut it from rerelease prints.)

Altogether *The Freshman* is especially replete with scenes straight out of nightmares. In addition to the discovery that all the people he thought were his friends only want to exploit and ridicule him, there's the earlier scene of his arrival on campus in which the same pack leads the unsuspecting Harold behind the stage curtain of the auditorium and then opens it in front of the assembled student body. Lloyd fills this scene out with business involving a kitten stuck inside his sweater, but the scene holds us mainly by virtue of the bad-dream setup: Harold has no material, but he can't just walk off; he can't save himself. And then at the Fall Frolic, before the revelation, we have the famous scene in which Harold's cheaply basted suit comes apart. As Lloyd explained the construction of this scene:

> I wanted to be not too old-fashioned and I didn't want to pull my pants off. I said, "Everybody pulls their pants off in a scene. Let's not do that old, corny, lose-your-pants situation." So the first two previews I never lost my pants, but there was always something wrong with that section. One of the fellows said, "Harold, you've got to lose your pants." So I did and from then on it went fine. The audience loved that section. I had lost everything else and they wanted me to lose my pants.

This shows that there are two layers to the way in which comedy is about conforming, as Bergson outlines it. Harold Lamb, of course, has to grow up enough to avoid the disasters caused by his youthful eccentricity. But Harold Lloyd the director can't buck the mass audience's expectations. Harold has to lose his pants because Lloyd has to accommodate the demands of the form.

In fact, Harold has to fail all around in order to spring-load the comedy, and it gets to us although in this respect *The Freshman* is pointedly not autobiographical. When he reminisced about the time he spent finishing high school in San Diego while playing with local stock companies, Lloyd claimed jocularly, "The captain of the football team and I were the two most prominent men in school. I remember the girls used to leave notes in my Latin books. . . . I was playing the gay young dog to the best of my small town ability, and I treated 'em all alike." Young Lloyd and the football player were both sexually successful in their respective lines; in *The Freshman* Lloyd shows himself as helpless on both stage and playing field, because that is what slapstick storytelling requires. And if we don't recognize the elements of the form, then it won't seem like *our* comedy. Thus he has to stand tongue-tied onstage, blow his football tryout, and lose his pants for formal reasons; these disasters seal Harold's experiences as forms of communal dread. Lloyd realized that the universal-adolescent material has to sink its bucket into the elemental well. And he had an unbeatable instinct for what makes material function within the conventions and yet feel confessional. It's the impersonal confessional—the timing of the slapstick somehow ensures the detonations of psychological exposure, if not the full power: colored skyrockets, not A-bombs. But that timing also prevents the pathos from making the fuse sputter.

The Fall Frolic is an orgy of mortification beyond anything else in Harold Lloyd's features in scope, though not in kind. He had come close to going this far in *Girl Shy* when a publishing-office reader entertains the stenos with Harold's ludicrously boastful manuscript *The Secret of Making Love*. When Harold walks in on this scene, the girls garland him, sigh as he passes, and lead him on to say more dumb-cluck things about sex. And he's already been publicly exposed on the train into town for having his pockets stuffed with ladies' undergarments. (He'd hidden them on himself thinking he was emptying his own grip to gallantly make room in it to hide Jobyna's dog from the conductor.) In Lloyd's movies, the fantastically disquieting scenes are more upsetting because of their integration into the movie's overall air of harmless fun. The current in-your-face way to make a scene nightmarish, by having ugly people poke their noses into a wide-angle lens, would ruin the everyday dread of public disclosure of our weaknesses that Lloyd dramatizes. It is important for slapstick to stay close to the kinds of things we feel happen to us too often. Generally speaking, it isn't as fantastic in substance as the average straight melodrama.

Furthermore, the nightmare scenes in *The Freshman* are so pungent because the audience is in an ambiguous position. Like the college kids, we, too, are laughing at Harold, though at the same time we're identifying with him. Buster Keaton's mother, Myra, described one of her husband's famous stunts:

> [He] started doing a trick that if he ever missed, nothing saved his shins. He began jumping from the floor clear up onto the seat of a chair that stood on top of his table right at the edge. . . . When he got tired he missed and his shins scraped on the chair rungs and the table edge. . . . Six shows a day . . . were almost more than he could stand. Our hours were from three P.M. to three A.M. But the crowd hollered for that jump, *hoping he'd miss.* (italics mine)

This specialty of Joe's was an acrobatic feat, but what Myra felt the audience wanted was slapstick. We feel that we knock our shins, both literally and figuratively, all the time, so we pay to watch it happen in a spectacular form to the star of the show. Thus, in these scenes in *The Freshman*, there's a combination of masochism and sadism, in a general, rather than clinical, sense. And Lloyd understood at some level that the masochism and sadism could be intensified by making his stories romantic comedies. Sexual maladjustment so extreme that it threatens the hero's ability to find a partner hits us where we'd all like to live. There are parts of us more sensitive than our shins.

The Kid Brother is in some ways an even more arresting example than *The Freshman* of the not necessarily personal self-exposure in Lloyd's work. Harold Hickory lives with his father and two older brothers who farm, haul logs, and act as the local sheriff and deputies. In stark contrast, Harold, living with three rugged men, has to replace the dead mother by washing the laundry and dishes, cooking, and keeping house. When the men are off the property, Harold puts on his father's holster and pretends to be the man; when they return, they're totally in charge. Entrusted with the community's funds for a dam project, the father and brothers sign a letter and blow smoke from their pipes on it to dry the ink. They laugh when Harold wants to sign; he writes his name bigger than theirs and steals a puff from his brother's pipe to round out the male formalities. Guns, logs, pipes, pens—in academic writing, all phallic symbols of male authority, power, and prerogative. But Lloyd's imagery is thematic to such an extent it's not really symbolic. He knows that real men haul real logs.

Some of this material is autobiographical; for instance, the fact that Lloyd had been such a tenacious tagalong that he once waited in the snow for his older brother until his feet were black with frostbite. He also remembered hating to do chores for his aunt, the most unpleasant he felt to be operating the mangle, a central prop in *The Kid Brother*'s opening sequence of Harold's domestic drudgery. He seems to have had a happy childhood but to have derived from it an understanding of greater confusions. One Christmas he received a box of toy soldiers, but instead of playing war with them, he used them as actors on a little rigged-up stage, letting "pink and blue and lavender pill boxes from the drug store" serve as actresses. He then admitted, "I would have died of shame if anybody had found me out"—transforming soldiers into mere actors, like he wanted to be. As an adult, Lloyd was able to let the identity of the boys he played slide around without agonizing over it, yet it's the traces of shame that prime us to laugh.

He does it best in *The Kid Brother* in two scenes in which he disguises himself from his brothers. First he brings a girl from the local medicine show home after he is involved in burning the show down. The brothers see her come in but aren't awake when a neighbor woman, the mother of Harold's rival, takes her away, clucking that it wouldn't be decent for a girl to stay unchaperoned in a house of men. Harold sleeps in the curtained-off cot he made up for the girl, and in the morning his brothers come and flirtatiously offer "her" breakfast in bed. Harold slips curtain rings on his wrist and with femininely curled fingers accepts their offerings. When they discover the ruse, they try to beat him up, but he's fast and clever. At one point in the chase, he puts on his father's coat and hat and sits in the old man's seat in the horse cart to fool the brothers. They eventually catch on, but there's a payoff moments later in the chase when they see the figure on the cart again and pounce, only to discover that this time it *is* their father, who dusts the dirt with them. Harold's two disguises—helpless girl and forbidding lawman-father—represent reality and fantasy for this runty wannabe who has to play housemaid to these big, rough men while longing to be like them. Harold's identity as a man in *The Kid Brother* could go either way, but either way involves him putting on items that don't fit, that don't make the man.

The pressure on Harold Hickory is not something Lloyd was likely to have felt with respect to his own father. Lloyd saw his parents' marriage come apart as his father's diminishing business success met with his mother's contemptuous disappointment, but he leaned toward his father. When he was sixteen, Harold decided to move with him to one of the two coasts. Father and son flipped a coin and so came to California, and Lloyd became by profession the first member of his family "connected in any way with the theater," and also, eventually, an exponentially more reliable breadwinner than his father.

The familial material of a movie like *The Kid Brother* translates Lloyd's need in life to make something of himself, his lack of male inheritance, into slapstick and romantic comedy terms. The end of *The Freshman*—a football game in which Harold Lamb talks his way onto the field and, after nearly losing the game, wins it—derives from the general requirement that this boy prove himself among the other boys. The end of *The Kid Brother* is more acute because it involves Harold Hickory seeking out and physically beating the villain who has stolen the funds for the dam that the townspeople have arrested his father and brothers for stealing. In his silent features, Harold Lloyd is often downright desperate to succeed, even when he plays rich boys. In *The Kid Brother* his desperation stems explicitly from his family relations. But Lloyd doesn't have to treat this material as personal because it's a stepped-up version of all boys' striving to live up to their fathers. It's already personal, for the audience as much as for him.

Family plays an even larger part in Keaton's pictures than in Lloyd's. The casts of both his shorts and his features include actors playing mauling in-laws, disapproving fathers and brothers of his girls, emasculating mothers, and one overwhelming father. He most obviously sketches from life in his 1922 two-reeler *My Wife's Relations,* in which he makes a joke out of the bossiness of his matriarchal in-laws, the Talmadges. And as late as the 1930 talkie *Free and Easy,* Buster is still semicovertly having at his wife and her relations. Keaton and Trixie Friganza, as the loud-voiced, ill-tempered stage mother of the girl he loves (and loses), sing "Oh, King! Oh, Queen!" a number that solves the problem of Buster's aversion to comic dialogue by having the queen and king whisper to each other how they like to pet. When Friganza's queen whispers what she *won't* do, their spooning turns into a battle royale in which they tear each other's robes off. Natalie Talmadge and her mother Peg—the uncongenial wife, who had turned Keaton out of her bed after the birth of their second child in 1924 and less than three years of marriage, and the dynastic mother-in-law—merge. In this number, Buster both acts out how the home situation made him feel and gets some back from this megaphonic materfamilias.

However, at the same time that he drew more freely on his personal experiences, he relied less on emotional effect to stir his audience. He took tempestuous family relations offered as entertainment for granted. For his family's vaudeville act, in which father was both teacher and partner to his son, Joe had Myra sew a valise handle into the back of Buster's coat so that Joe could more easily throw the boy about the stage, into the scenery, and once into a row of heckling Yalies, breaking one undergraduate's nose and another's ribs. "Arrested many times," the family "always managed to get around" child labor laws designed to keep youngsters off the stage "because the law read, no child under the age of sixteen shall do acrobatics, walk wire, play musical instruments, trapeze, and it names everything"; but as Keaton pointed out, "There was not one word that made it illegal for my father to display me on the stage as a human mop or to kick me in the face."

As a kid Buster was exactly the package his father wanted him to be, and the brutality that was the focus of the act—and that shocks us in descriptions—was, as Keaton always maintained, part of the fun. Although Buster was known as "Mr. Black and Blue," inspection by child protection authorities proved that he was an acrobat trained in taking spine-jamming falls without getting hurt. Yet the fun and the glory of their vaudeville success made Joe loom that much larger in Buster's imagination.

The secret of the Keatons' appeal was related to the fact that the parents themselves didn't distinguish between hitting Buster on- and offstage. As Keaton remembered:

When I disobeyed orders I got a good clout over the backside. Nobody expected me to like it, or cared whether I did or not. The clout told me in the one way a normal and mischievous boy understands to behave myself. When I failed to get the point I got another clout.

After I was seven, Pop would punish me for misbehaving while we were working on the stage. He knew I was too proud of being able to take it to yell or cry. I don't think my father had an ounce of cruelty in him. He just didn't think it was good for a boy as full of beans as I was to get away with too much.

A contemporary review of the Three Keatons suggests whom the act was aimed at: "The two chief performers, representing themselves as a proud but very abusive father and a solemn child . . . keep the audience, or at least the male part of it, heartily amused." All the same, the rough handling caused Alfred Butt of the Palace Theater in London to inquire of Joe during the Three Keatons' run there whether Buster were his own son; Butt's response was, "My word . . . I imagined he was an adopted boy and you didn't give a damn what you did to him." But the popularity of the act depended on thinking that they were blood relations. The giddy, guilty thrill of seeing a father and son have it out drew big crowds to see their own private behavior amplified in public; by all reports, it busted men's guts with laughter.

As he got older, Joe's drinking made him kick harder, more angrily, and less accurately onstage and made him an even more overbearing tyrant offstage as well. (Buster's assertion of his father's total lack of cruelty contradicts most other accounts.) Buster first went out on his own after he and Myra, having put up with Joe's drunken violence as long as they could, simply didn't show up for a grueling three-a-day engagement in Los Angeles, sneaking off without leaving Joe a note. Buster got a role in the Shuberts' musical revue *The Passing Show* of 1917 and had to come up with solo routines, which proved difficult for a twenty-two-year-old with eighteen years' experience exclusively as a member of a team. His biographer Rudi Blesh reported: "He set up obstacles, with hotel chairs and tables as props, to stumble over and get tangled up with. He would think up a task for them to interfere with; but, more important, first he must create a fate for himself by setting up its inanimate pawns. Joe Keaton was gone. Someone—better, something—had to take his place."

Buster had to find a way to replicate the intensity of his physical exchanges with his father without having his father onstage. He did it most literally in *Steamboat Bill, Jr.* by casting as his father the golemic

Ernest Torrence, who makes up in size what he lacked in actual relation. Even the tornado that ends *Steamboat Bill, Jr.* is surely a reference
to the stories that Joe always told about the baby Buster being sucked
out of a rooming-house window by a tornado and deposited safely in
the middle of the street. The movie is bookended by Buster's going up
against overwhelming natural forces (father, tornado) that Keaton
identified with Joe; the whole movie is a tempestuous vernacular fairy
tale about Buster's precociously joining Joe's world as a full partner.

Keaton's most startling, distinctive intuition was to make his slapstick opposition simultaneously particular to the story and general. He
had to work out the details of the gags with the house or the boat or
the train or the wind or the father figure, but the details couldn't get in
the way of our feeling that he was facing something bigger—House,
Boat, Train, Wind, Father. Perhaps from a childhood of watching audiences explode in laughter at the sight of his violent physical combat
with his actual father, Buster knew how much primal material can intensify comedy. His great move was to respond to all forces as if they
were primal. He formalized the opposition that we feel we face all the
time, in part by the deliberateness of his subdued reactions. His characters respond with the same blend of stoicism and frantic effort to all
opposition regardless of its nature. Keaton, playing the boy trying to
become a man in nearly paralyzing awareness of the full range of
forces working against him, like Lloyd, treats the personal impersonally, only more closely to his actual experience—and his shrimpiness
takes on jumbo dimensions.

Unlike Lloyd, Buster Keaton had a successful father, one who
trained him in the skills on which he built his adult success. Keaton's
father *was* a self-defeating star, toppling from a higher level than
Lloyd's father ever attained. But for both Lloyd and Keaton, their relationships with their fathers were much more formative than Chaplin's
was: he scarcely knew his father, who almost never lived with him and
died of alcoholism when Charlie was twelve. Lloyd was close to his father, but Buster was cast in his father's mold: when he was a child in
the act, father and son wore identical costumes, including a bald-pate
wig with a ring of red hair and a red beard. Lloyd was supplementing
his father's income as early as age nine and eventually more than made
up for his father's wipeout as a provider by, among other things, making his father and older brother officers in the privately owned Harold
Lloyd Corporation. Buster had to cooperate with a domineering father
to help him provide. And when Joe wiped out, Buster took over the
role of head of the family, housing and feeding his mother and father

and grown sister and brother until 1956, right through his own career's zenith and nadir.

But even when replacing his father, Buster was also his father's negative image, maintaining a reactive, receptive, passive role in both his career and his marriage. At his peak of artistic productivity and control in the twenties, with his own studio, he had simply shifted his weight from Joe Keaton to his movie mogul brother-in-law Joe Schenck, who handed him Arbuckle's old studio, set up his production company and distribution deals, and paid his salary directly to Natalie. (Schenck was married to Natalie's older sister, the dramatic movie star Norma Talmadge, who called him "Daddy.") As Tom Dardis has pointed out, "Amazingly enough, Buster owned no shares in the production firm that bore his name. He felt that if he acquired shares, he would be obliged to worry about how the firm was doing, and he was confident that Joe Schenck would always take care of his best interests." The son of a failure, Lloyd's basic story in his features is about making success from nothing. What's most significant for Keaton's pictures is his relationship to a father who rotted as he himself ripened, and his own hesitations about taking his father's place.

In *Steamboat Bill, Jr.* the enormous Ernest Torrence as the father of the slight, college-educated boy, a father who has to fold his son's hand in a ball and push it in another man's face to get him to fight with his fists, dramatizes the way that sons always feel belated. Lloyd's father was not a very high mark for a son to test himself against, which may be why in his features he almost never has to overcome the objections of the girl's father. In *Steamboat Bill, Jr.* Buster has to deal not only with the girl's father but with his *own* father's skepticism about his manliness, and in both that picture and *College* with his mother's deleterious influence. When Bill Jr. arrives from college to learn how to run his father's paddleboat, he hasn't seen the old man in so long that he needs to wear a white carnation to identify himself at the depot. Of course, that day everyone's sporting a boutonniere. Bill Sr. finds his son when he stumbles over the boy's valise and looks up to see him skip dancing to his own ukulele accompaniment. Approaching from around the corner of a building, the father can't see that Buster is trying to calm a baby whose carriage he's bumped. He just thinks his son is a prancing girlie and says to his first mate, "If you say what you're thinking I'll strangle you." Such vignettes couple the son's inadequately impressive masculinity with an outright fear of effeminacy. This is not a plea for tolerance; it's worrying a wart. Keaton himself said that he, Arbuckle, and Al St. John found a "sissy type Romeo who was paying court to beautiful Anita King" "sickening"; they punished him for entering their field of vision by "accidentally" hitting him with a pie. If Bill Jr. falls short of his father's model, he's female, but the father is the gruff, bossy type next to whom almost any son would seem like Franklin Pangborn Jr.

Sons often find to their dismay that it doesn't matter how successful or even physically big they get; their fathers, grandfathers, uncles, and older brothers always got there first and are somehow part of the definition of what it means to be a man. And little Buster is all but helpless in the meaty hands of this father, who leads him around town to remake him—at one point, the distracted Buster stumbles at the foot of a series of steps and, dangling from his father's grasp, looks like a rag doll. Bill Jr. has shown up with what he must think of as a dashing little mustache; Keaton referred to it as a "'baseball mustache,' so-called because it has nine hairs on each side." Bill Sr. disapproves and so takes him to a barber, who requires two swipes with a razor to remove it. Buster's father rejuvenates him by having his mustache shaved off, but the barbershop is also where Buster discovers the girl (whom he knows from his effete college days), the daughter of Bill Sr.'s wealthy rival. The father can boss him around, but independence and sexuality will out, almost despite Bill Jr. as well as his father.

Then, in the legendary central routine of this sequence, the father insists that Buster get rid of his suspect foreign beret, and we watch as Buster tries on a succession of hats. Buster likes a motoring cap and adjusts it so as to get an approving nod from his father. But as his father turns toward him, the cap pops up into a ridiculous position, and Bill Sr. nixes it and makes him try on some more appropriate styles. In the accelerating flurry of headgear, the salesman hands Bill Jr. Keaton's signature porkpie, and the son grabs it off his head and hides it in terror before his father can see it, as if he couldn't face the response it would evoke. What's the "in" of this in-joke? It could be just a throwaway, but if you blur the distinction between Bill Jr. the character and Buster the man and movie star, it looks as if Keaton feels that the fact that he's so famous an entertainer his hat is instantly recognizable to the public is an affront to his "father."

This, too, the Keatons acted out onstage. One of the great difficulties for Buster growing up had been that "by degrees, Joe became his straight man." The rave clippings claiming that Buster was "the whole show" must have been welcome as enthusiastic endorsements of their act, but also disturbing for family relations. Joe never could "accept the fact that Buster had grown up and was no longer a child; . . . he

continued to call him 'Bus,' or 'Bussy'" into adulthood. And the violent nature of their act enabled Joe to take out on Buster, in a semi-
seemly theatrical format, his rages over his son's catching up to him.
One of the incidents Buster mentioned to his biographer occurred when
Joe found a pipe in Buster's jacket in the dressing room. Buster said to
one of the actors, "Now I'll catch it. If you want some excitement, just
watch from the wings." Keaton then specified the number of chairs
and brooms father and son broke over each other's head and back.

A son's search for identity within his father's domain can provoke
almost ironic acts of defiance. It's worth contemplating that Joe was
helpless with anything mechanical and that he particularly loathed the
movies, even passing up a lucrative offer from William Randolph Hearst
in 1914 to star with Myra in a series to be based on George McManus's
cartoon strip *Bringing Up Father*. After Keaton's now famous first day
on a movie set—dropping in as a guest to watch Roscoe Arbuckle
shoot the two-reeler *The Butcher Boy* and then suiting up to play a bit
part, in 1917—he either, according to legend, learned how the camera
worked by taking the Bell and Howell home that night, breaking it
down, and putting it back together (not altogether implausible, since
he was an amateur inventor from adolescence) or, as he said in his autobiography, learned it all from Arbuckle: "Roscoe . . . took the camera
apart for me so I would understand how it worked and what it could
do. He showed me how film was developed, cut, and then spliced together" (a likelier version, since it doesn't rely on Keaton's having figured out in a night what it took any number of men in several countries
decades to invent, and we know the two men hit it off). Either way, in
The Playhouse and *Sherlock Jr.* he devised the most startling in-camera
effects of their day or any other.

However, devoting himself to a medium Joe despised, as Keaton did
with film, still kept him solidly in an adversarial relationship with his
father. And Joe made the relationship unpleasant, taking Buster's entry
into moviemaking as "a blow." He warmed to the idea only when
Buster got him bit work in some Arbuckle pictures, but Joe predictably
brought the family tradition of comic child beating with him. When
Arbuckle tried to direct Joe, the former star of a specialty called "lego-
mania," how to kick Buster for the 1917 two-reeler *A Country Hero*
(now considered lost), Joe exploded, "I've been kicking that boy's
ass . . . ever since he was born, and now you tell me how."

Keaton told how his mother had explained Joe's changing personality to him:

Myra told me, "Joe's not punishing you."

I said, "It *feels* like it."

She said, "No, he's not mad at you or anyone else. It's old Father Time he'd like to get his hands on. Man or woman," she said, "some can take getting old, some can't."

That Myra personified Joe's aging as *Father* Time is perfectly apt. Joe seems to have personified it in Buster's growing up, getting more skilled and successful, and receiving more attention—in the son's having the power that belongs to the father. And then, to complete it all, Buster, whose given name was, after all, Joseph, never really thinking he'd get any older either, became ever more like the original, and drank his own success away.

Buster couldn't live up to a father who had tested his mettle on the legendary frontier, and yet by the late 1910s he had surpassed the old man. His diffidence in this repeated comedy-drama of trying to find the body language for successfully assertive manhood draws on this primal guilt over the way in which sons do their fathers in without trying—in *Steamboat Bill, Jr.* while trying to do the opposite, in fact. Bill Jr. rescues both fathers from drowning during the climactic windstorm by stringing ropes to the steamboat controls so that he can operate the boat while steering from the bridge. He saves the day and earns the right to the girl, but he does it not by running the boat according to the normal procedures his father tried to teach him (and at which he failed) but in his own idiosyncratically maladapted manner (the best way to resolve the boy's rigid foolishness, in Bergson's schema, without violating the nature of the comedy). What's significant is that Bill Sr. doesn't transmit anything to his son, yet Bill Jr. has his way nonetheless and will push the old generation into the background by producing a new one. As close as this material is to Keaton, it's close to us all, because growing up in our father's shadows is every son's lot—we come into *their* world, especially if they're famous or very successful—and eclipsing his father is any son's fate, if he lives long enough. (Even effeminate sons "win" in the end.) Fathers are archetypally titanic figures in both senses: preemptively powerful and foredoomed.

Northrop Frye has written that "comedy often turns on a clash between a son's and a father's will," and it's this troubling aspect that Buster was able to turn to advantage most in *Steamboat Bill, Jr.* According to Frye's formulation, the son fights with the father and, by winning out, replaces him, so that romantic comedy draws its charge from this very succession of the generations on which the conflict in

Steamboat Bill, Jr. centers. Clearly, this isn't exclusively a comic pattern. As Dreiser wrote about Hurstwood's decline:

> A man's fortune, or material progress, is very much the same as his bodily growth. Either he is growing stronger, healthier, wiser, as the youth approaching manhood; or he is growing weaker, older, less incisive mentally, as the man approaching old age. There are no other states. . . . Given time enough, however, the balance becomes a sagging to the grave side.

It's taboo for a boy to kill his father, but it has also been decreed by nature that the father will nonetheless most likely decline and die before the son, who, coming into his prime as the old man sinks down, will incur the guilt for what he didn't do but was done "for" him. (For all the good it does him. As Faulkner put it in Quentin's words in that most vexed of paternal sagas *Absalom, Absalom!*: "A man never outlives his father.") Buster may not have known more about this than the rest of us boys, but it had a theatrical form in his life that it doesn't in most of ours, as Joe discovered when he forgot to insert "the felt pad he had been wearing under his trousers ever since [Buster] had got strong enough to hurt him when [they] did [their] anvil-chorus work on each other with the brooms." Joe turned "green with pain" at the first blow, bellowed, "Christ . . . I left the pad off!" and, as Keaton related it, asked Buster,

> "Are you going through with it?" . . .
> "Sure," I [Buster] said, as he [Joe] winced, "it's part of the play."
> I socked him again. "Going through with it?" he asked once more.
> "Yes," I said. This time he gave me an appealing look, and remarked,
> "But remember I'm your father."
> And Pop did go through with it, although I showed him no mercy.

Naturally, this is not a turn of events that fathers can find much cheer in; Mack Sennett's father is reported to have lamented with respect to the maturity of his three strapping sons that "the saddest moment in a man's whole life is when his son gets big enough to lambaste him." But neither is physical superiority something the son wants once he gets it; Buster Keaton broke up his act with his alcoholic father because, as he said, "I was not prepared to watch my father go to pieces" (though walking out on the act only accelerated Joe's disintegration). The fascination of Keaton's melancholia has a lot to do with the fact that the material another kind of storyteller would have turned into Greek tragedy Keaton plays as slapstick romantic comedy.

Lloyd hit his stride in feature films by starting to play inexperienced youths on the verge of manhood. And Keaton played a kind of innocence that went beyond Lloyd's, as Lorca's stage directions in his surreal fantasy "Buster Keaton Takes a Walk" indicate: "Adam and Eve would run in terror if they saw a glass of water, but on the other hand they would stroke Keaton's bicycle." When Lloyd stutters in the presence of flirty females in *Girl Shy,* one of whom asks him to darn the stocking she's wearing, or when he crashes out of the dining car at the beginning of *The Freshman* because an older woman takes him and Jobyna for sweethearts, he's so jittery *because* he knows of the physical requirements of romance (as we know in *Girl Shy,* for example, from the two vignettes he writes about *The Secret of Making Love*), and they scare him. By contrast, at the close of *Sherlock Jr.,* when the girl has solved the crime and comes to find Buster in his projectionist's booth, Buster has to look out at the happy ending lighting up the screen to get his moves—clasping then kissing the girl's hands, putting a ring on her finger, kissing her. But then the movie he's copying cuts forward to the hero dandling the couple's two kids, and Buster can only scratch his head. The joke springs from a kind of narrative parallax—Buster's movie isn't like a movie; he doesn't know how to produce kids that fast. But this is just a way to complicate the basic innocence of the character, make it more than just a treacly convention.

Keaton never milks his innocence or treats it as a sign of moral superiority (Chaplin does both), though he can display the defensive sensitivity of a child: when the Confederate induction board rejects him for service in *The General* without telling him why, he says, "If you lose this war don't blame me." He never moves as far down the maturity scale as Langdon, who will clap his hands with eerily infantile helplessness, but there's a similarity among these grown men acting at times like tykes. Watching Chaplin, Lloyd, Keaton, and Langdon, it's easy to assume that innocence is a necessary feature for a slapstick hero. As Pauline Kael observed in "The Man from Dream City," her 1975 essay about Cary Grant, "The screwball movies brought back the slapstick tradition of vaudeville and the two-reelers, and blended it into those brittle Broadway comedies. When it was joined to a marital farce or a slightly daring society romance, slapstick no longer seemed like kid stuff: it was no longer innocent and was no longer regarded as 'low' comedy." Kael's description of the screwballs seems exact, and it conforms to people's notions about silent slapstick, but slapstick didn't have to be all that innocent.

In the little-seen 1926 feature *Hands Up!* Raymond Griffith plays a

Confederate spy assigned by Lee to capture a Union shipment of gold needed by Lincoln to continue the war effort. This puts Griffith in a position similar to Keaton's in *The General*, but Griffith is sexually ambivalent in a much more commonplace, heterosexual way. Griffith has no devoted attachments; he is in fact a rake. He sneaks aboard a west-bound stagecoach to eavesdrop on the manager of the Union gold mine in conversation with the Union officer in charge of transporting the shipment. The manager and officer are driving up front; when they stop the coach to take the manager's daughters on board in back with Griffith, Griffith dallies with both of them at once to get an in with their father. The girls hesitate to respond to his merest advances because they haven't been introduced. Trying to think how to break the ice, he pulls two dice out and gives them a prospective rattle and then grimaces as he immediately realizes how inappropriate *that* instinct was. Next he pulls out cards to introduce himself but grabs them from the wrong pocket and whips out two aces. Sporting New Orleans's idea of Parisian evening dress, he's experienced in the ways of a rowdy, corrupt, man's world—a slapstick Rhett Butler.

At the action climax, when Griffith is trying to make off with the coach now heaped with sacks of gold dust, one of the sisters comes in on him, and he proposes to her to get rid of her quick. When she exits, the other sister comes in, and he proposes to *her*. But they've detained him long enough that he never does get away with the gold. After an ingenious chase, he gets caught and is about to be strung up from a tree limb when the first daughter slips a ring on her finger and runs out to stop the execution, telling her father he can't hang Griffith because she's his wife. The manager relents until the second girl comes out and pulls the same act. In these scenes of comic bigamy, Griffith thinks more daringly and calculatingly about the slapstick *uses* of heroines than any other slapstick star, including Keaton.

In the 1921 two-reeler *The Playhouse*, Buster never can distinguish between the girl he loves and her twin sister. To avoid a mix-up on the way to the preacher, he marks an X on the nape of his girl's neck with a grease pencil. Keaton is bizarrely phlegmatic in the face of his own confusion; his solution is funny because it's so objectively practical. But that's very different from the hint of debauchery in the way Griffith flirts with actual male fantasies: when Lee's surrender abruptly terminates the story in midclimax, Griffith takes *both* girls to Utah. He doesn't come across as fully corrupt only because he's so accommodating. But he does trespass a step or so, assuming that the male audience for slapstick will happily wink.

Not even slightness itself is necessary for a slapstick star, as the career of the 266-pound Roscoe Arbuckle shows. (He was even with Chaplin for popularity from Chaplin's appearance in 1914 until Arbuckle's plummet in 1921.) Arbuckle could play innocent and prided himself on his "clean" pictures, but his size, somewhat counterintuitively, also gave him the benefit of a wider range of character possibilities. In the 1916 Triangle-Keystone three-reeler *Fatty & Mabel Adrift*, he plays a friendly, open-faced farm boy—the kind of kid who's actually called Fatty. But in the 1915 Keystone two-reeler *Fatty's Tintype Tangle*, flipping pancakes up over his back into a skillet, and tossing his bowler from the toe of his shoe onto his head, which he shakes to get the sit just right, he could also be an attractive comic hero. He could, in fact, be as dazzling in his way, even as a henpecked husband and son-in-law, as Cary Grant was when drawing on *his* vaudeville background to play piano and make a strolling musical exit with Constance Bennett in *Topper*, or to tumble with Katharine Hepburn in *Holiday*.

But Arbuckle's girth was also fantastic enough to allow him to give a totally idiomatic performance as a seedy bum in the 1915 Keystone one-reeler *Fatty's New Role*, in which he stumbles into a momentarily deserted saloon and rolls the bar dice against himself for drinks, stealing a snort only when he wins. When he mixes himself a cocktail, he tops the booze with a cigar butt and a slice of cheese and does a classic shake shake shake. His new role is Chaplinesque in its skankiness, but even more cut off; Arbuckle has no qualms about going all the way with this dissociated character by croaking at the end. And he dies funny, not pathetic.

In a completely different register, he's a sybaritic mama's boy in the first reel of the 1915 Keystone two-reeler *Fatty's Plucky Pup* who falls asleep smoking in bed and sets fire to his room. He then languidly gets up to put the fire out with teacups of water; satisfied that the first cup has doused the flames, and thirsty after such exertion, he drinks the second cup. And he's also the premier female impersonator among silent comedians, displaying a fabulous burlesque kittenishness in the 1915 Keystone one-reeler *Miss Fatty's Seaside Lovers* and the second reel of the 1917 Comique short *The Butcher Boy*. In addition, though a little man has an advantage in being able to take pratfalls without hurting himself, Arbuckle was an exception, taking "falls no other man of his weight ever attempted," "Brodies that shook buildings." (He was no sedentary sitcom daddy like Vitagraph's John Bunny.) Arbuckle had the same physical skills as the small guys, and since his size itself served as his trademark, he was able to vary his roles more than any other star. He's not as distinctive as a result—more of a good host, adaptable to circumstances, standing bodily for slapstick's accommodation to physical existence (grossness and all in his case, as in Falstaff's).

Littleness and innocence may seem to be essential aspects of great silent slapstick for contingent reasons: perhaps Lloyd, Keaton, and Chaplin were the most consistently inspired makers of slapstick features. It's a mistake to confuse what was with what had to be. Roscoe Arbuckle's career was cut short just as slapstick feature making got under way, and too little of Raymond Griffith's output survives to judge why he never gained the public's affection as the top three did. However, in the long run, innocence proved a trap for Lloyd and Keaton— only Chaplin was able to sustain it, and it isn't a consistently pretty sight.

Buster's premature decline came about because he transferred his practical reliance from his father to Joe Schenck, who profited by having his brother-in-law Buster produce popular shorts and features while Schenck angled to become a wheel. When Keaton made the suicidally expensive *The General* and couldn't recoup the losses with the less ambitious *College,* Schenck sold Keaton to his brother Nicholas Schenck at MGM. Keaton's lack of concern for business was in the long run a personal disaster—he never saved any of the millions he made when he was a top star. And despite warnings from Lloyd and Chaplin about what would happen to his pictures when he worked for a studio, Keaton didn't have the connections or business head to set up his own production company and distribution deals.

But if Buster's business headlessness brought calamity when Joe Schenck unloaded his contract, it made Keaton, during his great run from 1920 through 1928, the purest of commercial directors in the silent era, and perhaps up to the present day. This is a strange thing for a man who considered the audience the only valid critics of his work and who believed in the prerelease screening system. He dismissed to the end of his days the idea that he was an artist, curtly dismissing what he called "that genius bullshit." Keaton could maintain this attitude in part for a reason that also ensured his downfall—as his friend Buster Collier put it, "As a rule, you came out of vaudeville hard as nails," but "Buster didn't have that hard shell of ego."

Keaton quickly found at MGM that Irving G. Thalberg, the head of production, would not allow the time-tested improvisational style of developing a slapstick feature, since it didn't fit with his autocratic industrial system of moviemaking. Though Keaton ignored this for *The*

Cameraman, which made money and which even Thalberg admitted was a classic, the star was brought into line in short order. He had to shoot from scripts concocted by staff writers who transformed his screen character from a young man who is dawningly sexual, and who combines childlike passivity with adult stoicism, into a late starter who says, in the 1931 *Parlor, Bedroom, and Bath,* "Oh gosh, no—never had a love affair with a woman," and faints when Reginald Denny offers to arrange things so that the girl he's infatuated with could be the mother of his children. Buster's ignorance about what the hero should do with the heroine at the close is charming in *Sherlock Jr.* (like us, he takes his cues from the movies), as is the awkwardness of his all-night hug in *The General.* But his inability to hug and kiss in 1931 is ruined by the spoken insults heaped on him for his lack of virility.

And besides, he doesn't look too fresh. He's clearly too old to be as innocent as he is, and his persona goes sexless; he mutates into a toy donkey. Buster's Eeyore voice is thus fitting but too specifically uncultured. In the silents, everyone could fill in his own voice for the star; in the talkies, Keaton's voice and the dialogue supplied for it make him into a hick, which is too limiting. (It also doesn't help that it scrapes like a gin-rusted hinge.) His silents have a fairy-tale quality, even the 1920 two-reeler *The Scarecrow* and the 1925 feature *Go West,* set on a farm and a ranch, respectively. The way his character is written in his talkies, he brings a whiff of bucolic comedy in with him, even in urban-set farces. You can't blame the MGM writers, who must have looked at the face that Keaton's hard living had given him and realized he could scarcely play a juvenile anymore. But all the same, MGM extinguished his aura with inappropriate names (usually Elmer), story lines, and dialogue that turn him into a rube, a forerunner of Red Skelton, for whom Keaton supplied gags in the late forties.

Harold Lloyd didn't have Keaton's business problems because, as he put it, "Whatever I have been able to accomplish in pictures that the public has liked, has been made possible, I believe, by one thing—my independence. I have never been forced to make bad contracts." He was always in a better bargaining position than Keaton, as well, not only because Lloyd's pictures made more money but because he saved much of what he earned. When Lloyd built *his* Beverly Hills mansion, he could afford it.

But he did have a similar dilemma in terms of how to transfer his evergreen persona to talkies (starting with *Welcome Danger* in 1929, a silent substantially reshot for sound, made in his thirty-sixth year, and ending with *The Sin of Harold Diddlebock,* written and directed by

Preston Sturges in 1946 when Lloyd was fifty-three). Hal Roach said, "Harold Lloyd . . . created a character that I helped him develop, the young man. He couldn't grow old with that character. Every action, every bit of his character was based on his youth. The things that were funny for a boy of twenty were not funny for a boy of thirty-five." Roach's rivalry with a former partner whose success outran his own made him set the upper age limit a bit low, but the basic insight is sound.

However, Lloyd, who remained a star to the end and never filled a supporting role in the talkies, found several happy solutions for the incongruity of a man his age playing an innocent. My favorite comes in *The Cat's-Paw* (1934), in which Harold is the son of a missionary in China who comes to America speaking a formal speech that makes everything sound translated. His version of "Hello" is "A cordial greeting, my worthy friend," and when he has to use the telephone, he says, "If you would excuse me, I'll hold a brief discourse over the instrument." It's as if W. C. Fields's ornate locutions were being uttered unironically by the "young man who might have quit divinity school to hustle brushes" that James Agee said Lloyd resembled.

In this way, *The Cat's-Paw* turns the mysterious fact that popular fashions of the preceding decade look hopelessly square to us as we shimmy down the century into an advantage. Lloyd makes his character as mulishly innocent as possible by surrounding himself with the cynical commotion that thirties audiences liked in their newly talking pictures. Harold gets involved in corrupt local machine politics, falls for a knowing but gold-hearted working girl, and gets taken to a nightclub where a moll involves him in her striptease act. He trails the stripper as her dress comes apart, gallantly picking up the fallen pieces as if he were trying to prevent this distaff remake of his nightmare high point in *The Freshman*, not ten years old at that point. *The Cat's-Paw* has the gangsters that audiences would have known from Warner Brothers headline movies and a fast-talking comic cynicism about corrupt politicians that falls midway between *The Front Page* and Sturges's *The Great McGinty*. With this potpourri, Lloyd acknowledges his obsolescence as a way of keeping up, and the movie is unjustly forgotten.

But the differences in their business acumen made no difference in the long run. Keaton was an important star at MGM making pictures he hated, while Lloyd sank down losing his own money on pictures he was proud of. But Keaton washed out of MGM on a tide of booze whereas Lloyd retained a large fortune when he faded into an active retirement. Keaton never retired from show business, hiring on as gag consultant, taking commercials and small roles in movies, appearing in European circuses, right up to the big exit. Keaton and Lloyd replaced their fathers as heads of the family and then as stars inevitably suffered the fate of all "fathers." We're lucky to have all of their silent features, which preserve them at their peak of adult power playing the eager juveniles they had even then ceased to be.

CHAPTER FOUR

Girl Heroes

Theodore Dreiser's 1928 interview with Mack Sennett produced the following exchange:

> One of the things I [Dreiser] was moved to ask at this point was, slapstick being what it is, was there any limit to the forms or manifestations of this humor? And to my surprise, yes, there was, and is.
>
> "No joke about a mother ever gets a laugh," he [Sennett] insisted most dogmatically. "We've tried that, and we know. You can't joke about a mother in even the lightest, mildest way. If you do, the audience sits there cold, and you get no hand. It may not be angry—we wouldn't put in stuff about a mother that an audience could take offense at—but, on the other hand, it is not moved to laugh—doesn't want to—and no laughs, no money. So mothers in that sense are out. You have to use them for sentiment or atmosphere in burlesque."
>
> "In other words, hats off to the American mother," I said. . . . "But not so with fathers," I added, after a time.
>
> "Oh, fathers," he said dryly. "No. You can do anything you want to with them. Father's one of the best butts we have. You can do anything but kill him on the stage."
>
> "And as for the dear mother-in-law," I interjected.
>
> "Better yet. Best of all, unless it is an old maid."
>
> "No quarter for old maids, eh?"
>
> "Not a cent. A free field and no favors where they're concerned. You can do anything this side of torture and get a laugh."

Are there any mothers in slapstick? Not many, but the few there are adhere fairly nearly to Sennett's comments: Arbuckle's in *Fatty's Plucky Pup,* Lloyd's in *The Freshman,* and Langdon's in *Fiddlesticks* all worry over their boys in a way presumed natural. Buster Keaton's 1927 feature *College* is a particularly complicated example because we can see there's a problem with the (presumably widowed) mother, who has unsocialized her son, encouraging him in both his studies and his disdain for sports. In this way, she's come between Buster and his girl, who's humiliated in the opening sequence by his valedictory speech "The Curse of Athletics." (When the speech is over, only Mother is left in the auditorium.) The climax of the picture comes about when the girl, who's not really likable, is resisting a disreputable jock's advances. Buster is charged up enough by her distress that to save her he's suddenly able to pull off all the sports that, thanks to Mother's influence, he had earlier failed at (e.g., he pole-vaults into the window of the room where the villain has locked her).

Thus, to win the girl, and so make her into a mother, the story requires Buster to overcome his own mother's influence, but this doesn't make the mother a legitimate butt for jokes. The only joke the mother is involved in physically comes after Buster's disastrous commencement speech in the first sequence: standing in the rain on the steps outside the high school between the defiant mother and the angry girl, Buster holds the umbrella over his mother's head, thinks, moves it over the girl's head, thinks again, and moves it back. Mother doesn't have to move for the joke to work, she just has to magnetize that umbrella.

Later at college when Buster has botched a tryout for the baseball team, some of the players toss him in a blanket, right by the window of a big matron in dishabille. She sees his head bobbing up by her balcony and thinks he's a peeper, so she takes up *her* umbrella and wallops him each time he pops back up. To save his skull, Buster grabs the umbrella, which opens, and in one of Keaton's incomparable camera tricks, we see him fly up at the usual silent speed and fall in slow motion. On the final ascent, the lady grabs him, and he pulls her off the balcony on top of himself. Cut to ground zero, and we see her sprawling but can't see Buster, until his head pops out from between her legs. His reappearance is jocularly shot as a rebirth, and the umbrella connects the earlier, calm scene of clamp-jawed motherly displeasure with this wild scene of matronly outrage. Keaton flirts with violent physical comedy aimed at the sissifying mother, but displaces it so we can *enjoy* the shattered taboo.

This kind of displacement could also reflect the heroine's parlous moral state. For instance, in the 1925 romantic comedy *Sally, Irene and Mary,* Sally O'Neil and William Haines are Irish sweethearts who live across the air shaft from each other. They both have battle-axe mothers who accompany Haines to O'Neil's opening night in a *Follies*-like show. Haines and his mother are shocked by O'Neil's scanty costume and then bitterly disgusted when she doesn't come home that night. *We* know she's being a good, if impetuously (and, to be blunt, tiresomely) rambunctious girl, but they assume the worst. At this point, while Haines's mother launches a somewhat comic tirade against the absent girl, O'Neil's mother across the way becomes a slapstick monster, a toothless dragon. Haines's mother calls out an insult, and O'Neil's mother angrily pulls down her rolling paper shade, which, having failed to catch, snaps back up with her hair snagged in the string. When she tugs on the string to pull the shade back down, the whole contraption comes down on her head. The next day, Haines's mother, in a flower-print dress and white apron, spots O'Neil's mother in a tight shift doing morning exercises and calls out, "Her with the body of a truck trying to make it look like a ukulele." The movie-makers never stripped and ridiculed the mother of a girl less reckless with her reputation. Underlying this displacement is a direct objection to questionable female behavior. But what's most important is that Sennett's rule against ridiculing mothers applies to the *boy's* mother. That's what "mother" means; the girl's mother is a "mother-in-law," fair game in duck *and* rabbit season.

Still, mothers aren't indispensable figures in slapstick, but female costars are. Can Sennett's rule be expanded to include them? Comparing the male and female roles in Chaplin's 1921 feature *The Kid* certainly bears Sennett out. In it, Edna Purviance, Chaplin's costar in his most productive period (from 1915 through 1923), plays the wayward artist's model who gives birth to the title character. Her troubles are recounted in the drippy opening, which includes a shot of her standing in front of a church window that lights up like a halo behind her. Even when she abandons her child, she does it with the best intentions—she stashes it in a town car to give the child a better start in life. The mother instinct causes her to repent immediately, but when she goes back for the baby, she finds that the car has already been stolen. She's purified even more by this added disaster: she devotes her life thereafter to charity work among poor children.

Only when Chaplin, the male star, finds the abandoned love bundle does the movie switch to slapstick storytelling. We know from a scene of the Tramp flirting with a married woman that his sexual morals aren't necessarily any better than Edna's, but he doesn't have to pine or repent. And even his response to the infant is mixed. For instance, having been unable to dispose of the swaddled infant by returning it, as he thinks, to a momentarily empty baby buggy, he sits on the curb and offhandedly lifts the gutter grate, which signals to us that he's considering tossing the kid down it. Nothing like this thought ever occurred to Edna, or to any female character in any of Chaplin's movies, though when the Tramp entertains the idea, we readily recognize it as a stray impulse, not a deep taint. But Chaplin (at his best) assumes that the audience can identify with the full range of his male characters' impulses.

By contrast, when Chaplin pays any attention to developing his costar, she's typically idealized to such a point that she's scarcely comic at all. The exceptions come after 1921: Phyllis Allen as the laborer's overwhelming wife in *Pay Day* (1922); Purviance's melancholy, flighty society mistress in *A Woman of Paris* (1923); Paulette Goddard's spirited street urchin in *Modern Times* (1936); and, funniest of all, Martha Raye as the hard-nosed, unkillable intended victim in *Monsieur Verdoux* (1947). The point is that none of them is an exception to Sennett's rule: Allen is a gorgon, Raye a goon, and both are childless; Purviance doesn't get either man, and Goddard is presexual, so in the movies' terms they are not set to become mothers. Furthermore, though critics have pointed out that in *City Lights* (1931), beautiful, adult Virginia Cherrill gets in on the comedy when she empties a pot of flower water in the Tramp's face, she doesn't *take* it in the face, which makes all the difference. And of course she and the Tramp are only loosely associated at the end of the movie.

This last point is important because Sennett's rule also applies to the hero's girl, who is either married to the male lead or will presumably become his wife and the mother of his children after the resolution of the plot. Once Harold Lloyd began making romantic comedy features, he integrated the heroine into the story more than Chaplin, but his women are even more domesticated than Chaplin's. They have to be because they'll become the heroes' wives. Purviance is a fallen woman in *The Kid,* and in the 1915 short *A Woman,* she sees Charlie in drag and literally falls on the floor laughing. She may be bland, but she's not always virginal or even prim, as Lloyd's silent heroines are. Here's how a title card in the 1920 two-reeler *Haunted Spooks* introduces Lloyd's costar Mildred Davis on her third outing opposite him: "THE GIRL. Her life is bounded on the four sides by dimples, smiles, sunshine and kindly deeds."

Davis appeared in eleven Lloyd shorts and was working on what would become the first of four features with him before he took special notice of her off the set, though not for her kindly deeds. Lloyd fell for the teenage Davis only after watching her win over the hostile navy officers present while shooting the 1921 extended short *A Sailor-Made Man* on navy battleships in San Pedro harbor, thereby gaining the crew "permission to do things [they'd] never hoped to do." As Lloyd wrote with awe, "She certainly knew how to handle them." Lloyd the suitor was spurred on by Davis's coquetry and, once he started dating her, by the fact that "she had a lot of beaux." Clearly Davis could broadcast her sex appeal rather capably in life, which Lloyd acknowledged in her updated introductory title in *A Sailor-Made Man:* "The Girl—She averages six proposals a day—Including Sundays and holidays." But he always cast her, with her blonde ringlets and clear, innocent eyes, as a "big French doll."

Lloyd was impressed by Davis's way with the fleet but nonetheless continued to conceive his female costar's roles—both those played by Davis and the six played by Jobyna Ralston after he married and retired Davis—in line with Sennett's comments to Dreiser. A card in the 1925 feature *The Freshman,* for example, tells us that Ralston's character Peggy is "the kind of girl your mother must have been." But though we have reason to suspect a hollow ideal, Ralston unexpectedly fills it out: a wonderful Correggio Madonna type, placid and sweet and promising to mature into a rich womanliness. She's not a partner in Lloyd's stunts but a counterpoint to them. For instance, Harold carries her off bodily from her wedding to a bigamous rival in *Girl Shy,* but he still can't stammer out his proposal without her help. She knows his uncle has trained him to stop stuttering at the sound of a whistle, so standing on the sidewalk, she looks for the mailman, frisks him for his whistle, gives it a toot, and answers, "YES!" She enters the slapstick antics just enough to help Harold emerge from them into adult sexual life, the rewards of which she suggests in every liquid-ginger movement and glance.

The romantic suspense gives Lloyd's movies opposite Ralston the stirringness of borderline situations, and she's especially good at providing an emotional ground against which the slapstick is stitched. However, the suspense doesn't involve her disposition, but only Harold's exertions to prove himself, which are usually unnecessary because in most of his features he has only superfluous rivals—that is, other boys who also want his girl but to whom she clearly prefers Harold—and sometimes no rivals at all. Generally Ralston is already Harold's for the asking if he'll just wriggle through his growing pains. She embodies what the boy struggles to manhood for, but this can leave her on the sidelines, literally in *The Freshman,* cheering Harold on during the football game climax. She's important as an encouraging witness, but her worth can't be in contest as Harold's must be for the story to have tension.

Ralston acts out what these potential wives-and-mothers mean to Lloyd, which restricts her actions, unlike Bebe Daniels in Lloyd's 1917 two-reeler *Lonesome Luke on Tin Can Alley,* in which she plays a strolling, belt-hitching tomboy who scratches her shoulder blades against a telephone pole, punches a masher, grabs Luke's loot, and out-runs him. This short suggests a more aggressive pretty-girl character than any other silent slapstick movie. However, the role isn't central to the action, and the action isn't coherent anyway. And because so few of the *Lonesome Luke* shorts survive, it's impossible to say what Daniels's roles were like overall; this role is exciting, but it's too small a pinhead to paint a theory on. In any case, it doesn't quite indicate a new attitude toward a *romantic* heroine because Daniels plays a tom-boy; she can be funny in this way because she's acting like a boxing gym loiterer. She's certainly nobody's mother. Unfortunately, Lloyd never worked with Daniels after 1920. However, he did realize that he needed more active, ambiguous heroines for the talkies, hence Constance Cummings's worldly, emotionally confused actress in *Movie Crazy* (1932), Una Merkel's tangy, wised-up counter gal in *The Cat's-Paw* (1934), and Phyllis Welch's bright, forward runaway heiress in *Professor Beware* (1938). (Ironically, just at the point in his career when he needed, but was unable, to evolve a new character for himself.)

Keaton had a few simple criteria for leading ladies: that they not make him look short, be able to take the punishing pratfalls, and cost as little as possible. In his autobiography, he said bluntly about his two-reelers, "There were usually but three principals—the villain, my-self, and the girl, and she was never important." Sometimes he would include his heroine in the tumbling boat or the spinning house, but while the house spins on its foundation in the storm in the 1920 short *One Week*, Buster is outside alone with the camera trying to get back in, making a leap for but missing the front door. The girl is just one of the party inside the centrifuge. Keaton wanted his girls to be able to take pratfalls, but there's nothing in his movies comparable to the stun-ning shot of Virginia Vance knocked off her feet by a custard pie in the 1926 Lupino Lane two-reeler *His Private Life*.

There is more variety among Buster Keaton's heroines than Chap-lin's or Lloyd's, but what's most eyebrow raising in his pictures is that he almost never idealizes his relationship to his costar. The exceptions, Marion Byron as the rival ship captain's daughter in the 1928 feature *Steamboat Bill, Jr.*, and, even better, Sally O'Neil's mountain girl in the 1926 feature *Battling Butler*, are sweet without being cloying. But they don't swim in his mainstream. From Virginia Fox's haughty, spurning object of desire in *Cops* and Kate Price's burlesque Bluto of an immi-grant mate in *My Wife's Relations*, both 1922 two-reelers, the tension grows and then nightblooms into Dorothy Sebastian's contemptuous, bitchy Circe in the 1929 feature *Spite Marriage*.

Keaton used the tension between the boy and girl most fully in his 1927 feature *The General,* in which the idyllic courtship of Keaton's Johnny Gray and Marion Mack's Annabelle Lee is interrupted by nothing less than the Civil War and wrecked by the Confederate induction board's rejection of him because they feel he's more useful to the war effort as a railroad engineer. When Johnny's beloved locomotive *The General* is stolen by Union spies, he heads north to get it back. In the process, he happens to find Annabelle being held captive; he rescues her, and they make a dash back south together on the recovered locomotive. Feeding the train's furnace becomes the second source of discord between the couple, but Johnny is no longer in the supplicant's position. In this section of the picture, Keaton seems more adult, less of a stunned baby, because he's so much more capable than the girl. For instance, she exasperates him by sweeping up the engine floor. He tells her that what they need is fuel, so she picks up a wand and tosses it into the inferno while he looks on. In response he picks up a splinter and hands it to her, as if to crack, You forgot *this* log! She misses the sarcasm and promptly opens the grate and throws it in, at which he shakes her by the throat, then kisses her. Keaton, at this point unhappily married for five years and with his wife on the location shoot, here etches the simplest of all can't-live-with-'em-can't-live-without-'em cameos in movie history.

Marion Mack complained that during shooting Keaton "ignored and slighted" her, sticking "to the job and to his little clique." But though the picture, like any other slapstick star's feature, was unambiguously conceived as the protagonist's, Johnny's, from start to finish, the alarming laughs Keaton gets from his hero's discord with the nice girl makes her more important than the usual heroine. In fact, her very incompetence makes Johnny into her straight man. At the same time, she's unambiguously virtuous and funny only in this one sequence in relation to what the hero is trying to accomplish.

Some women could be funny on their own initiative, but only on the other side of the line from the nubile girls. For example, in Harry Langdon's 1926 feature *The Strong Man,* directed by Frank Capra, Langdon as a Belgian soldier comes to America looking for his pen pal sweetheart Mary Brown (Priscilla Bonner)—he's never met her but has sighed over her picture and letters. She turns out to be everything he imagines, though she hasn't let on that she's blind. This makes her more ideal, since her handicap makes him a relatively stronger man than he would be opposite an unimpaired girl.

However, while still searching for her in the city, he's grabbed by Gertrude Astor as Lily, a tall Broadway character with a thick neck and tigerish eyes who, to avoid arrest, has secreted a wad of dough in Harry's coat pocket while standing next to him on the sidewalk. The money slips into the lining of his jacket, and so to get her stash back, she pretends to be Mary Brown and seductively frisks him in a taxi on the way to her apartment. Needless to say, brisk, open sexuality isn't what appealed to Harry in the letters written by the blind girl, who turns out to be a preacher's daughter. When he tries to get away without going up to Lily's room, she pulls a faint; she's so big that to carry her up the marble staircase to her apartment, little Harry has to bump up the stairs on his butt with her slung across his lap. At the landing there's a stepladder aligned with the top step so that he backs the two of them all the way up the ladder, and off the other side. You know they'll go off the far side of the ladder, but you don't realize they'll flump like beef carcasses. It's as pungently indelicate a handling of a woman as slapstick offers.

Astor's role derives from her build. Gloria Swanson felt like a dwarf when the five-foot-eight Astor costarred with her, and it's perfectly in keeping with Astor's screen persona that she once played trombone on a Mississippi showboat. (The physical limits on stardom were so openly known and accepted that a *publicity* photo of Astor blandly bears a caption informing us that she's "beautiful and clever, but just three inches too tall to be a star.") Bonner, by contrast, has been described as "delicate and soft-spoken" and "almost timid by nature, [having] been brought up in a home where voices were never raised," and she related that her virginity made her the company joke when she worked for Marshall Neilan. The necessary split between the big, promiscuous broad and the helpless dear is also a split between a woman who can get in on the pratfalls and one who is kept clear of them. (In fact, Bonner thought Langdon cast her *because* she wasn't a comedienne.) In *The Strong Man* the independent funny lady is experienced to the point of criminality (as she is in Langdon's next picture, *Long Pants*). This is a paradigm of the way in which female roles divide between good and bad, marriageable and sexually active, sweet and sexy, nice and funny girls. Thus Sennett's dogma also means you can't joke about the kind of girl your mother must have been.

You can see this division even in the movies of the Marx Brothers, the least sentimental of all slapstick stars, both before and after the

Production Code, and before and after their move to MGM. In *The Cocoanuts, Animal Crackers, Monkey Business, A Night at the Opera,* and *A Day at the Races,* the ingenues fret and trill while the big ladies—including Margaret Dumont (who also frets and trills, but in a style that the movie easily turns into towering camp), Margaret Irving, Thelma Todd, and Esther Muir—get to play. In a Marx Brothers picture, it's to an actress's advantage to be pushed out of a canoe as Todd is in *Horse Feathers* or stuffed under the couch cushions as Muir is in *A Day at the Races.* Who wouldn't rather tussle with Groucho than wait for him to rescue her, since he likes tangling with dames and openly ridicules his own melodramatic plots? Dumont assumes her unassailability—always a way of asking for it in slapstick, for men and women alike—but Irving, Todd, and Muir are sexual in the manner of *The Strong Man*'s predatory Gertrude Astor. In the Marx Brothers' movies, "gentlemen" prefer broads who get involved in physical comedy precisely because it's associated with sexual activity and independence and all kinds of out-of-bounds traits that indicate a girl isn't nice enough to marry. And from the boisterous broads' side there are plenty of things they might be after besides marriage and motherhood. If one of those things is memorable screen time, then they haven't misspent their energy.

Naturally, slapstick comedians didn't invent the feeling that mothers should be pure vessels. First of all, there's the notion that, apart from unmistakable resemblance, our mother's purity is the only assurance we can have that our father is actually our father. And then there's the feeling attendant upon the realization that we are an outgrowth of our mother's body: since we come out of this vessel, we'd rather it were the Holy Grail than a spittoon. In 1926, when John Gilbert tried to get story approval from Louis B. Mayer for his next picture, Mayer shouted in objection, "Only you, you bastard, would allow a whore to enter a story about a beloved mother and her young boy!" Things got worse when Gilbert replied, "What's wrong with that? My mother was a whore!" Mayer screamed, "You should have your balls cut off for making such a remark!" and slugged Gilbert; as he was being restrained from attacking further, Mayer yelled, "I hate that bastard . . . He doesn't love his mother!" There is probably a little Louis B. Mayer in most men. Certainly, people have traditionally had very different attitudes toward male and female promiscuity, and slapstick comedies, which in this country have always been highly conventional and totally commercial, are not about to violate this sort of social norm.

What's strange is that for female characters, physical comedy itself is seen as a form of impurity, as if pratfalls, even though at the level of character and story they are clearly unintentional, imply that the heroine is altogether too physically available. Falling on her ass appears to make people wonder what else she might do with it. This isn't as idle a comment as it might sound. Miriam Cooper said that in the silent era, "all those girls who did comedy were tough," and then tells of how Mabel Normand shocked her and two other dramatic actresses visiting Cooper's hotel room by lifting the back of her skirt in front a full-length mirror and whooping, "My ass is open to the world." This implication is what forces female characters in slapstick movies to choose between comedy and motherhood, that realm "ideally" impregnable to laughter. The choice occurs as part of the plot but also reflects the moviemakers' a priori judgment about how the audience feels about the actress. Either way, the pattern is the same and nearly as Sennett described it.

Still, in the movies that focus on female characters, there's some room for play in Sennett's dogma: when the heroine is young, the audience enjoys laughing at her up to a point. But then she needs to be rescued from the possibility of ridicule if she is to have a happy ending as a wife and mother. This isn't the case with heroes. Think of Harold Lloyd on the rooftop in the final shot of *Safety Last!* walking with and cuddling Mildred and leaving first his shoes and then his socks in a patch of tar. Or of Harry Langdon telling his girl in the final scene of *The Strong Man,* "Run along home, honey. I don't need any help," and then tripping over a rock.

All of this is connected to the common observation among the people who made a living from it that women tend not to enjoy slapstick as much as men. Sennett referred to his audience as "the average working guy," which makes sense considering that the last jobs held by Sennett and Hal Roach, the two most prominent producers of silent slapstick, before going into theatrical work were as an ironworker and the superintendent for a long-line mule team freighting company, respectively. (One interviewer has said of Roach, "When he laughed, it was deep and about as masculine as laughter can get.") Harold Lloyd chose his most famous costume to get away from "low-comedy clothes" in order to "permit enough romantic appeal to catch the feminine eye, usually averted from comedies." Groucho Marx proclaimed, "Women don't understand crazy humor," and Irving G. Thalberg, thinking along the same lines, added an ingenue with a straight operetta love story and songs to *A Night at the Opera* to attract female moviegoers. It's even the case that all the major Warner Brothers cartoon characters are male.

In addition, it's apparent that men don't like to laugh at women, certainly not the women they're attracted to. When Mack Sennett tried to transfer Gloria Swanson from "sweet, homespun [Keystone] comedies with Bobby Vernon" to rougher slapstick entries opposite Mack Swain and Chester Conklin, she protested that she didn't like pictures "where people throw pies and spill soup." Sennett countered, "Nobody's thrown any pies at you, have they? . . . I wouldn't allow it. It's not funny with a pretty girl." Too often the girl merely provides, as Gilbert Seldes pointed out, "serene, idle beauty" for the wilder male comics to play against. Most female stars are good-looking, so the persistent scarcity of full-on slapstick leads for women, which goes all the way back, shouldn't come as a surprise. There were always some female slapstick stars, but they were funny in a much narrower and gentler range than the male stars, who could be utterly ridiculous and still end up married . . . or dead.

Mabel Normand, a lovely young woman, was one of the biggest slapstick stars of either sex, but in her shorts and in the Sennett features *Tillie's Punctured Romance* (1914) and *The Extra Girl* (1923), she engages more sporadically than male stars in acrobatic mayhem. Of course, she wasn't a stage-trained comedy kangaroo like her frequent costars Chaplin and Arbuckle; she had been successful as an illustrator's and photographer's model (for Charles Dana Gibson and James Montgomery Flagg among others) when she started as an extra girl with Biograph in Manhattan in 1909. Her function in her Keystone shorts is to be peppy, more of a morsel than average, and to suffer outrage when slapstick sweeps her in its wake. When the action starts, she typically looks out at us and mouths, "Oh!" as if the rumpus threatens not her bones but some conception of herself. Her baffled clown grimace is at times so expressive you can feel her sigh sneaking out of *your* chest, but she doesn't really get to work her conflicts out bodily. She will slap mashers and even other women when they go after her man, but she didn't have the vaudeville training to improvise routines in response to mischance and affront. She's the motive spirit in almost no fully-developed sequences.

For instance, at one point in the 1915 Keystone one-reeler *Wished on Mabel,* a bee lands on her nose. Frantic, she crosses her eyes, shakes her hands, and steps backward, plumping herself down on a strange man's lap. Remaining thus seated, she smiles at her misstep, but when the man chucks her under the chin, she starts whamming him. The bee gag per se and the way it leads to the mashing joke, as well as Mabel's contrary responses to the stranger, are arbitrary and don't add up to anything. The scene keeps moving forward, but like a jet trail that dissipates as fast as it progresses. In the 1914 Keystone one-reeler *Mabel's Married Life,* she buys a punching dummy—the kind set on a round bottom so that it always rises from a punch—to make Chaplin as her sotted husband think a lover has followed her home from the park. At one point, Chaplin drunkenly throttles her, but when he has his memorable confrontation with the dummy, he's solo. Mabel reenters for some more tumbles at the end, but she doesn't have the same clarity in the slapstick that Chaplin has. Her pratfalls aren't physically characteristic, as even the dummy's are.

Normand *is* lively, however, as you might expect of a girl who had been proud as a child of outswimming all the local boys her age. *Wished on Mabel* starts with her being bored by her mother's reading fairy tales to her in the park; she runs off to frolic with Fatty, acting out the audience's urge for less innocent amusements. In the 1915 Keystone one-reeler *Mabel's Wilful Way,* she's even friskier. She sneaks off from her parents at a beer garden and goes to a refreshment kiosk where she steals candy from a jar and starts gobbling it. The clerk catches her, and so she puts it all back—not just the candy in her hand but the piece she's been chewing on as well.

However, such promising comic impulses don't evolve because in these pictures there are limits to how far a girl can break out from parental guidance. For instance, *Mabel's Wilful Way* doesn't offer a specific motive behind the daughter's wish to break out. It takes it for granted but thereby makes Mabel, who's run off with no money in her pocket, seem kind of dopey. You wonder what she's after, which you don't wonder when Fatty sees her predicament and steals money from the clerk's register to "buy" her an ice cream. These movies are unambivalent about male horniness but hedge about why a girl would seek adventure. They had a reason to hedge. The early Raff and Gammon short subject called *The May Irwin–John C. Rice Kiss* had drawn fire specifically in relation to young girls in amusement parks, as a letter to the editor of the *New Orleans Daily Item* in 1896 attests: "But permit me to suggest that the too suggestive kissing scene be dropped. This may capture the fancy of the lascivious, but it is actually repulsive to the clean of mind. I am sure that the young ladies who resort to the park, and all careful parents, must prefer not to have this scene produced any more." And Sennett was probably alert to the more recent criticism of Normand's earlier character Vitagraph Betty, who was considered too "free in her hugging and kissing." So Mabel wants to flirt and neck, but we sense she wouldn't go as far as it's implied the men would. The men's roles are thus more coherent, despite the brief development of character possible in slapstick shorts, because their baseness is commonly understood.

These movies, which kiddies could be sent off to by themselves, never draw on the actress's real experiences in the boomtown of Hollywood—for instance, the spring chicks Mabel Normand and Adela Rogers St. Johns prowling the Vernon Country Club without dates because they "thought it would be more fun to see who was around than to go with someone [they] already knew." Though Normand and Arbuckle formed the only remotely equal boy-and-girl team in silent slapstick (equal in terms of screen time and importance of their characters to the story), this reticence in their movies derives in part from the double standard of the men making the movies. Arbuckle "did not like dirty stories told when women were present. He adored Mabel Normand, but there were times when her uninhibited use of four-letter words and salacious antics such as flipping up her skirt to reveal her lack of underwear, made him uneasy and embarrassed." In response, Normand recruited a gang of girls from the Keystone ranks, dubbed them the Dirty Four, and claimed "equal rights for the girl comics. [They] declared war on the exclusive right of men to talk dirty." Normand was wittily self-aware of her outrageous image. For instance, one day while working for Samuel Goldwyn, who was smitten with her, Normand fumed to Goldwyn's scenarist Frances Marion: "'I'm mad at him now. . . . Look at him,' stabbing her finger in his direction, 'that stuck-up bastard! That—' and she let fly a string of cuss words that no longshoreman could improve on. Finally out of breath, she turned to me apologetically: 'Excuse me, Frances, for pointing.'"

Men tend to be suspicious of the idea that women, like men, might want excitement for its own sake. And women themselves tend to go back and forth about their own motives. Thus the confusion about the modern girl's impulses, reflected in Normand's Keystone shorts, is genuine, but these shoestring moviemakers didn't know how to use it for their art. They end *Mabel's Wilful Way*, for example, with Mabel's father turning her over his knee and spanking her.

The happiest exception to the wispy underdevelopment of Normand's roles is the 1915 Keystone one-reeler *Mabel and Fatty's Married Life*, like *Wished on Mabel* and *Mabel's Wilful Way* directed by Arbuckle. *Mabel and Fatty's Married Life* is such a good opportunity for Normand because the story arises entirely from her (admittedly basic) character, a wifey so overexcited by melodramatic crime books that she almost shoots her husband when he comes home during the day and she thinks he's a robber. He insists that she stop being so paranoid and leaves, after which she finds herself alone again, busy at her worktable, trying to pretend that the curtain by the window isn't moving as if someone were hiding behind it. Sennett's people add to the joke by making Mabel's hat jump around on her head—unaccountably, not only does she wear her hat while sitting at home, but we see her put it on as she sits down to work. This sloppiness doesn't matter, however, because this is Normand's most inventive stretch of pantomime. As Mabel is increasingly unable to suppress her hysteria, Normand lets go, mugging while squashing the jumpy hat back down. It's a slapstick version of what would become typical Lillian Gish material—the orchestral surge of female panic.

This overlap makes sense because Sennett and Normand had both worked with Griffith at Biograph in New York. Despite the differences in their temperaments, both men saw Normand as a sensual troublemaker: Griffith cast her as a restless, kohl-eyed rural home wrecker in the 1912 Biograph one-reeler *The Eternal Mother,* and Sennett cast her as a niece who sneaks out of her seaside hotel room to show off her skintight bathing leotard for the boys on the diving platform in the 1911 Biograph split-reel romp *The Diving Girl.* Griffith, the conductor of Gish's first great performances, also gave Normand a mini–mad scene in the 1911 Biograph one-reel melodrama *Her Awakening* after Mabel's public shame over her mother's tatty apron has so dazed the old lady that she gets run over by a car. Sennett didn't go in for this kind of thing, preferring instead to play moralistic melodramas for laughs. And Normand gets more out of hanging on to her hat as if to her sanity in *Mabel and Fatty's Married Life* than any male star of the era got from having his hat leap in fright or his hair stand on end. I think *Mabel and Fatty's Married Life* works so well for Normand because the wife's fear of burglars is classic female material in popular culture—even if it's corny and perhaps patronizing, it has a definite shape. In *Mabel and Fatty's Married Life* Sennett and Arbuckle didn't just take their girl star for granted but fashioned the logic of the vignette around her. The pleasure we get out of it is magnified by its rarity.

As Sennett affirmed, men don't want to laugh at pretty girls, not convulsively anyway, and so the actresses who specialize in all-out slapstick tend to be women like Marie Dressler, Phyllis Allen, Louise Fazenda, Polly Moran (all four worked for Sennett), Dot Farley, Charlotte Greenwood, Martha Raye, and Judy Canova, whom the average male wouldn't ordinarily think of romantically anyway. And with the occasional exception of Dressler, the careers of these women were limited to shorts, and after the demise of shorts to supporting roles. But what happens to female slapstick leads in features, which are much more likely to be romantic comedies? In the Sennett feature *The Extra Girl*, Mabel Normand plays Sue, a girl who's in love with Dave (Ralph Graves), her small-town boyfriend, but whose father wants her to marry a far less appealing candidate (Langdon's future foil Vernon Dent). However, Sue wants to be a movie star even more than she wants to marry Dave, and so she plans to mail her photo to a Hollywood studio. A rival substitutes a fashion photo in place of Sue's, hoping to get her out of town, and Sue does win an invitation to Hollywood. But when she arrives, the disappointed studio head makes her an assistant in the wardrobe department. To justify the slapstick treatment, the movie has to pretend that Normand, the former model, isn't the looker she clearly is.

The story is lumpy, not really an organically developed series of slapstick episodes or a romantic comedy with its own momentum. But it does have a number of knockabout scenes—Sue's escape from her own wedding, climbing in and out of her second-story window on a ladder and racing on a horse cart to the train to Hollywood; scattered bits of Sue working in the wardrobe department; the screen test that Sue is allowed to make; and a long sequence in which Sue leads a lion through the studio thinking it's a Great Dane in a mangy lion costume. The screen test, in which Sue plays an antebellum scene in a short hoop skirt with ruffled pantalets, is most revealing, so to speak. Before going on, Sue unwittingly sits on a workman's greasy glove, which leaves a black handprint on her otherwise crisp white drawers. During the test, in which the character displays no remarkable acting talent, she bends over, exposing the stain on her rump to the camera and crew, who laugh.

Sue doesn't know why they laugh, until four years later when she has married Dave and he projects the test for her and their young son. The boy watches the test and asks, "Daddy, who is that man kissing mama?" which suggests that when Sue was away from her parents, unmarried and living on her own in a rooming house without Dave's protection, she was unsettlingly out of conventional bounds. The fact that while on her own she meets a shady financier who swindles her parents out of the proceeds from the farm they sold to come live with her in L.A. further formulates her danger as melodrama.

So while Sue is trying to have a career of her own, the movie puts that slapstick handprint on her ass. It implies that Sue has strayed from the pure romantic comedy realm, in which she and Dave would have merely to overcome her father's objections (an emphasis that would bring the male costar forward), into a vaguer slapstick realm, in which the strange man's handprint suggests she's not merely evading a good reputation but actively acquiring a bad one. At the private family showing of the screen test, Normand has a funny reaction shot in several steps—slowly closing her lids in retro-humiliation and then compulsively lifting one; her transitions are superb—but her character has been saved from the consequences of foolishness.

If my interpretation of the handprint seems overelaborate, compare *The Extra Girl* to Gloria Swanson's 1924 working-girl comedy *Manhandled*. Swanson plays Tessie, a department store discount-basement clerk whose boyfriend Jimmy (Tom Moore) works day and night to pay for the development of a fuel-saving engine he's designed. Jimmy is so busy he's never available to take Tessie out, leading her to accept an invitation to a party from the department store heir and his novelist friend. Her comic impression of a Russian aristocrat, Countess Offernutski, charms the playboys at the soiree and leads to her getting better jobs, which we follow in pay increments up from $18 per week, to $60 as a romantic sculptor's model, to $75, with clothes thrown in, as a couture boutique hostess. (The hitch of the boutique job is that Tessie has to play the Russian countess when greeting the clientele—even extravagantly homesick White Russians who long to speak in the mother tongue. Tessie's panic upon "hearing" Cyrillic intertitles is perfectly timed.) Jimmy is off in Detroit making his breakthrough while Tessie is back in New York making the rounds, though not "enjoying" them the way a former coworker is. Each man Tessie charms warns her against the others, but they all want the same thing. On the night Jimmy returns unannounced, Tessie gets in late, with bruises on her arms where the retail heir has grabbed her in the back of his limousine. We know that Tessie is crazy about Jimmy and not even tempted by the other men, but we also see how bad those traces of another man's hands look to Jimmy.

Swanson is extraordinary in this uncharacteristically unglamorous role. No actress ever chewed gum with a more convincingly unselfconscious comic slovenliness; her defensive look when the store manager gives her a demerit because it's not appropriate at work perfectly establishes Tessie's adolescent cluelessness. And for a star who hated slapstick, Swanson more than "manages" the opening slapstick of the footsore worker's subway ride home. (Two tall men keep lifting her cloche hat off her head between their elbows, and she keeps resentfully snugging it back down. Then they knock her purse to the floor and, in bending over to help her pick it up, accidentally interlock arms with her; when they straighten up, they lift her off her feet.) Despite her dislike of slapstick, Swanson shows the benefit of her experience at Keystone, where, as she later recalled, "We made up our own stories as we went along. . . . It was a wonderful way to earn a living." The slapstick is at least as good as what Langdon and Lloyd came up with for their subway rides in *Feet of Mud* (a 1926 two-reeler) and *Speedy* (a 1928 feature), respectively. And though Lloyd Hamilton's sequence in *Crushed* (a 1924 two-reeler) is more inventive, Swanson's is better in that it's linked to her character as a tired working commuter.

Furthermore, Swanson shows Tessie's frustration with her situation without ever giving us to understand that *her* dignity, that is, Miss Gloria Swanson's, is inviolable. (Director Allan Dwan made her ride the subway at rush hour to break her down for the role.) She's Tessie to the core, which gives her actions startling impact; for instance, when she teases a man by dropping her hankie and grabbing it herself in midair just as he's starting to stoop for it.

However, the movie lets us know that this kind of physical assertiveness, even though satirical and self-protective, is the wrong kind of skill for Tessie. The movie does understand that a woman can be wised up without necessarily "knowing" more than she should, but it also accepts frankly that only in chivalrous romances can a woman accept gifts from a man without being expected to give something in return. In other words, Tessie's morality has to be beyond *possible* reproach. (In Hollywood, Louis B. Mayer applied this moral like a showman to his daughters' public turnout, legislating everything from their nail polish to their facial expressions, "because in Mayer's eyes appearances both reflected an inner reality and helped create it; there was no sense in being virtuous if the virtue didn't show.") So Tessie has to learn to appear as chaste as we in the audience, who follow her when Jimmy's away, know she is. When Jimmy sees the black-and-blue finger marks he calls Tessie "manhandled," like the clearance goods she sells. The story and dialogue of *Manhandled* thus make explicit the symbolism of the black handprint on Sue's underwear in *The Extra Girl*; they're further linked by the fact that Tessie, like Sue, is involved in slapstick only when she's out of the house, whether she's working or partying. And both the handprint and the bruises help turn the pictures toward resolutions that take Sue and Tessie out of the dangerous workplace and into the home.

Diana Trilling wrote of her mother when she first came to this country from Poland in the early 1890s, "While she learned English, she worked as a model in the garment district. Her employment as a model soon turned out to be too morally hazardous for her and she apprenticed herself to a milliner." Such hazards were also associated specifically with the movies. As the future Pat Nixon wrote her brother Bill in 1933 about being scouted by Paramount for a movie contract: "I went down to the Paramount Theatre (by request) and they photographed me, etc. etc., then offered me tryouts for stage dancing, etc. then modeling too. But that life is too tough, and unless you are featured the pay is low—one of the reasons why girls are tempted to accept presents and attentions—sheer necessity." These anecdotes, in which young women working outside the home face the temptation to trade on sex, indicate that these movies about the testing of a girl's morality reflect actual experience.

In fact, Swanson's experiences while developing *Manhandled*'s screenplay helped mold the story along these lines. She and Dwan were given the title by a Paramount vice president who was eager to flirt with a list of Hays Office proscriptions—you couldn't *show* "manhandling" on the screen, but the list said nothing about calling a picture *Manhandled*. Then the director and star simply had to come up with a story to go with the racy title. The staff screenwriter Frank Tuttle found an acceptable moralistic melodrama in the *Saturday Evening Post,* and the group headed to Florida to bang out a workable script. When they went down to Havana for better weather, Swanson found herself being courted by big Cuban plantation owners, who, to her dismay, assumed an actress would be as available to them as a prostitute. Swanson says she considered herself a "strait-laced American girl who made her own living," not the femme fatale that she usually played and that the Cuban men wanted her to be when they met her. She incorporated into the script what she learned from these misadventures, which culminated just like *Manhandled* in the back of a Rolls Royce, but with Swanson in the grubby mitts of *two* men, who claimed to be father and son, no less. And the lesson was corroborated at the other end of the social spectrum when she worked for a day as a salesgirl at Gimbels in preparation for the part: "On my ten-minute breaks I would scoot to the ladies' room, and there I got a whole education in how to deal with guys who got fresh and took girls for granted."

All these working-girl comedies are in some ways truthful about our confusion over women's roles in the new century. Such confusion can actually be great for comedy; however, slapstick features resolve the way people feel about women's exposure to temptation by removing the heroine from open spaces, which is where the action takes place. In *Manhandled,* we know that Jimmy is deeply wrong about Tessie, but the movie unhysterically shows that both Jimmy and Tessie have to come to their senses about what she's been up to. The happy resolution is that Jimmy's success in Detroit will permit her to become a housewife, which is all she wanted in the first place. But the movie ends before she actually gets her wish, which would be less fun than seeing her dangle.

Thus *The Extra Girl* and *Manhandled* both end with the heroines safely hitched, though only the former includes a coda of domestic security. As for Normand, when she made *The Extra Girl,* she had never been married and had had a hugely successful career in slapstick comedies. And it isn't correct to give the impression that her movies were completely shaped by Sennett and Arbuckle, men with Victorian notions about female behavior. From early on, Normand "had Sennett's ear, and often was able to persuade him, against his stubborn Irish will, to follow her . . . instincts." But more than being just the power behind the throne, Normand "again and again proved able to come up with useable picture ideas" and in fact was directing her own movies at Keystone by 1914, when she was twenty-two. (She directed Chaplin before Sennett let him direct himself.) So it makes sense to presume that she would have worked up the material for *The Extra Girl* along with Sennett, who produced it.

Sennett made *The Extra Girl* to help Normand after she had left his studio (and bed) to work for Samuel Goldwyn, who unsuccessfully cast her in a drama. When it had to be reshot and still failed at the box office, Goldwyn had her start churning out formula slapstick romances much like her earlier Sennett feature *Mickey* (1918). But before she went back to Sennett, she'd already been sideswiped by the unsolved William Desmond Taylor murder. Though, according to Robert Giroux's account, Normand was the cause of Taylor's death, she wasn't even remotely guilty of it. All the same, the effect of the scandal on her career was not a hailstorm from a blue sky: her energy as a star personality had gone largely to living it up as a bad girl. She had been a respectable working-class model by the age of sixteen; to switch into movie work required overcoming her religious mother's objections, and the reports of her carryings-on make you think her mother was right to worry. In Hollywood, Normand was one of the few unchaperoned girls, and she "liked to run wild because it shocked the stage mothers and delighted their daughters. [She] liked to be the scandal of the town." Thus it's perfectly in keeping with her personality that when she acts out the classic Cinderella scene of hurrying from a midnight party in the 1921 Goldwyn feature *What Happened to Rosa,* she doesn't leave her slipper behind, she leaves her dress. By this time her off-screen skirt flipping could often be attributed to narcotics, and her youthful high spirits had become plain old unfunny drunkenness. She didn't help her career by making it difficult for the publicity men to get printable quotations from her, all the while ignoring the tuberculosis that would kill her before the age of forty. Being a bad girl can seem liberating to the daughters of vigilant stage mothers even as it immolates their idol.

If I speak of *The Extra Girl* exclusively in terms of how it pegs Normand's "likeable 'she-ro,'" to use a contemporary critic's coinage, it's because the movie isn't very successful as a comedy. It calculates audience response with too little finesse and isn't headlong or instinctual as even a second-string Keaton picture like *College* is. *The Extra Girl does* have the perfect Normand moment, when she's trying to sneak upstairs past Dent, who's waiting for her in the parlor with her mother. Halfway up, her bag of apples busts; Dent comes to see what's going on, and Mabel, with her adolescent girl's comically wistful blend of compliance and defiance, kicks the apples at him as she comes back downstairs to join him. But overall *The Extra Girl* feels becalmed by its agenda to counter the tattle that Normand had skipped off from "parental" restraint in decadent Hollywood.

To restore goodwill toward Normand, the picture rewinds her career to a position lower than any she'd had in the movies and then saves her from Hollywood altogether by marriage—but as a slapstick story, the ending would be the same in any case. Swanson had a successfully daring screen image in romances, but when she worked out the comic story of *Manhandled,* she brought it home to the same harbor as *The Extra Girl,* at the end of which Sue has to forswear her career to reassure the audience about her playing slapstick in the first place. At the same time, you could say that slapstick dramatizes the girl's fear that she won't find a mate and have children (true as recently as the 1997 romantic comedy *'Til There Was You,* starring Jeanne Tripplehorn). This internal view of slapstick matches the external view Swanson put into words when she said of Sennett's casting her in that knockabout production, "It was somehow not respectable." Sennett himself changed the last intertitle of *The Extra Girl* from the scenario's more neutral exchange between Sue and her son when he asks who the lady on the screen is, and she answers, "Why that is mama . . . acting in the movies when she was young and foolish," to Sue's more orthodox avowal to

Dave, "Dearest, to hear him call me Mamma means more than the greatest career I might ever have had." Either way, by having Sue settle down at the end, Normand was trying to extend her success with the kind of stories her audience wanted to see. Normand was an entertainment businesswoman hoping to revive a profitable movie heroine, who'd never challenged the boys on-screen as Normand herself had delighted in doing behind the scenes, anyway.

Frederick Lewis Allen wrote of women in the twenties that they "worshiped not merely youth, but unripened youth: they wanted to be—or thought men wanted them to be—men's casual and light-hearted companions; not broad-hipped mothers of the race, but irresponsible playmates." However, the movies, like the confession magazines popular in the era, avoided censorship by insisting on moralizing endings to their racy stories, a bastardizing commercial creed that could be stated outright without shame by an editor in the following rejection slip published by the Lynds: "*Live Stories* is interested in what we call 'sex adventure' stories told in the first person. The stories should embody picturesque settings for action; they should also present situations of high emotional character, rich in sentiment. A moral conclusion is essential." The women in the popular audience wanted to see their way of life as respectable mothers threatened with irresponsibility and danger but not fundamentally challenged. That is, they enjoyed the excitement of someone shouting "fire" in the theater as long as the exits weren't locked. As Colleen Moore wrote:

> For all that women in the roaring twenties believed themselves to be emancipated, free to smoke and drink and—most of all—to discuss right out in the open the great taboo of sex, the vast majority of women did nothing of the kind. Nor did the lives they led resemble even remotely, for the most part, the romances fed to them in movie theaters.
>
> Feed on those romances they could and did.

Adela Rogers St. Johns, the ultimate twenties career girl, estimated that at the time, 90 percent "of the women who were wives and mothers did NOT have nor wish careers or jobs." Female moviegoers, the majority of the audience overall (Iris Barry estimated 75 percent in 1926), though not for slapstick movies, expected a sort of cultural exchange. In the movie magazines, they saw stills of popular actresses like Moore "cooking, sewing, playing tennis, swimming, gardening." But Moore let the paper doll apron slip off: "I didn't have the vaguest idea of how to cook or sew or garden, and had no time to learn, but such pictures of cozy domesticity went over big with the fans, who were always looking for some link between their lives and the lives of their favorite movie stars."

The story of *The Extra Girl,* a technological updating of Cinderella that flirts with the possibility of female independence, became standard early on. Colleen Moore's 1926 feature *Ella Cinders* is also about a small-town Cinderella who gets to Hollywood by winning a studio-sponsored beauty contest. The contest turns out to have been a scam, but she knows that if she goes back, the whole town will laugh at her, so she pushes forward, sneaking onto the studio lot to search out her chance. Ella becomes a star, as Sue never does in *The Extra Girl,* but then makes the greater sacrifice by giving up her achieved stardom for marriage and motherhood.

Ella Cinders is much funnier than *The Extra Girl* in a very available way—it has a Top Ten lilt. I think that Moore felt she could afford to be funny because although she suits up in flapper wear very fashionably, unlike Normand's, Moore's looks are middling—she could be Louise Brooks's sister, but she could also be ZaSu Pitts's sister. In-between looks are an advantage for slapstick. That's in fact why Ella won the "beauty" contest: a fly landed on her nose during her photo session so that in the stills she submits her eyes are crossed. As one of the judges says, "Beauty means nothin'. . . . The movies need newer and funnier faces." Moore has agreeably loose standards when it comes to her looks and poise. She's willing to play a scene with her face covered with coal dust or soap (or flour in the 1927 *Orchids and Ermine,* which isn't otherwise a slapstick movie, or motor oil in the 1928 *Lilac Time,* which is a romantic melodrama), to undermine the very possibility of Ella's being glamorous by parodying the fey poses of ingenues while sitting for the photographer, and to perform a long bit of hilarious, impossible eye tricks (accomplished by immaculate double exposure).

More important, *Ella Cinders* is structured around slapstick in a way that Normand's movies were only fitfully. In silent movies, slapstick riffs were often used to show a young heroine's high spirits, but there are almost never full-on routines like those in *Ella Cinders,* devised by director Alfred E. Green with former vaudevillian Mervyn LeRoy as his head gagman. For instance, there's a routine in which Ella, sent to slave in her wicked stepmother's work shed, punches a hole through a blocked-up window and sticks her head out to get a peek at the iceman she loves. Blocking the window is a billboard; from his side, the iceman sees Ella's head on the neck of a babe in arms, and laughs. The stepmother comes in, scolds Ella for lollygagging, and sticks her head through the hole to see what her stepdaughter was gandering at just as a bill sticker who has noticed the hole slaps the board with glue to repair the damage.

Even better is the centerpiece sequence of Moore slipping onto the studio lot. First she has to get past the guard, with such tricks as stacking a mannequin's head on her own and draping her shoulders with a blanket to make herself look more sleekly actressy. She never fools the guard, but she almost outruns him as he chases her onto the stages where, not understanding that the crews are in the middle of shooting, she interrupts three pictures. It's a clever series that includes some Harold Lloyd–like false assumptions, both on our part and on the characters'. In the second of these inset pictures, she comes upon Harry Langdon trying to hold a door closed against several men on the other side. Moore lends a shoulder, saying, "They're after me, too." Then, in an enticing matchup of talents—Langdon's fluster and Moore's spunk—they have a little routine together in which Langdon disguises Moore as his dinner table to hide her from the studio cop.

Moore's slim, lacquered flapper is one of Hollywood's first images of a modern gal. And behind the scenes she moved easily between male and female society in Hollywood, gossiping with other starlets on the Griffith lot and then learning to roll a cigarette with one hand and twirl a rope while on location with the cowboy actor Buck Jones. She explained why her career had stalled in 1923, despite her natural aptitude for the wide-eyed, so-called "Papa, what is beer?" expression:

> I just wasn't the accepted—and acceptable—model for a sweet young thing in the throes of her first love. The necessary curls I could manage, the same way Mary Pickford and the others did, with time and effort. But no amount of either could make my five-foot-five boyish figure into a curvy, petite five-foot-two or transform the sauciness of my freckled face with its turned-up nose into the demure perfection of a Mary Pickford.

She solved the career problem by noticing the girls her younger brother brought home from college, who

> didn't look any more like the sweet young things I was playing in the movies than I did. They were smart and sophisticated, with an air of independence about them, and so casual about their looks and clothes and manners as to be almost slapdash. . . . I shared their restlessness, understood their determination to free themselves of the Victorian

You can't leave accidents to chance: slapstick stunts took more work than we tend to think. Harold Lloyd at work with assistants during the shooting of *The Freshman* (1925). Courtesy of the Academy of Motion Picture Arts and Sciences.

Lloyd taking a fall with the help of an off-camera assistant during the shooting of *The Freshman*. Courtesy of the Academy of Motion Picture Arts and Sciences.

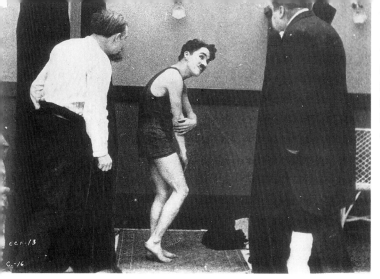

The protean poseur: Chaplin in *The Cure* (1917). Courtesy of the Museum of Modern Art Film Stills Archive.

Chaplin in *The Great Dictator* (1940). Courtesy of the Museum of Modern Art Film Stills Archive.

Left to right: Chaplin with Henry Daniell and Jack Oakie in *The Great Dictator.* Courtesy of the Museum of Modern Art Film Stills Archive.

Father and son in matching outfits on stage: Joe, Myra, and Buster Keaton in vaudeville, circa 1900. Courtesy of the Museum of Modern Art Film Stills Archive.

Ernest Torrence about to refashion Keaton, his college-educated shrimp of a son, more to his own liking in *Steamboat Bill, Jr.* (1928). Tom Lewis looks on and sympathizes with the old man. Courtesy of the Museum of Modern Art Film Stills Archive.

Father and son in matching outfits on-screen: Keaton and Torrence in *Steamboat Bill, Jr.* Courtesy of the Museum of Modern Art Film Stills Archive.

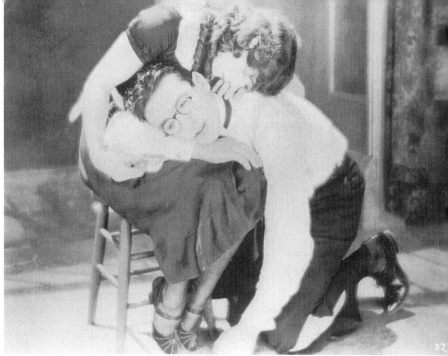

The comedy of sexual maturation: the girl holds the boy up and leans on him at the same tim
Jobyna Ralston and Harold Lloyd in the scene that Lloyd cut from re-release prints of *The Freshman* (1925). Courtesy of the Academy of Motion Picture Arts and Sciences.

Why choose? The slapstick comedian does not have to be an innocent, as we see in the movie
of Raymond Griffith, who in *Hands Up!* (1926, with Marian Nixon and Virginia Lee Corbin)
played on men's sexual fantasies as much as their dread. Courtesy of the Academy of Motion
Picture Arts and Sciences.

The Kid Brother, after Harold Hickory fools his brothers by pretending to be the girl, he
~retends to be the father. Courtesy of the Museum of Modern Art Film Stills Archive.

~rold Lloyd in *The Kid Brother* (1927). Courtesy of the Museum of Modern Art Film Stills
~chive.

Amazons are funny: a publicity still of strapping Gertrude Astor, the lewd, comic villainess of Harry Langdon's *The Strong Man* (1926). Courtesy of the Academy of Motion Picture Arts and Sciences.

Virgins are not funny: a publicity still for demure Priscilla Bonner, the blind preacher's daughter Harry tumbles for in *The Strong Man*. Courtesy of the Academy of Motion Picture Arts and Sciences.

abel Normand takes a spill in *The Extra Girl* (1923). Courtesy of the Museum of Modern Art
m Stills Archive.

Mabel Normand is saved from slapstick because she's pretty enough to catch a husband
(Ralph Graves). Courtesy of the Museum of Modern Art Film Stills Archive.

By dressing down, the comic actress can play physical comedy. Colleen Moore with wicked stepmother Vera Lewis in *Ella Cinders* (1926). Courtesy of the Museum of Modern Art Film Stills Archive.

Moore in *Ella Cinders* also shows that the comic actress can parody the kind of beauty that must be taken seriously in romances. Courtesy of the Academy of Motion Picture Arts and Sciences.

Moore suits up elegantly in *Ella Cinders*.
Courtesy of the Academy of Motion Picture
Arts and Sciences.

inally, the comic actress is an acceptable candidate for marriage and motherhood, though nce she's attained them, her slapstick days are behind her. Moore with Lloyd Hughes in *Ella Cinders*. Courtesy of the Academy of Motion Picture Arts and Sciences.

Beatrice Lillie and Harry C. Myers in *Exit Smiling* (1926). Courtesy of the Museum of Modern Art Film Stills Archive.

Lillie lacks the physical beauty to win Jack Pickford, here staring at her in his dapper villain's costume in *Exit Smiling*. Courtesy of the Museum of Modern Art Film Stills Archive.

William Haines, Polly Moran, Marion Davies, and King Vidor on the set of *Vidor's Show People* (1928). The heroine takes herself seriously in front of the camera while the hero cuts up; the plain-faced supporting actress can appreciate the joke. Courtesy of the Museum of Modern Art Film Stills Archive.

Preston Sturges and Betty Hutton in a publicity still around the time of *Star Spangled Rhythm* (1942). Later that year she would have reason to hug him when he directed her in her best role: Trudy Kockenlocker. Courtesy of the Museum of Modern Art Film Stills Archive.

All exceptions admitted: Hepburn, the most beautiful of all slapstick heroines, gets her man playing slapstick—and enjoying it—to the very end. Courtesy of the Museum of Modern Art Film Stills Archive.

Cary Grant and Katharine Hepburn in *Bringing Up Baby* (1938). Courtesy of the Museum of Modern Art Film Stills Archive.

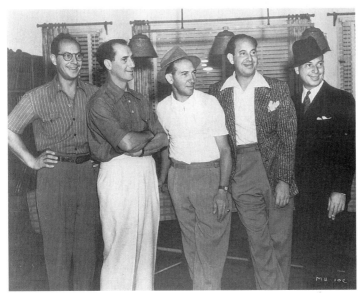

Brothers Zeppo, Groucho, Chico, Gummo, and Harpo Marx, in 1938.
Courtesy of the Museum of Modern Art Film Stills Archive.

Brothers Chico, Zeppo, Groucho, and Harpo Marx in *Duck Soup* (1933).
Courtesy of the Museum of Modern Art Film Stills Archive.

William Demarest and Betty Hutton in Sturges's *The Miracle of Morgan's Creek* (1944). Girls should *listen* to their fathers. Courtesy of the Museum of Modern Art Film Stills Archive.

Jimmy Dundee, Eddie Bracken, and William Demarest in Sturges's *Hail the Conquering Hero* (1944). The suit doesn't fit, but you have to wear it anyway. Courtesy of the Museum of Modern Art Film Stills Archive.

Publicity shots of Bracken and Hutton for *Morgan's Creek* indicate some understandable confusion about how to characterize the movie. Courtesy of the Museum of Modern Art Film Stills Archive.

die Bracken and Betty Hutton in *Morgan's Creek*. Hutton's sober expression is appropriate the story; her amused glimmer is definitely not. Courtesy of the Museum of Modern Art Film ls Archive.

Strange bedfellows Jerry
Lewis and Dean Martin
in *The Stooge* (1953).
Courtesy of the
Museum of Modern Art
Film Stills Archive.

Martin and Lewis: it
couldn't last. Courtesy of
the Museum of Modern Art
Film Stills Archive.

shackles of the pre–World War I era and find out for themselves what life was all about.

Moore felt as if she'd been "emancipated" when her mother cut her long hair in preparation for a screen test for the lead role as the flapper heroine of the best-seller *Flaming Youth*. And she further demonstrated her unladylike professional aggression by saying to John McCormick, her manager-fiancé, "Get that part for me for a wedding present, or else."

She got the role and so married McCormick, who went on to become production head at First National, Moore's studio. Yet her absorption in her career left her with this feeling: "I had everything a woman could ask for, except the one most important thing in a woman's life." If you just chalk this statement up to socialization, you then have to explain how even as a teenager Moore had sought out and fought for the career she'd wanted from childhood. She certainly assumed there was an internal source for her dawning perception: "It is the woman who keeps a marriage together, whose job it is—and a full-time job—to make a home a place of warmth and refuge for a man, and a place of security and inspiration—and fun—for their children. . . . the rewards are a companionship and a feeling of belonging worth far more than all the fame in the world." It's a difficult issue because in movies this is the form of convention; for example, it's exactly what Sue says at the end of *The Extra Girl*, though it wasn't true for Normand herself. Regardless, Moore was able to churn out conventional romances because at some level, and for whatever reasons, she shared her audience's feelings. Clearly, the magazine spreads were not entirely commercial-minded fabrications.

As Neal Gabler has written with respect to William Fox's rehabilitation of a dilapidated and disreputable Brooklyn burlesque house into a "family theatre," "Fox succeeded in part because he drew on his own life experiences and knew how to translate his own inchoate yearnings for entertainment and respectability into those of the audience." This seems to be the dynamic of Hollywood dream manufacturing at every level of involvement, so much so it almost doesn't seem strange that Carl Laemmle, the founder of Universal, collected movie star autographs. Thus, after laboring to provide female moviegoers with both disrupting and reassuring fantasies, Moore took her place among them as a private person—one of the major silent stars, retired for good at the age of thirty-two, without regrets. Of course, she became not just a housewife but a prominent social figure in Chicago, a *star* wife and stepmother. And her new role had some leeway to it. In addition to her autobiography, she published several books about her extraordinary aluminum-and-jewel dollhouse and one advising *How Women Can Make Money in the Stock Market*. Part of her remained a girl-child, but not the part that became a partner in Merrill Lynch.

Beatrice Lillie was entirely a creature of the theater and was considered goofy looking, so her 1926 silent vehicle *Exit Smiling,* directed by Sam Taylor from a story by Marc Connelly, opts for slapstick over romance. Alfred E. Green, the director of *Ella Cinders,* had started out directing two-reel comedies before "graduating" to features; Sam Taylor was one of Harold Lloyd's veteran gagmen and that same year received the directing credit on Lloyd's *For Heaven's Sake.* And Lillie was even more willing and able than Moore to work in the established method of improvising gags around a basic story framework. In *Exit Smiling* she gives the most full-scale female lead performance in a silent slapstick picture that I know of.

Lillie plays Vi, the stagestruck drudge of a bottom-scraping theatrical touring company who cooks and serves the troupe's meals, does their laundry, plays walk-ons, and understudies the leading lady, who's never quite drunk enough, however, for Vi to get her shot. Vi especially wants to play the scene in which the virginal heroine of the show they're flogging through the sticks has to vamp the villain for an hour to ensure that her lover will be saved. Lillie gets her most distinctive laughs from serenely stylish straight-faced parody of a bad fledgling actress practicing bad scenes from bad plays. She has Chaplin's precision of gesture, but with the distancing effect of Keaton's deadpan. Lifting her great comic mask of a face, with its hint of ambiguous amusement, she offers us a slice of Vi's hammy theatrical acting as if on a silver salver; she's able to make you like Vi without rating her too highly.

Keaton's face, with those nearly Asiatic cheekbones and heavy-lidded eyes, is a masterpiece of design, but it isn't necessarily a clown's face. It's both cool as a mandarin's and unaffectedly expressive as a monkey's. But Lillie, with her punching-bag jawline and pulled-taffy nose tip, did feel that the mirror had fated her to be a clown. As she said in her autobiography, "It's great to be laughed at, but just think, if only my nose had been a quarter of an inch *shorter* I could have been a *femme fatale.*" At times Lillie resembles glamorous Norma Shearer, except that Lillie has the eyes of an imp, seemingly unconcerned about her image.

Lillie's looks enable her to go all out with her conceptual pantomime and thus to keep Vi's innocence from congealing because she's innocent of dramatic taste as well as meanness. But *Exit Smiling* does have its sentimental side. Jack Pickford plays Jimmy, a boy who has to leave his job at a small-town bank and his girl, the banker's daughter, when he's framed for embezzlement. When Vi's troupe plays Jimmy's hometown, she spots him waiting for a train and falls for him at first sight. Knowing nothing of his predicament, she coaches him so that he can get a job with her company. The plot's kicker is that when they play Jimmy's hometown again, Vi overhears the man who framed Jimmy talking to a man who in turn is blackmailing *him;* if the embezzler doesn't cough up some money by midnight, the blackmailer will tell the banker who really stole the money. Vi, who pines for Jimmy without knowing that he has a girl waiting for him to clear his name, gets to act out the good-girl-as-vamp role from the troupe's melodrama, keeping the villain in her clutches until midnight so that her beloved will be saved. But in doing so, she clears his name, enabling him to stay in town with his girl.

In the service of this ultimately weepy plot, Lillie brings her gift for nearly exquisite theatrical parody as well as a talent for silent slapstick, and the movie is very funny in both styles. *Exit Smiling* goes farther than *Ella Cinders* in developing gags from the props appropriate to the story, even at the expense of the gentler romantic comedy elements. Working in what was a male tradition, Lillie comes up with specifically female business. There's Vi dressing for the street after a performance, adjusting the lay of her hat and flinging a feather boa all the way around her neck and down her back where it catches on her skirt and draggles like a tail as she sashays out of the dressing room. And there's Vi serving the troupe their lunch: an actor helps himself to all the bacon, and when he looks away, Vi simply picks up his plate and serves the rest of the members from it. And then there's Vi ironing: mis-singing a current popular love song while thinking of Jimmy ("You are the ordeal of my dreams!"), she burns a shirt; without a trace of distraction she carefully folds the shirt and feeds it into the stove.

It is true that Lillie's acting, and even much of the slapstick, may be too fine lined for people who have a taste for the rougher male style of silent comedy. But the climax, in which Vi uses her secondhand wiles to detain impatient, unresponsive Harry Myers as the embezzler, combines Vi's major motivation, which is to be a great actress, with female slapstick that does get rough, and it's sensationally funny. Lillie really throws herself into this final tangle. She tries some alligator-wrestling holds when seduction fails, springs over a sofa onto Myers's back to prevent his getting out the door, and ties his jacket over his head to keep him from answering the phone. When the time has elapsed and Jimmy has been saved, Vi can't help taking a bow at the curtain to Myers's salon; drapes and rod come down on her head.

In *Exit Smiling* you get that rarest of senses, that the pratfalls complete the heroine, and Lillie even more so. Consider the much more representative situation of Marion Davies, the female star of King Vidor's 1928 silent *Show People*. Davies plays Peggy Pepper, a southern belle who comes to Hollywood to be a dramatic star and ends up a pie tosser in low-budget slapstick shorts (another girl Merton). The picture costars William Haines as Billy Boone, who'd also like to break into A-list dramas but who enjoys the bill-paying buffoonery. On Peggy's first day, the director doesn't tell her what kind of scene they're shooting, and so when she enters and gets a stream of seltzer in the face, she's too stunned to react, at first. When she does react, she cries and is furious. (William Randolph Hearst, Davies's lover and promoter, refused to let her stop a *pie* with her face. Vidor had to arrange with Davies to have Hearst called away to the phone to be able to shoot the seltzer scene without interference.) But working with Billy does make Peggy happy, that is, until she gets her break and becomes a romantic star in classy productions, is rechristened Patricia Pepoire, and no longer feels that Billy is socially adequate. However, her dramatic pictures are more expensive and less profitable than her comedies had been, and she's so far off her instincts that she gets herself engaged to a fake count. To prevent the marriage, Billy crashes the ceremony and sprays seltzer in Patricia's face to remind her of when she was happily Peggy.

Davies appeared in *Show People* to drag her reputation down to earth. She had the qualities to be a popular movie star, but Hearst, who overmanaged her career as part of his bid to extend his media empire into movie production, preferred her to play "old-fashioned, sentimental, ladylike roles" in lavish pictures on which he "spent so much . . . that even when they did well, the cost frequently couldn't be recovered." In *Show People* Davies ridicules the public image Hearst had created for her, but Peggy never really *likes* slapstick, which gives off a very different feeling from Bea Lillie as Vi. In this picture, Davies comes across not as a cutup but as a good sport, most famously when Davies as Peggy sees Marion Davies the movie star on the studio lot and mouths something on the order of "She isn't so much." It plays like a First Lady going along with her consultant's image overhaul.

It's the San Simeon bad boy William Haines who really gets to swing from the chandelier; when he's goofing around with corncobs in the studio commissary, using them as binoculars to eye Peggy, who's sitting next to him, he looks like he can't think of a better way to earn a living. *Show People* assumes that women naturally resent rough kidding, though the point is that they should get over it. *Exit Smiling* doesn't stand on female dignity, and Lillie alone among silent female slapstick stars doesn't seem exasperated by its loss. When Vi gets in the way of stagehands carrying the furniture off and is hoisted onto a couch, she rides it like Cleopatra on her barge. With Lillie, when dignity flies out the window, a superbly dry imperturbability comes in at the door.

However, in the final scene of *Exit Smiling*, when Jimmy, knowing only that he's been cleared but not how, says good-bye to Vi, he sweetly adds that he hopes she gets to play the Vamp role someday, oblivious that she's just played it for his sake. (Jack Pickford's earnest adolescent self-absorption makes perfect sense of both Vi's devotion and her disappointment.) He exits, and Vi opens her coat to look at the Vamp costume and then looks up tearfully at us. And fade. (The movie's title is thus bittersweet.) When Vi doesn't get the boy she loves, you realize that what makes the Vamp sequence ludicrous is the perception that Vi, and Lillie, aren't attractive. Through the eyes of nostalgia, Lillie's eccentric beauty looks positively platinum to us, even in her cotton pinafores with big bows in her hair. Still, with Franklin Pangborn as the effeminate leading man, Doris Lloyd as the listing and lewdly gum-chewing lead actress, and Vi playing for one performance the role of the villain in the melodrama in drag, this movie has the widest sexual range of any silent slapstick. You wouldn't expect it to have such a limited idea of what makes a heroine desirable.

But there's much more behind this unrequited ending. Lillie's mother, Lucie, trained her daughters Muriel and Beatrice to join her in a three-act singing teary, melodramatic songs. They performed locally in Toronto and then toured the provincial Canadian circuits before Lucie's theatrical ambition relocated the family to London. Seeking work in London theaters, Beatrice arranged her typical audition routine so that "with the last, plaintive note, [she] collapsed, sobbing" on the "big, battered suitcase" that she took to auditions, which to her mind showed "that you've left home, and you're on your way to somewhere that's going to make you unhappy." But when she went through a number like this for the revue impresario André Charlot, Lillie's "coat caught on a broken catch of one of the suitcase locks. The suitcase itself swung off the floor for a moment, then fell over, and [she] fell on top of it." This enabled Charlot and his office girls, a more cosmopolitan crowd than Lillie was used to, to vent the laughter at her histrionic somberness that they'd been half suppressing, and Charlot made her a comic singer. When Lillie said that her nose kept her from being a femme fatale, it was with a hint of real professional regret.

Her early success in Charlot's revues came during World War I, when the number of actors serving in the military left "roles open for girls to fill." She "quickly became 'one of the most dapper and accomplished of contemporary male impersonators,'" a huge hit as "what they called a girl hero." The great model for this kind of performance in England was Vesta Tilley, a music hall star for some half a century (roughly 1870 to 1920), who sang specially written songs, both clever and rousing, to fit the character she was playing, and who dressed so convincingly as a man that she influenced *male* fashions. Audiences saw each young masher or soldier, policeman or clerk, "not as we saw him in real life, or as he imagined himself, but as he appeared in the eyes of clever, critically observant woman." Tilley's audience laughed both at their recognition of the type she was portraying and at her cleverness. It may well be that this is the kind of response Charlot hoped for Lillie to win as well—perhaps somewhat friskier for the post-Victorian audience. Despite the suitcase mishap, he did *not* want her to get horselaughs, either by accident or intentionally. For instance, as Lord Lionel Lyonesse, she got endless curtain calls one night because she'd hurried into her tux without buttoning her fly, leaving her shirttail sticking way out; Charlot refused to let her incorporate the mistake into the number and fined her another night for taking a curtain call with a big false mustache.

Charlot wanted to maintain a certain sophistication in his shows, and it's probably because of these restrictions that Lillie's comedy became so marvelously arch. The *New York Times* described "the familiar Charlot note" in part as the ability to convey "a great deal of extravagance that the words [of a song] did not express." Lillie attained this not by donning a walrus mustache but rather by adopting a deadpan archness so impeccable—her mechanically apt gestures seem to glide on tracks—that she became equally elegant and ridiculous.

What needs explaining is that when Lillie did her transvestite act in *Exit Smiling,* some ten years later, she did it in the broad slapstick mode Charlot didn't care for. In the picture, Vi goes on as the villain for Jimmy, who's faking illness to avoid facing the audience in his hometown. It's a relatively standard joke when Vi as the villain is foiled: she curses and punches her fist down for emphasis, but her blocking is off, putting her too near the fishbowl. And Vi not only comes on in the mustache Charlot rejected but sneezes it off and puts it back on upside down. But there's something stranger about the bit when we see Vi in drag unable to keep herself from playing the girl. As Doris Lloyd, the female lead, goes into her soulful emoting, Vi, the stagestruck hopeful who has been used to imitating Lloyd in the wings for practice, reverts to habit: she mimics Lloyd's gestures, standing right behind her, but onstage and dressed as a man. The fact is that Lillie wasn't thrilled by her success in men's clothing; the slapstick mishaps Vi has onstage in drag could be said to express her ambivalence about it.

Lillie's mother certainly "didn't take at all to the idea" of her drag career, but we can glimpse the influence of her mother behind both Lillie's talent for male impersonation and her distaste for it. As Ruth St. Denis said to her dancers, including Louise Brooks, for whom her words "held special relevance," "a talented girl is the result of a mother who has been repressed and into whom goes all that mother's ambition and culture." Lillie described her mother as "a little bit terrifying, majestically poised with a will of iron." This formidable matriarch's combination of seemingly contradictory attitudes—restless ambition and propriety—is summed up in her exhortation to her daughters, "Work hard. Be charming, and always ladies. If you have talent, it will be discovered. Remember, *en avant*—ever forward," authoritative advice that fuses female decorum and male adventurousness. Stage mothers are legendary monsters mainly for satisfying their desire for fame vicariously through their kids. But the example of a mother as a rhino-hided hustler, promoter and survivor might well enable a girl to brave the minefield that is the popular audience's perception of female clowns.

Lillie had to stomach a lot because of her success in drag: the audience and her mentor-producer kept her in a no-woman's-land where she wasn't very comfortable. She considered that "the absolute, final, bloody end had come when [she] read the following [notice about herself]: 'I thought that in skirts she would be nothing. She was not at all bad. . . . All the same, she ought to be in a revue as a young gentleman.'" She saw her discomfort as typical, because, as she stated, "I've found that men as a rule resist laughing at women. The explanation can probably be found buried down deep in the general subject of s-e-x. I must confess that a woman clown in baggy pants and a putty nose has no particular appeal for me, either."

The last comment is of particular interest, because although I can think of women comedians doing some of their best work in onetime costumes (Carol Burnett yoked with the curtain rod in the "Went with the Wind" skit), I don't know of any top female clown who always appears in the same stylized makeup and costume, which is certainly not the case with male clowns. Mabel Normand and Edna Purviance could appear as quite fashionable young women, as did many of the heroines of thirties comedies. Even Dressler and Fazenda, who could dress up or down, dressed differently from picture to picture. (And Carol Burnett's scrubwoman is not her best shtick, by far). There has been no comedienne as identified with an outfit as Chaplin was.

When Judy Garland dresses as a hobo-clown for "A Couple of Swells" with Fred Astaire in the 1948 *Easter Parade*, she seems lost in the outfit in a way he doesn't, though it hardly suits his star persona. It may be simply that women haven't had the freedom of movement, literally and socially, that men have had, and that the loose-fitting tramp clothes suggest. Also, women are commonly associated with civilization because, with their physical and sexual vulnerability to men, they stand to lose much more than men by civilization's breakdown. Socially they have to represent the superego to counteract the male id. And baggy pants costumes, like clowning in general, are a form of id—I won't wash, I won't dress for church or school, I won't stop fidgeting and scratching, I won't be good, I won't grow up. In our tradition, these are all essential male attitudes, points describing the line of scrimmage between Huck Finn and the Widow Douglas's "sivilization." Camille Paglia has tried to co-opt for women the male tradition of the tramp who tramples polite boundaries. But as she points out, and we all know, the term "tramp" has had a very different meaning when applied to women. This should give women the advantage as comedians of breaking taboos. However, breaking taboos doesn't mean that the comedy will win approval from the popular audience who live by them. Not even Lillie knew where violating them left her.

Lillie got an eye-opening example of a spontaneous assertion of those taboos when she took her three-year-old son to the theater to see her perform for the first time:

> When it was over, he had only one comment, said with something that combined outrage and sorrow: "People *laughed* at you."
>
> Just for a moment, I wished that they hadn't. For future attendances at the show in which I appeared, he'd sit on the floor, out of sight of the stage, as soon as Mumsie brought him into the box.

A more extreme example was a number in which, "costumed like an Edwardian belle in a saucy pink silk dress with a froufrou skirt and lace-up boots," Lillie sang while sitting on a prop moon that swung over the audience suspended from a crane. Dangling, she would remove pink garters and toss them to men in the audience. She ends the story with the remark that her son "Bobbie, understandably, had some reservations about the whole act." The son's mother-love is as protective as it is limiting, and when it comes from a three year old, it's hard to think of it as anything but a primal expression. Lillie's response to it, "Just for a moment, I wished that they hadn't," is partly the key to the strange turn *Exit Smiling* takes in its last scene.

When I showed *Exit Smiling* to my class, they unanimously groaned at the unhappy ending, just as the 1926 *Variety* reviewer predicted. But it does make a certain kind of sense. Lillie remained indulgent toward the appeal of the suffering melodramatic heroines she had been drawn to when she was a girl in love with the movies in the first decade of the twentieth century: "Every little heroine was *me*. It was best of all if she was shamefully treated and wept a lot. . . . Such delicious torture. I invariably came away convinced that I could have done a better job." When she later made her debut on a London stage, she could still say of herself at the time, "I hated anything funny. The diet of weepy movies had left its dent. More than anything, I yearned to be *sad*. I wanted to cry, break a leg, knock my teeth out—whatever was required to win the sympathy of people watching me." Her spontaneous clowning during performances, for which Charlot always fined her, stemmed in part from his refusal to let her sing serious songs.

Thinking of how much Lillie had longed to be the heroine of a "weepy movie" made me think of the end of *Exit Smiling* not as a thwarted romantic comedy but as an example of the women's pictures Lillie loved as a girl. In *its* final shots, *Stella Dallas,* for instance, first filmed the year before, also glorifies the lone heroine rather than joining the young couple whose marriage she has helped to bring about. We see Vi miss her chance to become a mother, but in movies, as Lillie knew, anguish offers a nearly perverse mixture of misery and gratification, "delicious torture," for heroine and star alike. At the end of *The Extra Girl,* Mabel Normand—the rich, successful, unmarried, childless career actress—has settled down as a wife and mother. In *Exit Smiling* Jimmy gets marriage, like the vast majority of the moviegoers, and Vi gets a rusty halo for the very reason that no one knows what she's done—except for an entire house of movie patrons, showing after showing after showing. Thus at the end when Vi is alone, you may think Lillie wanted to reassure her son after the patrons have done laughing at her that she's not really a joke, but you also have to notice that she's *alone* up there. She no longer has to work to hold the screen—it's *hers*.

You may also conclude that *Exit Smiling* isn't a romantic comedy because Vi doesn't get the man. But structurally it *is* a romantic comedy—Vi simply isn't half of the couple. In Northrop Frye's analysis of comedy, he has written:

> The plot structure of Greek New Comedy, as transmitted by Plautus and Terence, in itself less a form than a formula, has become the basis for most comedy, especially in its more highly conventionalized dramatic form, down to our own day. . . . What normally happens is that a young man wants a young woman, that his desire is resisted by some opposition, usually paternal, and that near the end of the play some twist in the plot enables the hero to have his will.

He continues:

> The obstacles to the hero's desire, then, form the action of the comedy, and the overcoming of them the comic resolution. The obstacles are usually parental, hence comedy often turns on a clash between a son's and a father's will. Thus the comic dramatist as a rule writes for the younger man of his audience, and the older members of almost any society are apt to feel that comedy has something subversive about it.

In *Exit Smiling* Vi wants Jimmy, but her love story isn't the romantic comedy. Jimmy wants his hometown sweetheart, whose father objects because of the embezzlement charges; when cleared, Jimmy claims the girl—who isn't interesting enough to rate more than a minute of screen time—and they live happily ever after. Vi, in Northrop Frye's description of comedy, is an example of the archetypal crafty servant who helps his master get the girl he wants. This is a central-peripheral figure, "entrusted with hatching the schemes which bring about the hero's victory."

In *Exit Smiling*, however, Vi is a knot resolver who falls in love with the hero herself. In this regard, Lillie is less like Keaton than like Chaplin, who saw the Pierrot figure as "the solution" to the problem that "logically it was difficult to get a beautiful girl interested in a tramp," a corollary to Sennett's belief that it's off-limits to make a slapstick audience laugh at a beautiful girl. The solution rests on our accepting that the Pierrot will not be included in the central love story, as he sometimes hopes. (This is the plot of *The Tramp, The Vagabond, City Lights,* and *Limelight.* Even Gilbert and Sullivan went in for this kind of pathos in *The Yeomen of the Guard.*) Vi is like a barnacle attached to the love boat of Jimmy and his girl; but since Lillie is the star the picture is built around, the proportions are reversed—the barnacle is huge, and the boat tiny, irrelevant, unseaworthy as entertainment. I don't think that this kind of masochism is necessarily deeper than a conventional romantic comedy ending, but I do think it's too culturally persistent not to derive from some deep impulse.

Lillie became an international stage sensation when Charlot's Revue played Broadway in 1924. Her star persona was such that *Exit Smiling*, her debut picture, is capped with full-body-tackle slapstick, after which it swerves instinctively away from romantic comedy at the very end. This is only subtly different from *The Extra Girl*, in which the heroine herself swerves away from a career that has inevitably led her into slapstick, in order to have a happy romantic comedy ending as wife and mother. The choice between the two women's roles derives in part from looks—Normand was a beauty whereas Lillie's face wasn't considered right for a romantic heroine. But you also can't help feeling that Lillie was too unfazed by comedy to seem like wife material to 1920s moviemakers.

You will look long and largely in vain for movies that abandon these unspoken rules. You certainly won't find anything funnier or more exciting than the 1938 Howard Hawks picture *Bringing Up Baby*. This most physical of all the screwballs gets its drive from the fact that Katharine Hepburn's Susan is the protagonist of the romantic comedy in Frye's terms, in which protagonist equals successful pursuer, *and* is conceived as a slapstick heroine. (Though the slapstick is not the organic kind that we associate with the Chaplin, Lloyd, and Keaton silents.) In so many ways, Hepburn just crashes through the barriers—she's a predator, a stooge, and a glamor star.

Hepburn's self-assertion is the exception in romantic comedies. In movies it's much more common for women to be running (or backing away) *from* the altar, as in *The Extra Girl, Show People, It Happened One Night, The Philadelphia Story,* and *The Graduate,* and in the past few years *Mr. Wrong, The Pallbearer, That Old Feeling, Rough Magic,* and *Runaway Bride,* than to be setting their caps for men and tripping them so that they fall. In *Bringing Up Baby* Cary Grant's David, a repressed paleontologist who mechanically digs up fleshless artifacts from the past, is the sleeping beauty Hepburn kisses awake into the present. Susan meets David on a golf course when she plays his ball instead of her own, and in the last scene, she completes his work by returning the brontosaurus bone her aunt's dog has buried. The symbolism is not meant to be subtle: she steals his ball but gives him a bone, that is, usurps the initiative but makes him aware of his suppressed romantic feelings.

Lillie's background happened to prepare her for slapstick at the expense of romance; Hepburn's background, with a forceful pater-familias and a radical suffragist mother and aunt, doctrinally prepared her to have it all—the physical life and the emotional—and *Bringing Up Baby* uses this quality more than any of her other pictures. Hepburn paraphrased the "philosophy" her mother transmitted to her as a series of slogans similar to Lucie Lillie's *"en avant"*:

Don't give in.
Fight for your future.
Independence is the only solution.
Women are as good as men.
Onward!

Her father, a physician who'd been a college fullback, taught Hepburn and her older brother Tom acrobatics as well as sports, rigging up a tightrope on the front lawn of their Connecticut home for them to slide down on a trapeze, sitting or hanging from their knees. Dr. Hepburn coached his son and daughter alike, though with greater pressure on the boy. But his standards were probably fairly imposing for his daughter as well, since Katharine explained his admiration for his own mother in these terms: "She was his ideal—a fighter with the highest standards."

As a girl, Lillie "used to delight in dressing up in a shirt and a pair of trousers and insist on going for walks with [her] sister" simply to shock. Hepburn hacked off her hair and dressed as a boy when still in grammar school, played a male role in a play at Bryn Mawr and was reprimanded for wearing men's clothes off campus, and continued to gain attention for wearing men's clothes well into her forties. (In 1954 the management of Claridge's in London asked Spencer Tracy to tell her not to cross their lobby in trousers when she came to his room at night.) Her friend and frequent director George Cukor, who put her in drag in the unnerving lark *Sylvia Scarlett* (1936), perceived in her "a piquant quality he called 'garçonne.'" Hepburn developed her strapping androgyny from playing sports, especially golf, with her father and crafted it for theatrical use by watching Hope Williams, whom Hepburn understudied on Broadway in *Holiday* in the role she later played on film, and whom she referred to as "half-boy, half-woman." Her description of Williams could in most respects apply to Hepburn herself: "A forthright manner. Great good looks. A slim figure, a boy's haircut. And a walk. Her walk was an arms-swinging stride. . . . It was stylish and original." (In *Sylvia Scarlett* she even has the mannish do.)

Cukor's coinage suggests a proud ambivalence about Hepburn's athletic self-confidence—she seems to go a bit too far, to overmatch her mates. (This is the implicit theme of her pictures opposite Spencer Tracy, who strikes back.) But *Bringing Up Baby* was made just before the 1938 exhibitors' box office poison list that ended Hepburn's brief reign at RKO, and so the movie feels free to romanticize what's uncommon and even threatening about her. The screenwriter Dudley Nichols, who worked the script up with Hagar Wilde from her 1937 *Collier's* magazine story, often worked for John Ford and had witnessed Ford's infatuation with Hepburn dating from their collaboration on the 1936 *Mary of Scotland*. In *Bringing Up Baby* Grant wears Ford's round specs and is awestruck by Hepburn's vitality. Grant plays the academic eunuch more than gamely; he seems truly constipated by gray matter. He sputters with his whole body, the tall stiffness of which presents itself very differently when his instincts are blocked. (In *His Girl Friday* that body stands like a wall impeding Rosalind Russell's escape.) Hepburn's physicality, perfectly typified by her fairway stride, is more fluid and takes over the movie. Unlike her later pictures with Tracy, *Bringing Up Baby* has no hesitations about her dominant personality—or at least none that it can't use to generate more excitement. The movie is intoxicated by her potency.

And it's authentically potent. Dr. Hepburn, watching his daughter set out to seduce the poet Phelps Putnam, compared her to "a young bull about to charge." Female initiative was even an oral family tradition: when Hepburn's mother reminisced about her first meeting with her husband "she depicted herself as the aggressor." It's not for nothing that the leopard, which in Hawks's picture comes in both domesticated and man-eating varieties, is Susan's emblem.

Hepburn isn't all aggression, though: she stares adoringly at Grant and says, irrelevantly to the conversation, "Ohhh, you're so good-looking without your glasses," in her most lulling tones—all the while scandalously manipulating and baffling him. The extent to which the moviemakers realize that there's something against the grain about her is when they have Grant's David, whose clothes Susan has sneakily sent out to be cleaned, put on a woman's frilly dressing gown. That wrapper is the moviemakers' recognition that they shouldn't like what they like about Hepburn. But at the end, David can see that the maddening day he spent with Susan was the most fun he'd ever had. He hasn't developed a taste for sexual-upside-down cake, though. His manhood is saved at this final moment when Susan literally falls from a ladder and he saves her by grabbing her hand.

The screenwriters altered the original story, in which David and Suzan (as it's spelled in the magazine) are already engaged, so that Hepburn's Susan has to pursue David, who's always trying to get away from her. The story's David isn't a scientist but lives off an independent income. More important, he's the romantic protagonist, who single-handedly captures the escaped panther (rather than leopard) for Suzan's aunt so that Suzan will inherit enough money for him to be able to marry her. Thus, in the story, the paternal obstacle, in Frye's sense, is female. But in the movie, though Susan's aunt turns out to be the rich widow from whom David is trying to get a donation, he isn't interested in Susan herself—*she's* chasing *him*.

In a movie like *The Extra Girl,* though Sue is the starring role, Dave is the active role in romantic comedy terms. The happy ending makes them both happy, but he's the one who has pursued Sue unstintingly while Sue has wrongheadedly pursued a career. Sue's father objects to her marrying Dave, but she is partly an obstacle as well, in her single-minded chase after movie stardom. (The heroine herself thus becomes what Frye calls a "blocking character" in "ritual bondage" to a "ruling passion.")

In the movie of *Bringing Up Baby,* Susan may be deviant for going after David, but she never deviates from that desire, and she's (somewhat scarily) able to improvise ways to keep him near her. Hepburn's Susan also has a rival in Alice, David's fiancée, who doesn't believe even in *post*marital sex because it would distract them from his work. David, the reluctant object, is thus also an obstacle with Alice as the personification of his ruling antipassion. But you never doubt Hepburn's ability to leap all hurdles.

This reversal of the sexual roles of classic romantic comedy is in fact more startling than Hepburn's feminist pictures, *Christopher Strong* and *A Woman Rebels.* In the 1933 *Christopher Strong,* she plays a celebrated aviatrix who gets pregnant by her married lover and, since she can't have him honorably, commits suicide by removing her oxygen mask while flying—she passes out at the controls and crashes. Meeting the conventional end of a fallen woman, boy, does she fall. In the 1936 *A Woman Rebels,* she plays a Victorian daughter who struggles for a woman's opportunity to earn her own living, but she also has a child out of wedlock and sacrifices for the girl, who grows up not knowing that her old maid auntie is actually her mother. For all that these movies assume or promote women's independence and rights, they're conventional weepers, without the liberating impulsiveness of slapstick.

Because in movies aesthetics usually matter more than ideology, the risqué or progressive intentions of *Christopher Strong* and *A Woman Rebels* can't mask their conventional prissiness. They really look bad next to the brisk, forthright *Bringing Up Baby,* which provides as close to a passive rape fantasy as heterosexual males got in Hollywood comedy of the thirties. (This movie can prove off-putting for young men; several of the guys in my class heard Henry Miller's alarum: "When the female laughs the male had better scoot to the cyclone cellar.") I think that *Bringing Up Baby*'s failure upon its initial release (it lost $365,000 for RKO) indicates that it isn't just Frye's older members of the audience who find the aggressive heroine subversive. The younger popular audience did as well, and it is one of the few examples of a fluffy comedy achieving the kind of controlled unease that we usually get only from more ambitious works of art.

I can't think of another top female star of the era who was equally able to blend slapstick and sexual charisma. Even though Hepburn's sharp cheekbones and slim-hipped, statuesque figure make her look as if she were made of glass, she takes more pratfalls than any romantic heroine ever did—she has the back ripped out of her dress in a hotel bar, trips over a phone cord, falls down a bluff, gets dunked in a creek, and unknowingly tugs a mangling leopard around on a leash. For a while, Hepburn even worked on a caged set with a live leopard, until the "tame" Baby sprang for her back.

Hepburn's role isn't fully written as a slapstick clown, in terms of situations and props, as Lillie's Vi is in *Exit Smiling,* but it's more athletic, and more sexually determined, which adds another dimension to the slapstick romantic comedy. Bea Lillie shows no qualms about slapstick but doesn't get her man. Carole Lombard in *My Man Godfrey,* Irene Dunne in *The Awful Truth* and *My Favorite Wife,* Jean Arthur in *Only Angels Have Wings,* Barbara Stanwyck in *The Lady Eve,* and Lauren Bacall in *To Have and Have Not* are all likable comic heroines who pursue the hero, but none of their characters is conceived fully in slapstick terms. Lombard, a graduate of Sennett's silent two-reelers, might seem a more obvious choice than Hepburn as the foremost slapstick heroine of the first decades of the talkies, but her pictures aren't as all-out physical as *Bringing Up Baby.* And although Stanwyck's wicked sexual confidence games in *The Lady Eve* make Henry Fonda fall all over himself, *she* remains physically composed. There *is* Betty Hutton (see chapter 6) in *Star Spangled Rhythm,* but she's not Olympian like Hepburn; Hutton never landed a Cary Grant. Mack Sennett developed the Bathing Beauties because he "found that audiences enjoyed a certain amount of athletic girlhood, together with the comedy of the Keystone Cops"; Hepburn's training with her father enabled her to supply both pleasures to moviegoers herself.

Hepburn shared a taste for movies with her father but not her mother, who thought them "silly." (Once Mrs. Hepburn took her children to "a very sentimental movie" and got thrown out of the theater for laughing—a usable heritage for anybody.) At the same time, her father vigorously objected to her taking up acting, which he thought "a silly profession closely allied to streetwalking," whereas her mother "was all for it," just as long as she "didn't settle for the old routine of nursemaid to the rising generation."

However, slogans are one thing and life another. Bea Lillie's mother admonishing her to be a lady while muscling her and her sister into showbiz is like Katharine Hepburn's mother propounding radical reform and rushing home every day at five to serve her husband tea. Both suggest the comic perplexity of women seeking the initiative and independence men are expected to display. Not surprisingly, the career-versus-marriage dilemma, which Adela Rogers St. Johns called "the tug-of-war that is at the core of every modern woman," is a constant for comedies starring women, as it is for successful actresses in life, from *The Extra Girl* and *Manhandled* and *Exit Smiling* to the present, even though the "correct" resolution changes over time. The male slapstick stars have to prove themselves in the world, as stockbrokers, cowboys, boxers, locomotive engineers, athletes, steamboat captains, cameramen, just to list some of Buster Keaton's occupations in his silent features. As in life, women's roles have been until very recently much more restricted, and for women, workplace and home life represent conflicting demands (whereas men generally have to achieve something in the former to gain the latter).

Comedies have to stay close to life in some respects to get at what makes us anxious and convert it to laughter; this explains why only a rare bird like Katharine Hepburn could take the traditional male initiative, perform the slapstick stunts, and end up with a top-drawer romantic hero. She's miraculously funny in *Bringing Up Baby*—somehow both airy and unstoppable—but it's not really a shock that she wasn't popular in the role. She was subject to the same dilemma as merely mortal comediennes, nowhere as succinctly stated as by Philip Barry in the following exchange from his 1939 play *The Philadelphia Story,* which he finished with Hepburn in mind (and which salvaged her career from box office shipwrecks like *Bringing Up Baby*):

GEORGE KITTREDGE [who thinks he has been outraged the night before, expostulating with his wayward fiancée just before the ceremony]: But a man expects his wife to—

TRACY LORD [Hepburn's role]: —To behave herself. Naturally.

C. K. DEXTER HAVEN [Tracy's hopeful ex]: To behave herself naturally.

The audience wants the heroine to be a fun girl, but within definite, if unstated, limits. Working mother Adela Rogers St. Johns wrote that a "mother is what makes a home" and then cited Hepburn's explanation of why she, as a career woman, would not have kids, as authoritative corroboration. Men tend to look at women in a fairly narrowly circumscribed light in slapstick comedies, as Sennett's interview makes plain. But while comedies with female stars obey the same rules as those with male stars, they also get some drive from the pistoning Yes-No-Yes-No of the modern woman's feelings about the roles she wants to play.

CHAPTER FIVE

The Marx Brothers: The Buoyant Refuse
of Our Teeming Shore

Dryden wrote, "The true end of satire is the amendment of vices by correction. And he who writes honestly is no more an enemy to the offender, than the physician to the patient, when he prescribes harsh remedies to an inveterate disease." *Duck Soup* is regularly referred to as satire, but does it really seem as if its intention were to improve or heal the citizens watching it? Putting foolish behavior on display doesn't make a movie a satire. Satire is purposeful and usually compares its objects of ridicule to a norm of better behavior. It hopes to ameliorate. As C. L. Barber wrote, "A satirist at least pretends to an objective view; he implies that it is his subjects that are distorted, not his mood; however much he may in fact load his language, his attitude is that he is normal, ingenuous, an *honnête homme*."

But in *Duck Soup*, when we see Groucho as the head of state of a central European country playing jacks during a cabinet meeting, for instance, the intention can't be to satirize the way governments function. Groucho playing jacks presents *himself* as ridiculous, if anything. He's the movie's Lord of Misrule, overseeing a travesty of the operations of government much like the medieval and Renaissance revelry organized "under leaders, usually a lord and a lady or a king and a queen, with attendants who paralleled the functionaries of a castle or a royal court." Led by Groucho, who was most engaged in developing the act's material, the Brothers demolish various upper-crust institutions and figures—government, high society, art collectors, academia, grand opera—and stand tall in the rubble, having freed, in the manner of the older holiday festivals, "the vitality normally locked up in awe and respect" of their supposed betters. I don't think the Marx Brothers would still be so popular if they had gone in merely for topical satire. Rather, they follow in a long tradition of "festive abuse" that isn't so much aimed at a target as released and left free to radiate in all directions, even back on the clowns themselves.

The Marx Brothers' movies lack satire's concentrated, utilitarian purpose, but they're motivated by experiences in a way that we can reconstruct. And though you have to talk about Chaplin in segments because what he's about changes so much, the Marx Brothers are very consistent over time (with one significant alteration when they moved from Paramount to MGM). When you look at where the Marx Brothers came from, as a family and as performers—men and clowns, brothers and Brothers—you quickly see the impulses of boys who had been excluded by class, religion, opportunity, and measly physical gifts from the burstingly successful world around them. Jews of the Marx Brothers' era could feel set apart, dominated even in a democratic society, and yet this feeling itself links them to the universal comic impulse to balance complaisance toward rule with mockery of it. Even envy of rulers doesn't have to end in a revolutionary grudge match. Far from satirizing the concept of the man at the top, Groucho, making hash of all the sessions of government he attends, sees the fun in the unreasoning abuse of power.

In this and other ways, the Marx Brothers' attacks on the elite are the opposite of elevating, and audiences recognize their zany debasement in part as a plausible attitude toward modern living. Far more than any physical comedian, Groucho has served as a role model for a certain stripe of young man, but a role model without sanctimony, you could say, *because* he isn't a satirist. There's nothing like critique (radical or otherwise) in Marx Brothers movies, and in fact their careers always inch closer to the center of middle-class life, from vaudeville to Broadway to movies to television. Once, as a boy, my father didn't have money for a movie ticket and so tried to get into the theater by walking backward through the front doors, hoping to pass for someone on the inside making his way out. That's how the undercapitalized Marx Brothers insinuated themselves into the wider American culture and transformed it into the kind of club that would have them as members.

Groucho told the following story about the Marx Brothers' transition from the stage to pictures:

> Soon after we arrived I was called into a conference and informed that I would have to discard the black painted mustache. When I asked why, they explained, "Well, nobody's ever worn a black painted mustache on the screen. The audience isn't accustomed to anything as phony as that and just won't believe it."
>
> "The audience doesn't believe us, anyhow," I answered. "All they do is laugh at us and, after all, isn't that what we're getting paid for?"

This is a strange scene to have occurred in an era when male leads wore conspicuously dark lip rouge. But that was a mute convention; Groucho's greasepaint mustache and eyebrows practically yodel for attention. They had a chance origin when Groucho arrived at the theater too late one night to affix his usual crepe mustache, but by the time of their first feature, the greasepaint seems to have reached the level of an insight. This insight, based on the observation that obviousness doesn't jar the act, is the key to Groucho's "character."

He continued:

> On the stage I frequently stepped out of character and spoke directly to the audience. After the first day's shooting on *[The] Cocoanuts,* the producer . . . said, "Groucho, you can't step out of character and talk to the audience."
>
> Like all the people who are glued to tradition, he was wrong. I spoke to them in every picture I appeared in.

The aside, which breaches the counterfactual convention that the theater audience isn't there, is a less extreme device than an actor's speaking to a movie audience who in fact *aren't* there. Groucho readily advanced to the more startling form of attack.

Of course, no one in the movie notices his fake mustache or when he speaks to us, but he does ruffle Margaret Dumont's characters by the way he treats them. In *The Cocoanuts* Groucho is trying to land Dumont's Mrs. Potter, a wealthy widow, but can't say three lines without insulting her. No realistic interpretation—for example, that Groucho insults her to express his frustration at having to marry for money a woman he's not attracted to—can take hold because devices like the greasepaint and talking to the camera and, in later movies, his breaking out in the voice of a kid or a blushing maiden or an old darky ensure that there's no layer of believable representation for realism to sink roots into. There's something purer about Groucho's outrageousness. When Mrs. Potter says, "I don't think you'd love me if I were poor," and Groucho replies, "I might, but I'd keep my mouth shut," you wonder, Why can't you keep your mouth shut now?

The switch from courting to insulting has a source in the dread of saying the wrong thing, which we see in *Animal Crackers* (the Brothers' second movie, and, like the first, adapted from a Broadway hit of theirs and shot at Paramount's Astoria Studios in Queens) when Louis Sorin's millionaire art collector Roscoe W. Chandler is wooing Dumont's Long Island hostess Mrs. Rittenhouse. He tenders, "You are a beautiful woman," and she kittenishly demurs, "No, no, Mr. Chandler," and he, obsequiously willing to see things her way, retracts, "Well, maybe I'm wrong," at which she stalks off. But Groucho doesn't *blurt* his insults. His is a more brazen expression of ambivalence, which he picked up from having been in showbiz a long time.

Idealizing women and assaulting them are the boxing glove and the mitten attached to the ends of the slapstick string. Even Chaplin could be ungallant at Keystone; for example, in the 1914 one-reeler *Mabel's Married Life* as a husband on a park bench sharing a banana with his wife and then complaining about the size of the bite she takes. At other times, he undermines the reality of the romantic comedy in a more purely conceptual way. In *The Pawn Shop,* for instance, Charlie wins Edna's hand by foiling Eric Campbell's robbery. But earlier in the picture, he had saved his job by miming to Henry Bergman as the pawnbroker, and Edna's father, that he has six children, ranging in height from a toddler to a basketball star. Having children implies that he's already got a woman, unless of course he's a widower, but that's too elaborate a reconstruction of motivation for the amount of time given to the joke. It's clear we're not to believe anything, not to bother connecting anything, that Chaplin knows we know it's all a show.

Groucho strips the comic violation of gallantry to its core, which makes it more blatant than ever. His assaults on Dumont are openly counterproductive, with the illusion-destroying self-conscious prankishness of Chaplin in *The Pawn Shop* superadded. (Chaplin didn't mix them.) Groucho can turn eye-battingly coy as he flatters Dumont between insults, leading her on to more abuse. But this off-and-on verbal antagonism itself, like Chaplin's gestures, tosses the story away, right from the start, and not as casually as in Chaplin. Groucho's performance style suggests that no affect, no matter how simple or direct, could ever be maintained with a straight face. Unlike Chaplin, he almost never participates in pathos, and he sustains the disposable tone over the length of features. More resolutely than any other film comedian, Groucho doesn't follow through on any lines, whether for or against his self-interest, insofar as that can be determined. It really can't, beyond the most momentary linking of dots. With Groucho at the center, the plots can never really build to anything. But then, with Groucho at the center, that lack of buildup seems coherent. Throwing away the possibility of realistic characterization helps turn Julius into Groucho; stepping out of character becomes his character.

Groucho's central instinct is to exploit the comedy produced by violating theatrical illusion, which allows him to be a government unto himself. He developed this act from theatrical sources at hand and from his own impulses and experiences: thus he'll come on like a haggling peddler, salesman, auctioneer, shill. He's the classically adaptable man, who always ends up on top because his fast-changing nature and tongue reset the terms of exchange while it's still in progress, updated to the idiom of an immigrant New York Jew. The type exists in Aristophanes (see Dikaiopolis in *The Acharnians*), but Groucho wasn't versed in the tradition. He reinvented what already existed, which is why his performances seem both modern and ageless.

Chaplin's evasiveness became a form itself whenever a picture ended with the Tramp scampering away from all entanglements. Likewise, Groucho's line "The audience doesn't believe us anyway" serves as the structural principle of the Marx Brothers' movies; they mock dramatic structure and theatrical affect by invoking them with an exaggerated, stylized lack of conviction. And they have no unifying central theme, certainly not a serious one, as Aristophanes's comedies do. The Marx Brothers walk away from their movies while continuing to caper through them, never lending the plots credence, until they landed at MGM, that is, and even then only intermittently. In general, the narrative frameworks barely hold their pictures together and are so riddled that it's not unusual for people to be confused about which movie a famous routine is in.

This is the opposite of sentimental; in the Paramount movies (*The Cocoanuts, Animal Crackers,* and after the move to Hollywood, *Monkey Business, Horse Feathers,* and *Duck Soup,* released in successive years from 1929 through 1933), Groucho never asks for identification, much less sympathy, and so the plot and his characters' motivations are constantly being exposed as preposterous and base, respectively. We *do* identify with him, but in his isolation from the concerns of plot and character. We don't care if he wins Dumont, and with the exception of the MGM features *A Day at the Races* and *The Big Store,* we don't even know whether he does. But even at the end of *A Day at the Races,* his successful proposal is rude: "Emily, I have a confession to make—I really am a horse doctor. But marry me and I'll never look at another horse."

Groucho's lack of conviction breaks out regularly in theatrical parody, either as a comment on his own dialogue in *Animal Crackers,* or on the action in *Monkey Business,* or as obviously fakey gestures such as running his hands over his hair and clasping them behind his neck as he moans, "Oh, the shame of it," in *Horse Feathers.* The most explicit, topical theatrical parody in all of the Marx Brothers' movies comes in *Animal Crackers* when Groucho steps downstage from Margaret

Irving and Margaret Dumont to speak his inner thoughts in an announced takeoff on Eugene O'Neill's *Strange Interlude*. O'Neill's technique in this 1929 play was to have characters alternately speak their "public" lines for the other characters in the play and their "private" commentary on what they'd just said for us, but not the other characters, to hear. In essence O'Neill elaborated the aside to make it as expressive as novelistic stream of consciousness. For the most part in this lampoon of O'Neill, Groucho doesn't speak his private thoughts—his lines parody bleak-lofty abstraction. (Woody Allen borrowed the joke for the ending of *Love and Death* and then played it solemn at the end of *Interiors*.) Yet the episode can be taken as a potshot at O'Neill for doing pretentiously what the weirdly uninhibited Groucho does all the time—speak the private underside of his public dialogue in the next breath.

Groucho never censors what he says out loud to Margaret Dumont, sugaring and salting her almost simultaneously. Thinking of Groucho as uncensored puts his scenes with Dumont in a different light. Groucho insults Dumont, and she lets him get away with it, huffily or happily, as if the good middle son Groucho had taken to imitating the prodigal oldest son, Chico, who got the most affection from their legendary stage mother Minnie despite, or because of, his delinquency. At moments there's something strangely maternal about the way Dumont suffers Groucho's incivility and comes back for more. In *The Big Store* she indulgently feeds him setups, pouting, "But I'm afraid after we're married a while a beautiful young girl will come along and you'll forget all about me," so he can reassure her, "Don't be silly—I'll write you twice a week." Here she takes his insults as flirtatious teasing, meant only for her. It's the left-handed flirting of a man who, when quite old, exploded in response to a question about his mother's favoritism among her sons, "My mother treated us all equally . . . with contempt!" He visits this treatment in kind upon Dumont's matrons.

Groucho's interaction with Dumont may have a personal source, but all the same, a lot of what spills out of him is pretty standard corn. Even his outbursts of cowardice are more wacky than confessional, which is how they seem when Woody Allen performs them. Groucho doesn't deny the moldiness of the jokes and puns—the eyebrow waggles acknowledge it. This by itself causes some newcomers to stare without laughing, because he's so famous for his wit they can't believe the zero entendre punning is what they've been hearing about. The senselessness of Groucho's gabble itself can be funny, but even when it isn't particularly so, Groucho is still funny to us because he doesn't pause for laughs. (Compare his so-far perpetually modern delivery to Eddie Cantor's sometimes forlorn, sometimes frolicsome, but always stagy pussyfooting.) Groucho's monologues, full of good and bad jokes run together without breathlessness but also without inflections, as if to underline the fact they they're memorized, help define his character further as the result of thirty years' experience, reeling off these endless sequences of free-associative jokes.

Still, Groucho didn't just pick up material that worked for him; he also learned to see through what worked and figured out further that seeing through the material could be put across to the audience as the entertainment itself. For instance, he's totally unconcerned about the abduction plot at the climax of *Monkey Business.* When he and Chico show up at the barn with a picnic basket to rescue the kidnapped girl, Chico says, "Hey, don't you think we oughta go look for the girl," and Groucho answers, "There's hardly enough for *two.*" He also refers to the whole scene as a "nice old-fashioned piece of melodrama." The Marx Brothers saw that the audience has to bring a lot to any situation to believe in it, but that their belief isn't necessary to their enjoyment. When Groucho later said that he hated "complicated, obscure non se-quitur plays," he was objecting to the obscurity of avant-garde plays that share his self-consciousness about theatrical illusion but don't relay it as an open joke to the audience. Treating his frank corniness as an insight into theatricality may sound forced, but if we combine the fact that Groucho was the reader of the family and that he was the only brother who "wanted to be in show business in the first place," it's not unimaginable that his on- and offstage interests would produce this kind of self-awareness.

It's not that far-fetched; for instance, all the Brothers conspire to parody bedroom farce, flurrying in and out of Kay Francis's hotel room in *The Cocoanuts,* Thelma Todd's sitting room in *Horse Feathers,* Margaret Dumont's bedroom in *Duck Soup,* and Groucho's hotel room during his assignation with Esther Muir in *A Day at the Races.* This activity, which generates suspense in farce, is meaningless in their movies because the Brothers don't care about the plot or their reputations, and we know nothing will come of the situation in any realistic sense. So the suspense of whether they'll be caught is nullified before it's played out; when it *is* played out anyway, it's not action but some distillate of fundamentally pointless hyperactivity.

The Brothers pinpoint this effect in *Horse Feathers.* When Harpo first enters Thelma Todd's room, he hands her a block of ice; she hollers that she doesn't want any ice, and he takes it back and throws it out the window and exits. Chico makes the same entrance and gets the same response and likewise throws the ice out the window, but he sticks around to romance Todd. Then when Chico and Groucho are both on the couch with Todd, Harpo comes in again with the block of ice, walks straight to the window without glancing at Todd, pitches it out and retreats, looking dazed. This bit of rote business tells you that they've exposed the machinery of farce for our enjoyment in the place of the farce, and this isn't as recondite as it may sound—my students thought this was the funniest gag in the whole movie.

You know the Brothers are aware of the conventions they're ignoring because in *The Cocoanuts* they had Francis come on to Chico by telling him he looks like the Prince of Wales, so that later when Chico, momentarily at rest in Francis's room, replays the line, "You remember me? Prince of Wales," and then Groucho knocks from the other side of the door and says, "It's me, the king of England," Chico yelps, "My father!" and skedaddles. Groucho had heard Chico's line through the door and so in a sense is mocking it in character by claiming to be the king of England. But when Chico runs from his "father," the movie is parodying the kind of risqué scene it hasn't stooped to create. It's a caricature of the outline of a shadow of something that was never there.

Harpo's specialty is to get at an even more basic form of rejection than parody. For instance, in *The Cocoanuts,* he slips behind Groucho at the hotel's front desk, pulls letters and telegrams from the room slots, and tears them up. If you buy the hotel setting at all, you can think of Harpo as anarchically severing the normal lines of communication. But the representation is hollow—the hotel is supposed to be all but empty, so you know the mail is there only to be shredded by Harpo. This second level sacrifices our expectations of consistency—as if those expectations were as artificial as words on paper, which they are—to unleash a deeper form of anarchy. The first level, in which we maintain a belief in the setting that is being attacked, draws on the child's anxious Cat in the Hat fantasy of seeing his own comfortable home destroyed. This fantasy rests on the same foundation as Tom Sawyer's ambivalence toward civilization and outlawry, a tension to which Jewish boys who hadn't had a stable middle-class upbringing could only aspire. In fact, the Marx Brothers, immigrant Huck Finns, had by 1929 reached the upper middle class financially but in their pictures consistently revert to the second level, where we find a foundationless world collapsing toward entropy but never approaching stagnation—nothing is constantly *happening.*

So when we watch Harpo in *The Cocoanuts* plucking a bellboy's buttons and eating them like nonpareils, or chomping the telephone mouthpiece and chasing it with ink, which he swishes in its well like a cocktail, he's breaking down his character's reality with physical jokes as Groucho does with verbal jokes. Harpo's shtick derives from theatrical traditions as much as Groucho's, but different traditions. Harpo, who never spoke on-screen, is obviously the most influenced by silent slapstick comedians among the Brothers. When a cop starts writing him a traffic ticket in *Horse Feathers,* Harpo, with a goonily angry expression, pulls out a booklet of his own and scribbles a ticket for the cop, in a superb variation on the fundamental antagonism in silent comedies of the 1910s and '20s. Harpo wrote that Chaplin was his "idea of comic genius," but this bit with the cop is more nuttily audacious than anything Chaplin ever did to a cop, because it doesn't involve making a getaway. In this semireal world, the cop still represents authority to be flouted, but the clown has authority, too, and it's more inescapable. If a comedian goes to prison, we always see how he gets out; in this sequence, Harpo locks the cop in his dogcatcher's wagon, and we never find out what becomes of him.

The most physically anarchic of the brothers, Harpo seems to have gushed out of the bottle after the cork—chasing blondes, hanging his leg on people's hands, picking pockets, and hiding silverware up his sleeve, or snipping everything in sight with shears (the same pair that the boys used to steal from their father Frenchy, who was a tailor, and hock?). In *Monkey Business* all four brothers imitate Chevalier singing "A New Kind of Love" to convince the customs officials that Chevalier's passport is theirs, but Harpo is the one who throws the immigration papers in the air, rubber stamps a bald man's head, and pretends to row with two pens in a stand.

At the same time, Harpo is the Brother whom children like most, and his borrowings from silent comedy often seem to understand it as kiddie fare. In *Monkey Business* Harpo, while running from the ship's officers, pauses to take part in a Punch and Judy show set up to amuse the kids on board. Harpo exits the puppet show sequence by escaping from the first officer on a toy train—which owes something to Hal Roach's silent shorts, both the Our Gang series and a trifle like the 1923 one-reeler *It's a Gift,* in which Snub Pollard powers his tiny missile-shaped car by holding a magnet up to passing automobiles—but ends it with an idea worthy of Keaton: to hide, Harpo lies facedown on the floor with only his head under the edge of a carpet.

Thus Harpo also gets at a more sophisticated level of perceptual gags; for instance, the Keatonesque double-take shot in *Monkey*

Business when a photographer goes to squeeze the shutter bulb, which turns out to be Harpo's horn—he's bent over under the black cloth instead of the camera. And when a lady harpist starts playing "O sole mio" she discovers that her right arm is in fact Harpo's; she shrieks and bolts, leaving the instrument to him. Because she obviously couldn't have ignored that her right arm was hanging idle, there's something pleasantly throwaway about this—it's just for us, like the false assumption shot at the opening of *Safety Last!*, which leads us to think Harold is going to the gallows, though no one in the movie could possibly make this mistake because it depends on camera placement and misperception of objects (station gate for jail bars; mail loop for hangman's noose).

And even Harpo's most childlike moments can turn into something else. For instance, when Margaret Irving, she-mashing him in *Animal Crackers*, asks him how old he is, his hand claims that he's five. But he's no sleepy kiddo. When Irving has managed to chloroform him, he wakes up as soon as the blonde he'd been chasing walks by. Harpo chases blondes without a segue to anything like the hallucinatorily raunchy gag he pulled in real life on a chorus girl in a dressing room, when he slipped a teakwood dingus into her without telling her he wasn't using the real thing: "Then it seemed a sudden thought came upon him. 'Gee, it's drafty here,' he told the girl. 'I think I'll close the window.' Without removing the wooden dildo, he got off the couch and closed the window. The girl fainted." In *Animal Crackers* we can only guess what he wants to do with that blonde, since in an irreducibly peculiar moment earlier, he had responded to Irving's coarse flirtation by slapping her hand, then kissing it, then trying to break her arm over his knee like kindling.

Harpo's crossbreed of imp and satyr is so antic he can be hard to figure. For instance, his expression when he's doing his gags isn't angelic, exactly. With eyes open round and an ambiguous big smile (naughty? crazed? imbecilic?), he looks like a face painted on a luminous balloon, the tumultuous, horny, larcenous spirit of mischief—at five years old. Harpo is lovable, but this mug isn't innocent, for instance in *Horse Feathers* when he nods yes in response to what Chico thought was a rhetorical question: "Whaddya wanna do, break my neck?!"

He can also be hard to take, especially when he attempts to express his serious artistic yearnings in his noncomic turns at the harp, which originally were a holdover from the Brothers' variety show days. He inadvertently got at the problem with his harp playing when he wrote, "If you've ever seen a Marx Brothers picture, you know the difference between him and me. When he's chasing a girl across the screen it's Him. When he sits down to play the harp, it's Me. Whenever I touched the strings of the harp, I stopped being an actor." Ceasing to be an actor in the middle of a picture is not a boast. But there's scarcely a clown you can name, besides Buster Keaton, or Groucho before MGM, who doesn't at some point fail to trust his material or persona to get *himself* across and so resorts to what he thinks are more direct means, but which may be less expressive, like Harpo's harping.

The accessibility of Harpo's comedy borders on fulsomeness, though I recognize in it a kind of birthday party clown generosity that you don't find in Groucho or Chico. The most extreme version of this comes in *Love Happy*, the 1950 movie that Harpo wrote, in which he undergoes a classic tragicomic ritual sacrifice for the group's regeneration: the mascot of a poverty row theater troupe, he shoplifts his pockets full of canned food and returns to the theater where the hungry actors swarm over him and, pulling the food from his coat, seem to devour him. It's an emblematic moment because Harpo always willingly serves himself up as a liberal feast, in a way very much along the lines of what he said about his childhood: "School taught you about holidays you could never afford to celebrate, like Thanksgiving and Christmas. It didn't teach you about the real holidays like St. Patrick's Day, when you could watch a parade for free, or Election Day, when you could make a giant bonfire in the middle of the street and the cops wouldn't stop you." For Harpo, comedy was a way to offer to the masses the festive communal cheer he'd found in the streets as a kid.

But the cannibalized clown in *Love Happy* isn't his *funniest* routine; Harpo's comedy is best when it flits too fast for the greater archetypes. Usually I find that the less sense his gags make, the funnier they are. For instance, the split-second insert when Harpo hayforks Groucho's library into a roaring fire in *Horse Feathers* is so good, and so superbly cut in, that knowing autobiographical sources doesn't explain what winds the gag's joy buzzer. (Harpo, when asked if he liked a stage production of *Pride and Prejudice* as much as the novel, turned to Chico and quipped, "Is that the book I read?" Burning Groucho's library, he's the older brother teasing Groucho for being a bookworm.) The delirious, unconnected bit in *Animal Crackers* before the card game when Harpo seems to sock Margaret Dumont in the gut, lifting her off her feet is one of the times when his uncontainable responses don't have anything precious about them. And the card game is pretty choice, too, even if at times it makes sense—not when Harpo shuffles the two halves of the deck separately but when he shows Chico the cards before he deals them to him, or tears up a spade from his hand because in the last trick he trumped spades. But it ends with a freaky capper: Margaret Irving discovers that Harpo is wearing her slippers.

This last bit is like something in *Un chien andalou* or *L'Age d'or*, which were first shown the same years as *The Cocoanuts* and *Animal Crackers*. Buñuel and Dalí came up with slapstick that ranges from the cartoonish to the exaltedly offensive, but their movies can't help being more than a bit studied, despite the volatile jokiness and unequaled dream logic. The Marx Brothers are studied, too, of course, but they studied in front of vaudeville houses how to reach as wide an audience as possible. Buñuel's anarchism may be assaultive but finally hasn't put him on the outs with the bourgeois cultural elite; the high modernist avant-garde can be taught in school. The Marx Brothers' movies are taught now, too, but whatever intellectuals say about them, they still make general audiences laugh, whereas Buñuel's movies have *only* an upper-class, educated audience.

Which is to say that the Marx Brothers' motives are trustworthily common. This isn't surprising when you read about their mother, Minnie, who when asked why she drove her children into show business, replied, "Where else can people who don't know anything make so much money?" In this respect, Chico *was* Minnie's son more than any of the other Brothers. Chico, who instructed Harpo when they were still children, "You don't *earn* mazuma . . . You *hustle* it."

Chico and Harpo started out playing piano in beer gardens, nickelodeons, and whorehouses, and Chico especially treats the audience as rowdy, commonplace clientele—he doesn't risk boring us. Minnie scraped together the quarters for Chico's piano lessons hoping it would deter him from gambling, but she hired a lady teacher who knew how to play with the right hand only, faking with the left. So Chico developed his showy style of tootling to cover basic deficiencies. (It was also the wow-'em basis of his early vaudeville career, playing blindfolded and with a bedsheet spread over the keyboard.) You don't have to know he was the champeen skirt chaser of the family (the reason his nickname was originally spelled, and always pronounced, "Chick-o") to see that he's flirting his way through his instrumentals.

It's most apparent in *Horse Feathers* when he's caught in Thelma Todd's apartment and pretends to give her a music lesson. She sits on the bench with him, and so instead of making his usual combination of sheep and wolf eyes at the camera—mama's naughty boy teasing us for being so susceptible to his charm—he smiles at Todd. He loves having this big blonde next to him, and his amused confidence is sexy. It's easy to see why his daughter said, "He knew he was irresistible," and you believe what Groucho said of him, that he could get a positive answer from asking a chorus girl bluntly, "Do you fuck?" Chico's lewd grin tells women how much they want it as he prepares to eat them up.

And it could be related to the reason he was such a good business negotiator—he never seemed hungry. Chico is the spirit of appetite without hunger, which is the truth of a lot of former poor boys riding high. He's also keeping himself interested in a racket that doesn't interest him: after Harpo played his first gig at a wake and "came home with a hatful of silver," he "now perceived what Chico saw in the piano, much as he detested it and much as he would rather be playing pinochle. There was money in it." How with this attitude Chico could be entertaining at all is the mystery, but it may be because he saw that performing facilitated the things he *did* enjoy—gambling and fucking and shirking responsibility.

I like Chico's routines with Groucho better than Harpo's routines solo or in any combination. (The great, riotous exception is Harpo's warning Chico in pantomime of the plot against Groucho in *A Night in Casablanca;* his subsequent speeded-up, condensed version for Groucho is even funnier.) But I realize that Harpo and Groucho created screen personalities in a way that Chico didn't fully. He came close with his Italian con man peddler. The Italian accent allows him to get in ludicrous but mechanical mispronunciations, malapropisms, and puns, which are funny because they're so obviously not genuine mistakes. To Chico a pun *is* logic—any connection that can be enounced functions. This is also true of Groucho, but there were differences. Chico could speak in puns because he was unconcerned with illusion, whereas Groucho actively undermined it. Also, Groucho can pun by himself in monologue, in his address to the faculty and students and his physiology lecture in *Horse Feathers,* for instance. Chico doesn't work solo— he's into pun-upmanship. There always has to be a game on for Chico, the compulsive gambler (when he finds himself in the barn at the end of *Monkey Business,* he spins a wagon wheel like a wheel of fortune), or someone to snooker. In addition, Groucho goes in for comic bathos, for instance, at the beginning of *Horse Feathers* when Groucho as Huxley College's new president begins to talk like a ragman and auctioneer. Chico is a peddler already, and so his recurrent puns about a coat and two pairs of pants tie him more directly to their childhood as a lousy tailor's sons.

Chico's very ability to do Italian dialect resulted from having grown up in the patchwork ethnic neighborhoods of New York's Upper East

Side, which were roughish and so required some ingenuity to survive in. Dialect offered the advantage of protective coloring: "Chico was quick of tongue and he had a flair for mimicking accents. In a tight spot he could pass himself off as Italian, Irish, German, or first-generation Jewish, whichever was most useful in the scrape he happened to be in." Groucho's wit is the kind a smart kid has to be careful about airing— he risks a pounding every time a bright thought occurs. This is why as a boy he called out insults to a prizefighter during a parade when the guy couldn't get at him. For a brainy runt, cowardice is a necessary corollary to lip. Harpo had his own resources, becoming a neighborhood character by "throwing a Gookie," the blowfish face we know from the movies, which was an imitation of a cigar roller who worked in a storefront window. And he always traveled well stocked for ambush ("The worst thing you could do was run from Other Streeters. But if you didn't have anything to fork over for ransom you were just as dead. I learned never to leave my block without some kind of boodle in my pocket—a dead tennis ball, an empty thread spool, a penny, anything"), clearly the origin of his crammed-full coats and pants pockets. Thus all their acts are based in part on childhood survival tactics. But Chico was the streetiest, a tough who ran with a gang, the one whose protective cockiness transformed his feathers. (My favorite line in *A Night at the Opera* comes when Chico and Harpo are wrangling with Sig Rumann. Harpo raises his shoe to clobber Rumann, and Chico says, "That's right, you go talk to him.") Chico is a mangy but spry little cartoon rooster, corrupt but not necessarily sneaky—like Groucho and Harpo, he can be oddly unhurried by conflict.

At their best, Groucho and Harpo are unpredictable within a certain domain; this is in the nature of comic personae. For the most part, Chico is just predictable. But since he's very funny, the only serious complaint against him is that when they get a big number, like the "Then It's War!" number in *Duck Soup*, he doesn't know how to flow with the material. He looks hunched and awkward when he's pretending to "hearken"—even Zeppo does it better. But you have to admit he's not vain, he's not fighting over seconds of screen time. Which leads back to the complaint that you wish he *would* push his personality forward more. It's odd, for instance, that although he was an incorrigible hound off-screen, he has few scenes with women on-screen, except as a sentimental protector of the ingenue in the MGM pictures (*A Night at the Opera* and *A Day at the Races,* both produced by Irving G. Thalberg and released in 1935 and 1937, and then *At the Circus, Go West,* and *The Big Store,* released one a year from 1939 through 1941).

Chico, who notoriously slept through rehearsals and failed to learn his lines, doesn't mind playing the sappy neuter Dad because of his basic indifference to the act. He had a shrewd business head and took over managing from Minnie with her tacky small-time advertisements and bribes and kickbacks to booking agents. But it was Groucho who sweated over their routines, constantly changing them and then trying to re-create what worked. (The funniest example is the report of Groucho coming offstage after a spontaneous stunt-and-quip and asking Margaret Dumont, "Do you remember what I said when I tripped you?" He kept a stenographer in the wings for the rest of the run.) According to Irving Brecher, Harpo worried only about his solo scenes, leaving the overall structure to Groucho. Chico's interest lay in wangling their way up from vaudeville to Broadway to movies and from Paramount to MGM by cultivating the men with the power to do them good. As a performer, then, Chico would do whatever was required to protect the deals he set up with the moguls during hands of poker and bridge; by the time shooting started, Chico had done his work at the card table. If Chico is underdeveloped as a comic star, he becomes fascinating the more you think of him half in and half out of the movies, which is biographically accurate. Harpo and Groucho both found him the most fascinating of the brothers.

Zeppo was their best face forward. Their assimilationist mother considered herself "more German than Jewish" and was so pleased by the coloring of her first two sons to survive—Chico with blue eyes and Harpo with green, and both blond—that she put peroxide in their bathwater to keep them fair. But Zeppo grew up to be the looker, with a V-shaped torso and "biceps like Charles Atlas." However, though Zeppo has the gear, his heart wasn't in performing, and so he doesn't dominate as a male romantic lead in their movies. None of them does; instead they come off as a game of four-card monte. Harpo wrote that on the provincial vaudeville circuit, they often played to a crowd of prostitutes and madams, who loved their shows, even when they flubbed up. Groucho said these gals were a great audience and that the Brothers were often invited back to the sporting houses after the show. He also thought the Marx Brothers were a "perfect act for these places," playing piano, cracking jokes, pulling stunts, and, no doubt, sampling the wares. In their movies, the open secret of burlesque, that everybody always wants it, is still open. And the Brothers all push forward some sexual aspect of themselves but don't give it any story development, not even Groucho, who keeps forfeiting the ground he gains with Dumont, often by making a pass at a beautiful young girl that he never follows up on either.

In *Humorisk,* the silent one-reel spoof they made in 1920, never released and soon lost, Harpo was the love interest and Groucho the villain, who ended "trudging off in ball and chain, getting his just deserts." Of course, in their minds, the romantic lead *can't* be Groucho—not just because he's a grotesque and too mouthy but because he wasn't the winning scorer, Chico was. Zeppo has the youth, face, and build, but not the personality or talent. On-screen Harpo is the most rampantly libidinous, but he's also a sweetie; Chico has the sexiest eyes and grin but seems both stunted and over-the-hill as a romantic lead.

A sense of grotesque singularity is part of what drives some clowns to slapstick. David Robinson, reading the prose treatment of *Limelight,* identifies as an autobiographical "reflexion" this description of Calvero's youth: "Another longing was to be a romantic actor, but he was too small and his diction too uncultured." It was probably his discomfort as a romantic hero that led Chaplin to experiment with the forms of his stories; he doesn't hatch romantic comedies, as the more confident Lloyd and Keaton almost always did. It could well be that Groucho felt too Jewish to play a plausible romantic lead. (Even his mother was disappointed by how Semitic he looked at birth.) One of the deftest jokes in *Monkey Business* is the cut to Groucho surrounded by beauties and coyly insisting, "No, you're wrong, girls. You're wrong. In the first place, Gary Cooper is much taller than I am." To compare Groucho to Cooper is supposedly laughable, yet Groucho is a much more attractive *performer* than the wooden Cooper, gorgeously carved as he was.

By sheer force of personality, Groucho would *have* to be the male lead, and by the 1970s, an assimilated era in which Dustin Hoffman, Woody Allen, and Richard Dreyfuss could get girls, Groucho probably would have been. He didn't derive his humor explicitly from his experiences as a poor, physically underendowed ghetto Jew—it's all unstated, *just*—and so he's not psychiatrically self-deprecating as Woody Allen is. But Groucho is more twisted, if anything, because he doesn't have an analytical open road to his sources. If he had, we might have lost the painted gargoyle with the spiked tongue, a more mysterious apparition.

So the upside may be that Groucho outrages Dumont so memorably only because his romantic drive is baffled. It's a kind of comic frustration—the defensive turns offensive. Groucho is far from seeming to want to be the romantic lead, however, and in fact shows the bait-and-snap cynicism of a man whose first sexual experience, at age sixteen, was with a prostitute who gave him the clap. What you find continually in movies, however, is that talent can hold its own against beauty, and so the Marx Brothers don't resolve which one of them is most presentable; they just keep shuffling the cards: in the "happy" ending of *Horse Feathers*, Zeppo marries Thelma Todd, but his three brothers leap on her at the close of the ceremony.

This gang bang ending also indicates how they developed their act out of the mischief of four rowdy brothers who as boys once disrupted a family wedding reception by jumping on a urinal (the first they'd ever seen) in the men's room, pulling it off the wall and making the busted pipes geyser, and who as young men in vaudeville handed chorus girls down from Chico to Harpo and Groucho. But in general, people can't tell the order of age and so can't see the significance of Chico being the oldest. Nevertheless, although *Monkey Business*, their first picture written directly for the screen, is the only movie that introduces them all at once, you do get a sense in all their pictures of the bonding and rivalry that siblings develop. In the first five pictures, they usually pair off in teams—the younger pair, Groucho and Zeppo, as hoteliers and the older pair, Chico and Harpo, as con men guests in *The Cocoanuts;* as hit men and bodyguards in *Monkey Business;* as college men and ringers in *Horse Feathers;* as government officials and spies in *Duck Soup*. There's a strange nebulousness to their relationships across this basic divide—each pair doesn't always know the other, but Groucho and Chico, for instance, slip immediately into routines. Also, Harpo quickly bursts forward as the pacemaker, and they all respond to his pulse regardless of their roles in the story.

They were lucky to be able to feed their inevitable competition back into the act to perk things up. When they were still in small-time vaudeville, Harpo remembered adding chords to his harp playing: "From the audience I got respectful applause. From Groucho I got dirty looks." But later Harpo first chased a blonde across the stage during the Broadway run of *The Cocoanuts* "trying to catch Groucho," whose scene he interrupted, "flat-footed." Groucho got off a good line, so Harpo chased her back across to see if he could come up with another.

Their movies aren't spontaneous even to the extent that their stage shows could be, but the sparring persists. For instance, the counterproductive insults that Groucho flips to women he also directs at his brothers, as in the opening of *Go West*. There Groucho is trying to sell a coonskin cap to Chico for Harpo; he puts the cap on Harpo with the three tails over his face. Chico says, "Isn't that tail supposed to be in the back?" at which Groucho lifts it, looks at Harpo's face, and says, "Not on him." The insult and the laugh it gets are more important to Groucho than the sale but don't impede it, though of course the big brothers Chico and Harpo cheat Groucho out of his money all the same.

This is the same scene in which Groucho asks if Chico loves his brother, and he replies, "No, but I'm used to him," which is exactly the feeling you get from Groucho's patience at being rooked by Chico. Groucho's exchanges with Chico seem to stem from the fact that Chico was the older brother and their mother's darling scapegrace. Chico is the only person who consistently puts it over on Groucho, just as Groucho does to the rest of the world. In their two-acts, Groucho becomes Sydney Chaplin in the guise of the food wagon proprietor in *A Dog's Life* who can never catch the Tramp, played by his younger half brother Charlie, stealing the muffins off the plate.

Groucho may have resented Chico for all kinds of reasons, but Groucho translated his feelings into their routines; for instance, the classic scam in *A Day at the Races* when Chico sells him a small library of code books containing the names of horses and jockeys. At the end of the scene, Groucho, now broke, is left with a bum tip, and Chico places Groucho's money on the horse Groucho had planned to bet on in the first place, and the horse wins. This scene plays out leisurely, as if Groucho can't avert his fate though he can see it coming. At one point Chico says, "You haven't got *that* book," and Groucho does a long take before saying, "You've got it, eh?" They slowly nod together, and Groucho says, "I'll get it in a moment, though, won't I?" The slowness itself, which could have been modeled on the attenuated pace of Laurel and Hardy's scenes of escalating payback, expresses Groucho's helplessness.

By contrast, in *A Dog's Life* Charlie steals from Sydney as if Charlie were the older brother. He can do this because he's the bigger star, though that was made possible in part by opportunities that Syd paved the way for and deals that Syd cut. Chico is also both the older brother and the deal maker, but it *feels* like it in his scenes with Groucho, who at times looks out at us as if exasperation or any emotion at all were useless—he knows he can't win. Chico's maddening slipperiness does set Groucho up to spike some zingers across Chico's net; as a pair, each is at once straight man and comic. But only Groucho needs the consolation that comes with the wisecrack.

Groucho would later "rail against Chico's selfishness and irresponsibility" all the while envying him sexually because Chico was married *and* loose, so loose that he capitalized on his resemblance to Harpo out of makeup by scoring girls while posing as Harpo in order to keep word from getting back to his own wife. Thus Chico was never the older brother in the protective sense as Sydney was to Charlie; he never went to sea and sent money home to keep his family from going hungry. More nearly the opposite: Chico stole nickels from them when all they had was dimes. Groucho does get the better of Chico in the famous password exchange at the door of the speakeasy in *Horse Feathers*—he gets inside, leaving Chico, who works there, on the outside, and then switches the password. But this can't last. Groucho forgets his own new password and so joins Chico on the outside. Older siblings exert a riptide that younger ones can't fight; Groucho and Chico's routines make drowning a deranging pleasure.

Fundamentally, as brothers and actors they shared the culture of being Minnie's sons. Typical of her command over them was how, when she needed a fourth for the act, she grabbed Harpo from his job playing piano in a nickelodeon and forced him that instant to go onstage, where he pissed his pants. As he described this landmark day, "When I arrived backstage at Henderson's [beer garden] Gummo greeted me with a soulful, brotherly look of commiseration. He didn't need to speak. His eyes said all he had to say: *So she hooked you too, huh?*" The Brothers were very close to Minnie and in awe of her: "Derision was as much a part of Minnie as the more physical, sensuous desire to have her bare feet rubbed, an act of obeisance her sons eagerly performed." Her barbed wit, a scary trait in a mother, provided a comic model for the boys' career, and she also held the family together with the earthy practicality she showed as the clan counselor and operator. Minnie was high-handed and self-centered, and though she nudged the brothers out into the world, she did it with maternal tentacles: she encouraged her boys to screw around with chorines rather than get married—that is, to remain *her* boys. And she disposed of them as she saw fit. For instance, she summarily ended Groucho's education after seventh grade, getting him a lowly job at a wig factory because the family needed the money. She didn't bother to inform him it wasn't a stopgap for the summer but the first day of the rest of his life.

The early act she developed with them was a highly conventional travesty of a grammar school classroom. Called "School Days," it featured Groucho as a German professor, with an accent, naturally (which he dropped during World War I), Harpo as a redheaded Irish cutup, like the boys who repeatedly threw him out the window in second grade until he simply stopped coming back for more, and Gummo as a Jewish boy. Chico later enrolled as an Italian boy, patterning his Italian accent after a barber he knew. They had to come up with something when bookings for their original singing act dropped off once they were too old to pass as the innocent "Four Nightingales." So they developed an act in which they never had to grow up.

As the Marx Brothers got more successful in vaudeville, they traveled with a big act including their own chorus girls. When they made the jump from vaudeville headlining to starring in their own show with *I'll Say She Is* in 1923, they simply expanded the act to take over the whole theater—they arrived on Broadway a stationary vaudeville touring company. And they carried this on in their next two Broadway shows, the movies made from them, and the subsequent movies written directly for the screen. The logic of the Marx Brothers' act was to turn an entire vaudeville program into a "story" that brings them on for their various specialties in quick succession.

But because the Marx Brothers are in almost all the turns (in the Paramounts, anyway), their pictures are more unified than most variety show features (such as the Warner's Gold Diggers series, MGM's Broadway Melodies, and Paramount's Big Broadcasts, as well as many musical theater biographies), even though the boys tatter the unifying story. While still at Paramount they managed to get rid of the love duets and the chorus kicklines you gawp at in *The Cocoanuts,* and for *Duck Soup* they even omitted Chico's and Harpo's instrumental solos, which helps explain why it hits a nonstop high like none of their other pictures. (Incredibly, *Duck Soup* was a career-altering box office flop.) Though the Brothers realized early on that by constantly sabotaging the story line they could make it another source of comedy, they couldn't get away with it at MGM, and back came the love interests' musical numbers. When Eve Arden as the bitchy aerialist in *At the Circus* snipes at the ingenue's number that opens the picture, "Who ever heard of anyone singing with a horse act?" it's like a second thought that somebody should have listened to.

Years later Groucho still endorsed their move to MGM:

I remember the first time we met Irving Thalberg. Chico, as usual, had arranged the meeting over a bridge game. Thalberg said, "I would like to make some pictures with you fellows. I mean *real* pictures."

I flared up. "What's the matter with *Cocoanuts, Animal Crackers* and *Duck Soup*? Are you going to sit there and tell me those weren't funny?"

"Of course they were funny," he said, "but they weren't movies. They weren't *about* anything."

"People laughed, didn't they?" asked Harpo. "*Duck Soup* had as many laughs as any comedy ever made, including Chaplin's."

"That's true," he agreed, "it was a very funny picture, but you don't need that many laughs in a movie. I'll make a picture with you fellows with half as many laughs—but I'll put a legitimate story in it and I'll bet it will gross twice as much as *Duck Soup*." . . .

It's a good thing we didn't bet. Our first picture was *A Night at the Opera,* and it doubled *Duck Soup*'s gross.

As hard as it is to fathom, Zeppo must in some ways have been the key Marx Brother to Irving G. Thalberg, because the way Thalberg saw to give them "legitimate" stories was to build up the juvenile lead to a singing, romantic comedy lead. Thalberg explained their problem as he saw it: "Men like your comedy, but women don't. . . . They don't have your kind of humor, so we'll give women a romance they can become interested in." He had the screenwriters pack in comic opera plots and family entertainment to get young women interested in the Marx Brothers, who otherwise didn't offer women any erotic focus.

Thus Thalberg's "genius" was to turn something funny into something "classy" and unthreatening and funny, though generally less funny. And not incidentally, profitable, though to be fair, Thalberg was willing to make movies that didn't recoup costs to bring prestige to the studio. But *A Night at the Opera* was to be a prestige picture not for MGM but for the Marx Brothers, who gained cachet by wearing the label of the blue-chip sausage factory. Thalberg wasn't evil, as studio chiefs go, and in fact his problem was perhaps that he *wasn't* a vulgarian. Buster Keaton, whose creativity plunged at MGM in the sound era under Thalberg, bore no grudge but said of his boss, "No truck driver ever guffawed louder at my better sight gags than did that fragile, intellectual boy genius. Nevertheless, he lacked the true low-comedy mind."

So at MGM Thalberg squared the Marx Brothers' circle. For instance, *A Day at the Races,* the second of the two Thalberg pictures, has a realistic opening at a train station, with extras and appropriate ambient sound. When Groucho sang "Whatever It Is, I'm against It" at the beginning of *Horse Feathers* during his installation as college president, the ranks of august professors formed a chorus, hands behind their necks and wagging their hips, but were then stuffily incensed when he ran down the line pulling their beards. That movie pulled the beard of the very idea of consistently realistic extras. In *A Day at the Races* Chico appears first, and though he's a bookie, he also runs a free bus to Maureen O'Sullivan's health spa, smiles sweetly to her, speaks optimistically about getting enough patients to keep the bank from re-possessing, and advises her how to get money from Dumont. This is what Thalberg thought of as a legitimate plot—the repossession of a young maid's property, granny's childhood favorite.

What Thalberg considered "real plots," according to Margaret Dumont, who, as if in character, approved, is the very kind of melo-dramatic hooey that the Brothers had always kidded. When Walter Woolf King, as an opera star who is helping Kitty Carlisle's singing career to further his designs on her, beats Harpo at the beginning of *A Night at the Opera,* Carlisle mothers him afterward. The scene is played for pathos, and Carlisle harks back to the deadbeat ingenues of *The Cocoanuts* and *Monkey Business,* only louder—she's an operatic soprano. Harpo bit his shoe while listening to one in *Monkey Business,* but now the boys expend their energy playing Cupid for Carlisle and Allan Jones, a replacement for Zeppo, who had left the act. Chico is now Jones's friend from their conservatory days and his promoter. The problem is that when Chico goes on to the great contract-dickering scene with Groucho, acting as an agent for the New York Opera Com-pany, it's hard to put together Chico's straight comedy friendship with Jones and his negotiating a ridiculously paltry sum and then shredding the contract paragraph by paragraph. You can't have a legitimate story featuring stars whose act consists in tearing up legitimate stories.

In *A Night at the Opera* the boys revert to their usual routines around the edges of the plot. Groucho has Dumont and Rumann to outrage and some classic routines with Chico and Harpo, and there's some fast-paced slapstick involving cots and a detective and the climactic ram-page through a performance of *Il Trovatore.* Working for Thalberg wasn't the almost unmitigated disaster for the Marx Brothers that it had been for Keaton. However, the legitimate story undermines the Brothers as much as the other way around, which becomes apparent early on in Groucho's scene with Harpo and King. After Groucho's line "Hey, you big bully, what's the idea of hitting that little bully?" Harpo knocks King out, then revives him only to conk him again. You find Groucho ad-libbing without jokes: "Ah, smelling salts. That'll bring him to," and then there's an absolute violation of Groucho's modus when he says to Harpo, "You're sorry for what you did. That shows a nice spirit." Even in the overrated stateroom sequence, Groucho's lines are peculiarly flat. It's hard to believe a veteran absurdist would have been satisfied with lines like "Say, is it my imagination, or is it getting crowded in here?" And when you know that there had been a road show on the vaudeville circuit to develop the script, with a lot of attention devoted to this sequence, and that at Thalberg's command the hired-hand director Sam Wood shot an unusually high number of takes for the Brothers' movies, it's odd that they couldn't have fashioned a line with a trapdoor in it, like Groucho's finest.

The Brothers' dislike of Wood and their weariness after all the takes may have made Groucho as indifferent as Chico. But Thalberg knew the mass audience depressingly well, as this praise for the preparatory tour of *A Night at the Opera* indicates:

> In past shows they always have been heartless clowns, perpetrating their gags on innocent and helpless victims. Movie audiences differ from stage audiences in mental attitudes and demands. They didn't like it. . . . So the Marxes and their writers reversed the players' personalities. They became sympathetic souls in the manner of Chaplin and Lloyd. The chill that had met them was dissipated and the picture audience liked them.

In the long run, I don't think people like the Thalberg pictures because the Marx Brothers are more likable in them. People like *A Night at the Opera* and *A Day at the Races* by forgetting all the "legitimate" connections that Thalberg insisted on and remembering the parts that remind them of the Paramount pictures.

The question remains why the Marx Brothers would have trusted Thalberg so implicitly, whereas they were less kindly disposed to Herman J. Mankiewicz, who oversaw *Monkey Business, Horse Feathers,* and part of *Duck Soup,* before being removed. First of all, Thalberg liked them. According to Groucho,

> Most everyone in [Thalberg's] employ was afraid of him. . . . But we had been successful in vaudeville too long to be impressed by this cathedral atmosphere, and in his presence we deliberately behaved like the Katzenjammer Kids. He wasn't accustomed to this rowdy familiarity from his hirelings, and I believe that was why he was fond of us.

Second, the MGM method of sending out road show versions of the movies to test the material was an industrial perfection of Groucho's own anxious attention to the act, which led him to keep that stenographer in the wings. But the number crunching during the road show for *A Day at the Races* is even more deliberate than having a steno at every performance. To perfect his punchline when Groucho looks at Sig

Rumann and throws his wristwatch in a surgical scrub basin, saying, "I'd rather have it rusty than missing," screenwriter Al Boasberg "made notes throughout 140 stage performances in four cities. Three words—*gone, disappear,* and *missing*—had been tried nearly fifty times each. Groucho was informed which words caused the most laughs." Furthermore, "One hundred gags were tested in each town and members of the audience filled out all 30,000 ballot cards taken along by the troupe. By trial and error, 175 laughs were selected, with the seventy-five which got the best reaction scheduled to be used in the picture." I wasn't kidding when I said they were "studied."

Thalberg wouldn't contract for any project he couldn't control and even predict the outcome of. Groucho and Harpo weren't averse to fine-tuning their spontaneity and so could work happily under him. And the Brothers would continue to throw him bouquets for most of the rest of their lives because his decisions were on the money, which is the third reason they liked him. Their deal with MGM was for 15 percent of the *gross,* which with Thalberg's tinkering was twice what their most successful Paramount picture had made. In fact, the two pictures Thalberg supervised, *A Night at the Opera* and *A Day at the Races,* were their biggest earners and enabled them to divvy up $600,000 from each in 1935 and 1937.

The financial failure of *Duck Soup* left the Marx Brothers, the performers with the most invulnerable personae, vulnerable to Thalberg's promises and also his pretensions—he was the man who had produced the movie version of *Strange Interlude.* Thalberg represented Hollywood's idea of quality. Even in *What Makes Sammy Run?,* a scabrous insider's view of Hollywood achievement, Budd Schulberg sees Thalberg as an exception, holding him up as the pinnacle of taste. However, Thalberg's runs to overstuffed department store taste. (His mother's family owned a large clothing store in Hamburg and then opened one in Brooklyn in the 1860s, which they later expanded into a department store.) At their most opulent *(The Barretts of Wimpole Street, Romeo and Juliet, Camille, Marie Antoinette),* his pictures put on display the sumptuous good taste of a Jewish kid trying to make movies that will appeal to the kind of people he fantasizes gentiles as being. Groucho said of him, "Thalberg was a strange man. . . . He was a Jew from a poor Brooklyn family. Yet he had elegance and good taste." That revealing "Yet" refers no doubt to "poor Brooklyn" but also to "Jew." However, "poor" doesn't apply to Thalberg's family of middle-class merchants, so Groucho here is identifying with the golden boy more than is warranted; he *wants* Thalberg to be more like him and thus rub some class off on him. And Groucho wasn't the only one: as Neal Gabler wrote of the Hollywood moguls of much poorer eastern European descent, "Thalberg was their Jewish American Prince."

The Marxes were nonpracticing German Jews who didn't speak Yiddish, just like Thalberg *and* Mankiewicz, whose father was a professor of languages. But unlike the producers' families, the Marxes were as lowly as the Orthodox Jews tamped into the Lower East Side. When Minnie and Frenchy married, they moved away from the bulk of eastern European Jews in Manhattan, but all the same, her boys grew up in a street culture barely distinguishable from that of a Russian-Jewish ghetto starveling like Eddie Cantor. Thalberg and Mankiewicz, in terms of middle-class style and education, respectively, both started on a higher social plateau than the Marxes. Comparing the movies that Mankiewicz and Thalberg produced with the Marx Brothers, it seems that Mankiewicz understood their comedy better while Thalberg understood a certain dimension of their aspirations better. And Mankiewicz's overriding self-contempt for wallowing in the golden trough of Hollywood probably didn't sit as well on the Marxes' stomachs as Thalberg's sincere enthusiasm, regardless of how much savvier Mankiewicz was about comedy. Groucho's awareness of Mankiewicz's underlying dismissal of their act may be reflected facetiously in the way Groucho signed a photo of the Brothers on the set of *Monkey Business* to their producer: "The only Marx who can spell Mankiewicz." In any case, after *Duck Soup* flopped, the Brothers, without a studio deal, weren't in a position to be picky about their producer's comic sense.

When Harpo once asked Mankiewicz about his character, the producer is said to have smacked him down with, "You're a middle-aged Jew who picks up spit because he thinks it's a quarter." This story suggests not only Mankiewicz's impatience with the Brothers but how conscious he was of their Jewishness. But what did being Jewish mean to the Marx Brothers, all essentially irreligious men? Groucho gave Chico credit for getting the act into the big time over his own resistance: "Look, Chico, we're not good enough. We wouldn't be a hit on Broadway. We're vaudeville actors. A Broadway audience demands class, and that's something we haven't got." And when Harpo wrote that their Spirit of '76 parody "was the only time we ever offended anybody" (in Cedar Rapids—it appears in the movie version of *The Cocoanuts*), he explained, "We never worked 'dirty.' We never used any Jewish expressions onstage. Our comedy may have been broad, and pretty hokey at times, but it was clean." The idea that they didn't work dirty seems not to have been true; Groucho couldn't resist double entendres even on "You Bet Your Life," knowing that they'd be cut before the telecast. But what's odd is the association Harpo makes between working Jewish and working dirty, as if they were comparable offenses to audiences. And it was probably also an element of what Groucho meant by not having class.

The ethnic caricatures that were at the heart of "School Days" show these Jewish have-nots using what they knew of the world. As Harpo recalled: "The toughest obstacles were kids of other nationalities. The upper East Side was subdivided into Jewish blocks (the smallest area), Irish blocks, and German blocks, with a couple of Independent Italian states thrown in for good measure." And they saw themselves as the underdogs occupying "the smallest area": when Chico caught the nine-year-old Harpo checking the empty Christmas stocking he had secretly hung in their tenement air shaft, Chico chided him in the terms of a streetwise gambler, "Figure how many airshafts on 93rd Street, let alone in the rest of the city, Sandy Claus has to shinny down in one night. Then you figure he's got to take care of the Irishers and Bohunks and Eyetalians before he gets around to the Jews. Right? So what kind of odds is that?"

Still, Chico's brotherly scorn voices no more resentment than the Brothers did in their pictures. This may be a result of the general, shrewd deracination of movies by the early sound era on the part of the largely Jewish movie industry, or it may be that by the time they were in pictures there was no sense of protest because they knew they'd made it. Irving Howe summed up the spirit of second-generation Jewish Americans who sought to assimilate: "What they were struggling for was nothing less than the persuasion that they had as much right as anyone else to feel at home on this earth, and what their parents were saying was no, Jews could not feel at home on this earth." And the Marx Brothers were second-generation *assimilationists*.

Even in life when Harpo received a cable from a Long Island hotel in 1927 reading, "RESERVATIONS CONFIRMED. TRUST YOU ARE GENTILE," he was upset but treated it farcically. He kept his reservation but when he appeared he "wore a tam o' shanter, smoked a pipe, walked with a crooked cane, and signed in as 'Harpo MacMarx.'" The Gentile friends staying with him got angry and insisted on switching hotels, to his relief, but he joked his way out again, asking the manager, "Lad, could ye dir-r-rect me to the near-r-rest Jewish temple?" He could respond to the world as a Jew, for instance, when he crossed Nazi Germany en route to a tour of the Soviet Union, an experience so frightening and depressing he couldn't eat. He wrote, "I hadn't been so wholly conscious of being a Jew since my *bar mitzvah*" (and all it took was the Third Reich). But then when the Brothers incorporated Nazism as a story element in their 1946 picture *A Night in Casablanca,* Sig Rumann, playing a master racist who calls Harpo an "inferior ape," is the same burlesque blowhard he had been before the Holocaust in *A Night at the Opera.*

The Marx Brothers don't present themselves explicitly as Jews, though they don't disavow their origins in the "uncouth ghetto world," as Meyer Schapiro nailed the Yiddish-speaking Bernard Berenson for doing. They kept their last name, and though their nicknames are not as Jewish sounding as their given names, they certainly didn't make them blend in. In any case, the audiences at the time knew they were Jewish because of Groucho's looks and accent (New York "neighborhood," though not Yiddish) and also because of the don't-try-to-impress-me cynicism about upper-crust culture. In fact, Groucho's role usually draws on the blatant incongruity of him as a person with authority, a major part of the joke of which is always, Imagine a Jew as a fearless explorer at a Long Island estate party *(Animal Crackers),* imagine a Jew as a university president *(Horse Feathers),* imagine a Jew as the leader of a European country *(Duck Soup).* And maybe even further, imagine a Jew *like me* as these important men. Yet his character isn't embittered by the social inequality that the joke responds to (as John Garfield's was), nor does he satirize the men who are more equal than he is. As a Jew inexplicably in charge, Groucho enjoys his power as irresponsibly as anyone could. In *Monkey Business* Groucho's position isn't specified, but since he's a stowaway, it obviously can't be much; so when he and Chico take over the captain's quarters to eat his lunch, the class climb is made explicit. Groucho badgering the captain's underling, "How dare you invade the sanctity of the captain's quarters?!" is skinning himself to reveal the interloper he must feel he is. But he's not at all anguished. When he issues orders to the engineer through a speaking horn and then ashes his cigar into it, he's making bubbly from sour grapes.

The Marx Brothers blast gentile institutions with abandon but without anger; they turn subversion into an improper frolic. It's important that this fundamental impulse is rendered not with the literary formality of satire but with the popular fun of blackout slapstick dialogue and stunts. They act out parodic versions of upper-class business and leisure and erase the distance not only between the participants, themselves and old money Long Islanders, for example, but also between the participants and the spectators, them and us. If, as C. L. Barber has said, "festivity signals the realization that we *belong* in the universe," the Marx Brothers' carryings-on signal the realization that they belong in American culture—they achieved what Irving Howe's second-generation Jews hoped for. But the "release" of the one festive day "was understood to be a temporary license, a 'misrule' which implied rule," which certainly applies to the Marx Brothers, who were liberals, but not radicals. A *Night at the Opera* shows this seeming contradiction: it features them as scroungers who don't fit into high society but was in fact their bid for the big time, and it worked. It was their number one hit and by consensus the movie that ensured that they and their funnier but less profitable Paramount pictures would not be forgotten.

Groucho was all over the map in his appraisal of their movies. In 1935 he said to Thalberg, "Our first two pictures were good because we played the gags hundreds of times on the stage. . . . The three other pictures weren't as good because we never knew if the gags were going to work out." As his biographer says, "By 'good' he too meant profitable." In October 1939, after the "mediocre reception" of *At the Circus*, Groucho wrote to Arthur Sheekman, "'A Night at the Opera,' for example, I always enjoyed looking at, and to a lesser degree, 'A Day at the Races,' but the rest sicken me and I'll stay clear of them in the future." By 1959 in his autobiography he had relented enough to write, "During our years in the movies we made fourteen pictures. Two were far above average. Some of the others were pretty good. Some were deplorable. The best two were made by Thalberg." And by the end of his life, in the 1970s, when the process of Jewish assimilation was nearly complete, he could look back with a calmer, colder eye and say:

> Women don't understand crazy humor such as that of Perelman or Benchley or even the early Marx Brothers. I think our earlier films were funnier than the later ones, but they didn't gross as much as those in which we dragged in a story and a love interest or "messages." We just set out to try and be funny. It seems we succeeded in being funny and making a little money . . . though one critic asserted that I was the symbolic embodiment of all persecuted Jews for 2,000 years. What sort of goddamned review is that?

At this late point, Groucho repeats Thalberg's coin-counting insight about comedy and the gender gap, but he's not confusing it with aesthetics anymore. He also denies the political aspect of his Jewishness, which is to deny by overstatement any statement on the topic. I've met similar resistance to *any* interpretation of the Marx Brothers as Jewish comedians from older Jews. Anybody can see that their comedy works by underlining and exaggerating incongruities, but maybe the older folks, like Groucho himself, perhaps, feel more comfortable assuming that the easygoing audience assimilates differences as much as it stands on them (as if refusing to perceive cultural differences might prevent pogroms, or something). True, any social commentary in the Marx Brothers' pictures works only indirectly and is pretty vague at that; however, their humor does have the turbulence that comes from merging with the mainstream. The comedy of these Jews, self-deprecatory at the same time that it deflates the high life of the dominant culture, became a cultural institution, an ambivalent model for a nation of immigrants pursuing happiness.

CHAPTER SIX

Preston Sturges: Girl in a Jam, Boy in a Jam

In 1890 Elbridge T. Gerry, the founder in 1875 of the Society for the Prevention of Cruelty to Children, explained his reasons for keeping child performers off the stage:

> The State as the sovereign protects each individual member of its future constituency in the enjoyment of health, vitality, and education, to the end that boys shall, on arriving at maturity, be physically capable of bearing arms in defense of the State and of intelligently exercising the elective franchise; and that girls, on becoming women, shall be so capable of properly discharging the maternal function and of educating their offspring that the physical and intellectual material of the body politic shall not be destroyed or impaired.

The direct beneficiaries of Gerry's vigilance included Buster Keaton, who loved his childhood on the stage and considered the SPCC "do-gooders" a "pain in the neck." (The results, according to Gerry's criteria, were mixed: Keaton went on to enlist in the army in World War I and "took being a soldier quite seriously, stud[ying] the Morse code regularly, also map reading and semaphore signaling," to become "the best-informed private in [his] outfit." On the other hand, toward the end of his life, he said, "I myself have gone through life almost unaware of politics," and, in fact, he never voted.)

Keaton's experiences slipping Gerry's net might make you expect that slapstick would lampoon these role models of the pure mother and the warrior son, but it doesn't, not when the hero is a young man. Slapstick is perhaps the least prescriptive of genres, but as popular entertainment it shares with the mass audience the values that Gerry stood for. Thus in silent slapstick you find that expectations such as Gerry's come as challenges to heroes who find distinctive ways of rising to them. In *Grandma's Boy* Harold Lloyd's grandmother tells him that her umbrella handle is the talisman that made her husband a Civil War hero; this belief enables Harold to defend the community against a marauding tramp and to pound his bullying rival, thereby winning the girl. In *The General* Buster Keaton is rejected for Civil War service because he's more valuable to the South as a locomotive engineer. However, his girl tells him not to come around until he's in uniform, and he spends the rest of the movie valorously taking on the Union army spies and infantry and defeating them, by ingenuity and a lot of luck.

The slapstick hero initially falls short of the military ideal but then grows into the role, even if by deception or accident. These movies don't satirize the ideal itself; they accept it while realizing that men's fear of not living up to it is a bottomless source of comedy. However, they take the inviolability of the girl (not to mention the grandmother) for granted. It took a sophisticate like Preston Sturges to distress both male and female archetypes, in two movies released in 1944, *The Miracle of Morgan's Creek* and *Hail the Conquering Hero,* and he did it during World War II, when the studios routinely glorified the boys sacrificing themselves for the noble women of the home front. Yet Sturges doesn't mean to attack these standards, either, which he more *consciously* shares. He knew even better than Lloyd and Keaton that what makes us squirm can also make us laugh.

Sturges's background was so different from every other slapstick artist's that it's astonishing he ever played the same games. Before he was three, his bohemian mother, Mary Desti, had run off with him to Paris to escape her bleak prospects in Chicago. Looking for rooms, she met the mother of Isadora Duncan, and when Mary met the dancer herself, they formed a permanent bond interrupted only sporadically by Mary's second marriage, to the Chicago stockbroker Solomon Sturges, the solid bourgeois stepfather whose family name little Preston was given. (He had been christened Edmund Preston Biden, in 1898.) Mary occasionally made a go of playing wife in Chicago but inevitably ran back to the life of the *presqu'artiste,* carting her son around the continent on Isadora's heels. Sturges was told about how when he was an infant, Mrs. Duncan had cured his pneumonia with champagne, and he could remember in his sixth year being dressed in a Greek tunic and sharing Cosima Wagner's lap with Isadora's niece Temple at Bayreuth.

Sturges also had his share of slapstick mishaps as a child, for instance, when at boarding school in Paris he was invited to accompany a professor on a visit to his rich relations. "Anxious to make a good impression [Preston] offered to carry the fairly heavy butler's tray around for [his] hostess." Not noticing that one shoe was untied he ended up tripping and depositing "the whole tray, the set of Sèvres, the boiling chocolate, the extra hot milk, the little buttered sandwiches, the plates, and the napkins upside down in Professor Azambré's lap." In a slap-stick movie, a fiasco like this would play out our fear of class deficit: us common folk don't have enough dignity to fit into the expensively breakable upper world. The difference is that Sturges is one of the few slapstick entertainers with any experience as a child of that upper world. He didn't finish high school, but unlike most entertainers from big cities, he was far from having what burlesque impresario Billy Minsky referred to in his own case as a G.E. degree—a gutter educa-tion. No other slapstick artist could have written *Unfaithfully Yours* with the conductor-hero hatching murder schemes stylistically coordi-nated to compositions by Rossini, Wagner, and Tchaikovsky. Only Carl Stalling and Milt Franklyn, the musical directors of the Warner Broth-ers cartoon unit, would have caught the jokes at all.

However, as James Agee pointed out, Sturges was also suspicious of his mother's beloved world of high-art bohemianism. He saw it as ef-feminate, and slapstick represented not only his distrust of anything "deep-dish," as he was fond of putting it, but also his desire to rough-house his way into a usable American identity, which he had found nec-essary when he returned from Bayreuth at age six and started school in Chicago. Living for a while with his adored stepfather, but still "wear-ing sandals and a little dress over short pants," he "became an object of derision" and, "of necessity, the best street fighter in Chicago."

Sturges always resented his childhood somewhat, but bohemian mores did prepare him for the hard-boiled Manhattan cosmopolitanism of the 1920s, where he made his name as a comic playwright, which led to his career in Hollywood. Sturges had a definitely male outlook, one he developed on the model of his assorted father figures. In 1916 one of them, Isadora's lover Paris Singer, reassured him after the al-most eighteen-year-old Sturges had set a former chorus girl up in a love nest and then come home from a vacation one day early to find her with another man. As he wrote, Singer "philosophically pointed out that I would probably be getting surprises of this nature for the rest of my life, so I might as well get used to them, and hardened to them, while I was young." Luckily the hardening was so comic and self-aware he never really crusted over. He certainly never stilled the unsettling comic convection of sex in his works.

The turbulent confluence of sporting sexual license and anguished cynicism is there in Sturges's career-making 1929 Broadway hit come-dy *Strictly Dishonorable*. Sturges sympathizes with the unhappy fiancée, Isabelle, but also has the older Judge note with discomfort how easily she dumps her ill-tempered, pompous fiancé, Henry, in a speakeasy surrounded by strange men. In the morning-after third act, Henry comes to the bachelor's apartment over the speakeasy where Isabelle has spent the night, and what seemed in the first act to be a mismatch of personalities and aspirations now exposes more sensitive sexual roots. Henry wants to reconcile but can't help asking with reference to the other man, an aristocratic Italian opera star who is the romantic hero, "Where did he stay last night?" Sturges, writing for the Manhattan audience of the late twenties, makes Isabelle the clear victor in this exchange when she accuses Henry of hypocrisy for making a "fuss" about her virginity: "As if it mattered to anybody but me. By the way, I forgot to ask you! Are *you* pure?" But not only would Sturges have to put such an attitude aside to write screenplays for the movies, it doesn't really represent his point of view: "It had always been [his] conviction that men and women are fundamentally different. . . . he insisted that it was man's 'natural penchant' to be promiscuous, while women were faithful."

He had in fact taken his first wife's decamping in 1927 very hard, though he credited it with improving his writing: "Whereas other people's troubles had always struck me as being very boring and only symptoms of weakness, I now had sympathy for people and their troubles. In other words, those three weeks, without teaching me anything about the craft, gave me the heart of a playwright." Yet he also says that this first breakup taught him a bloody lesson: "How completely through with a man a woman is, when she is through with a man. None of your masculine namby-pamby, none of that long-drawn-out, sentimental nonsense. She is as businesslike as a slaughter-house employee, scratching the calf's ears at one moment and taking its sweetbreads home for lunch shortly thereafter."

In *Strictly Dishonorable* Sturges struggles to give a sympathetic portrayal of this female disposition, but it's Henry who's really tormented. He's unpleasant, but more complicated and memorable than the bland fantasy lover who replaces him. In part, you feel that Sturges is trying to hide his identification with the rejected lover by siding with Isabelle against "himself." But the Judge's comment, "Cruel woman," when she sends Henry away tells you that Sturges can't fully go along with the woman's management of her emotions. Still, he never loses his sense of humor, even in the most bruising of reversals to male ego. Though his comic imagination bubbles furiously into language in the manner of Ben Jonson, Sturges as a writer lacks some final dimension of command. His work is neither focused enough nor broad enough in its outlook for him to rank as a truly great writer. But then neither does he consider off-limits any aspect of the forms of sexual warfare we think of as comic, and he even manages to keep the play of identification with male and female characters fairly mobile, despite his unmistakably male point of view.

Almost all of Sturges's movie career falls after the Production Code went into effect in 1934, and it's hard to think of anyone besides Mae West whom it would have constrained more. But Mae West characters live in a theatrical demimonde beyond middle-class decorum; they could get a lot looser if Joseph Breen of the Hays Office's Code Administration would permit. The protagonists in Sturges's scripts, on the other hand, like their author, uneasily occupy a middle ground. The major action shows them either on the outside sidling in or on the inside sliding out. And often enough they do one then the other. Sturges's movies feature people testing the limits of the codes governing their actions, sometimes wittingly and wilfully, sometimes not. The loss or gain of respectability or stability provides the basis of the drama, so Sturges's predilection for the risqué is really central to his movies. And like Mae West (and Oscar Wilde), Sturges might even have benefited from having codes to flout—it gives point to his perversity.

For instance, there's something gamy about the central situation in his screenplay for Mitchell Leisen's *Easy Living*. In this semiswanky Manhattan-set romantic comedy, Jean Arthur's Mary is a working girl whose life turns into a fairy tale when a sable coat lands on her head while she's riding to work on the top deck of a bus. When J. B. Ball (Edward Arnold), the millionaire who threw the glad rag off his penthouse roof to punish his spendthrift wife, takes Mary out to buy a fur hat to match it, the whole town starts talking about their nonexistent relationship. Mary arrives at her job as a staff writer for *The Boy's Constant Companion* swathed in fur and is fired because the editor and his wizened biddy assistant assume she can't have come by the windfall decently. But this very reputation for loose morals causes Louis Louis (Luis Alberni), the proprietor of a new deluxe hotel that Ball is about to foreclose on, to set her up in a penthouse suite for peanuts, in order to popularize the hotel as the vault where Ball stashes his mistress. By coincidence Mary winds up in love with Ball Jr. (Ray Milland), who, to prove he can fend for himself to his father, has taken a job as a busboy in an automat, where he meets Mary, who's unemployed and broke but well wrapped. The audacious thing is that Sturges has made Mary a courtesan in every respect except reality and set his nontramp between Oedipal noncombatants.

Sturges's instinct is that the audience responds to sexual misunderstandings more freely when they're presented in a comic vein, and that comic misunderstandings are more explosive when centered on the woman. This is the opposite of silent slapstick romantic comedy features in which the girls are innocent and the focus is firmly on the luckless but resourceful heroes. At the same time, Sturges did follow the traditional formulas governing the mixture of sex and slapstick. For instance, he begins *Easy Living* by involving Mary in slapstick with Ball Sr. when he drops the coat on her head; it's an accident that's funny in part because of the lack of sexual interest that the situation nonetheless implies to knowing New Yorkers. Then, when Mary goes to the automat where Ball Jr. works, and he falls for her, the resulting set-piece episode knocks itself out with slapstick all around her without ruffling her fur. Ball Jr., a banking heir in a workingman's uniform, is attracted to this working girl in a sable coat who doesn't have enough nickels for dinner, and so he unlatches some food doors to give her a free meal. He gets caught and in the ensuing wrestling match with his supervisor throws the switch that opens all the doors, leading to a stampede in from the streets. However, Mary remains calm at the center throughout, eating her free meal. In other words, when sex enters the picture, the girl has to be kept out of the roughhouse if we're to believe that she's "nice" enough to be the heroine—even in a picture that derives all its impetus from people's assuming she's a whore.

In *The Lady Eve,* which Sturges both wrote and directed, Barbara Stanwyck plays Jean, a cardsharp's daughter whose business is to seduce men on ocean liners until they're so addled that her father can fleece them. Jean is definitely not "nice." That is, until she's converted by her love for the latest patsy, an ophiologist named Charles Pike (Henry Fonda), but known as Hopsie because he's heir to a brewing fortune. Once she's smitten, Jean's corrupt skills enable her to protect Hopsie from her father. As she says to Hopsie one romantic night, "I'm terribly in love and you seem to be, too. So, one of us has to think and try and keep things clear. Maybe I can do that better than you can. They say a moonlit deck is a woman's business office." This is how the seductress-as-slaughterhouse-employee sounds when she's still scratching your ears.

Jean starts out mercenary and then reforms, but her plans go awry when the ship's purser clues Hopsie in to her racket and he won't listen to her explanations. Then her intentions become not so friendly as she contrives a revenge scheme to get Hopsie hitched to a *real* tramp, the Lady Eve, whom she plays herself, faking a British accent. On the first night of their honeymoon, the Lady Eve confesses to so many dalliances that Hopsie staggers out of the train in his pajamas. (He tries to run but falls on his back in the mud.) But when it's time for Jean, as Eve, to lower the boom for alimony, she won't accept any, a noble gesture Sturges later claimed to have made himself in his second divorce, from Post breakfast food heiress Eleanor Hutton (though it's possible he was embellishing his life in terms of his own movies). In any case, Jean, unlike Sturges, can in the end get her mate back by presenting herself as herself to Hopsie once again. This works because the grapeshot scatter of Eve's sexual corruption has pushed Hopsie beyond caring about Jean's morals. Jean at least fired only one bullet, straight at *his* heart.

Because Sturges concedes from the start that Jean isn't anything a boy's mother would hope for, he can let her in on the slapstick, but only as a cause. She initially gets Hopsie's attention as he's exiting a ship's dining room packed with gold-seeking missiles by sticking her shank out and tripping him. When she reenters his life as the Lady Eve, he falls over a sofa and pulls the drapes down on his head trying to figure out whether, in his valet's words, she's "the same dame." But Hopsie never does figure Jean's plot out; he just stops caring. Again, slapstick represents male confusion about, and submission to, sex, which obeys the female's command.

Sturges also keeps his heroine clear of the slapstick in *The Palm Beach Story.* In that movie, Tom Jeffers (Joel McCrea), an unsuccessful inventor, comes home to find that his wife Gerry (Claudette Colbert) has accepted seven hundred dollars from a millionaire who was being shown the town house apartment they were going to have to vacate for nonpayment of rent and who gave her the money just for the fun of helping a beautiful young woman. The sugar daddy is a nearly deaf old tycoon popularly known as the Wienie King, but Tom assumes the worst, or at least assumes that other people will assume the worst, and Gerry has trouble getting him in the right mood for the story:

TOM: Where'd you meet this Wienie King?

GERRY: You'll die laughing when you hear.

TOM: All right—convulse me.

GERRY: In the bathtub!

TOM: What kind of games do you play around here while I'm out?!

Gerry calms Tom down, but Tom blands out the story *too* much in order to be able to live with it. He's relieved to be able to say that sex had nothing to do with it, at which Gerry corrects him: "Sex always has *some*thing to do with it, dear. From the time you're about so big and wondering why your girlfriends' fathers are getting so *arch* all of a sudden. Nothing wrong, just an overture to the opera that's coming." The progression in Sturges's heroines from Mary to Jean to Gerry isn't a straight descent but follows the Goldilockean dialectical process: Mary is taken for a courtesan but is completely innocent while Jean *is* an "adventuress" who uses sex to take men at the card table; Gerry is more nearly "just right"—she wants to use her sex appeal on the rich men of Manhattan purely to help her husband's career.

Gerry is merely pragmatic about her allure, and it drives her nuts that her husband can't see how harmless it is for her to use her charms to help him get backing for his invention—a lulu: a metal mesh airplane landing strip to be suspended above the city so that an airport wouldn't have to be out in the sticks. She expostulates, "Can't you ever learn to be practical? Don't you know that the greatest men in the world have told lies and let things be misunderstood if it was useful to them? Didn't you ever hear of a campaign promise?" Gerry is mixed-up in her feelings for Tom, but she's not afraid of the world because she's not afraid of sex. However, there's a big difference in movies between male and female unscrupulousness. We admire Gerry for being able to say to her husband, "I've always been on the level with you and I always will be." But Sturges is probably reassuring himself, as much as he is adhering to the Code, when he suggests that Gerry could use her sex appeal so cleanly and efficiently to entice but never enjoy.

This angle brings out how most men feel about being supported by their wives. During his first marriage, Sturges had felt funny living in leisure with his wife, Estelle, on a Westchester County estate they bought with her inheritance. And he was "philosophically a male supremacist" as well, who felt that a wife is safest at home while her husband works, or that at least her being home will keep him from wondering what she's up to. The corollary fear, that if the woman goes out to work she'll be vulnerable to attack from all sides (and it won't be a fluke, as Gerry's profitable, though innocent, encounter with the Wienie King was), is a great raw nerve for slapstick to twang. (See the brilliant 1916 Keystone two-reeler *His Bread and Butter* starring the flourishy homunculus Hank Mann.) Gerry isn't safe even at home— the doors to houses open, after all, and a man like Sturges being by nature a worrier, enter the Wienie King (whose name makes explicit what's implied in jokes about the iceman). And Gerry can't wait to get out of the house, leaving Tom, in his pajamas and wrapped in a coverlet, tumbling down the stairs trying to stop her as she escapes.

The aging members of a millionaire's hunting club rescue the penniless Gerry at the turnstile to the train for Palm Beach, where she's fleeing to get a divorce, and give her a compartment on their private Pullman car. But in the picture's major slapstick set piece, when the swozzled coots blow apart the lounge car with their rifles, again Gerry isn't involved; Sturges's Snow Off-White flees these profligate dwarves as well. The closest she comes to participating in the slapstick is when she repairs to the sleeper car and steps on Rudy Vallee's pince-nez while climbing into an upper berth; unfortunately for him, he's wearing them at the time. But Gerry doesn't have the embarrassed reaction of a slapstick hero, and it doesn't keep her from getting what she wants. It symbolizes the effect she has on Vallee, just as the gun club's shooting spree is a volcanically blatant displacement of their attraction to her. Even when slapstick is symbolic of the effect that a free-range wife's actions have on her own husband, *she* keeps her feet.

In Sturges's most urbane movies, the men can't take sex in stride like the women, who seem born to it. Sturges admires his sophisticated, verbally skillful heroines in *The Lady Eve* and *The Palm Beach Story,* but the movies are exciting because he also shares the heroes' unease over the women's real or desired sexual independence. Gerry's epigrammatic arguments to Tom against their marriage in *The Palm Beach Story* are more convincing than Tom's commonsensical protestations because he's a financial failure. The ace-up-his-pant-leg, which he resorts to shamelessly, is that she can't resist his lovemaking; the problem is that she *wants* to because he's a flop. Men despair because financial and sexual success are linked but not quite synchronized. Financial success is far from assured, and sexual success may depend on it *(The Palm Beach Story)*; but even if a man is wildly successful, he may still be prey to sexual doubts *(Unfaithfully Yours)*. Male dominance always rings hollow to pricked-up ears.

These are Sturges's two major motifs: a man's attempt to make something of himself and his coping with the discombobulating subject of sex. Sturges identifies most obviously with the heroes who are trying to establish themselves in the world by their wit, skills, or valor. When he deals with sex the female characters are usually able to dominate, and Sturges splits his identification hectically between the dissatisfied women and the anxious men. He said that his first marital breakup gave him sympathy for other people's troubles and thus the heart of a playwright. However, what we find in his movies is not a unified response but both responses elbow to elbow: hypersensitivity to his own plight and a more general sympathy that extends to the kind of women who reject men. He's so good because he doesn't resolve the tension prematurely—he runs his movies off it to the end.

Sturges achieved his lowest boiling point with respect to sex and slapstick in *The Miracle of Morgan's Creek* (written and produced in 1942 and '43 but held up for distribution by censorship problems until January 1944), in which female waywardness produces the usual embarrassing results. After a framing sequence, the story proper opens with the peppery small Midwestern town constable Edmund Kockenlocker (William Demarest) directing traffic and getting into an argument with a brace of soldiers prowling the streets on their last day before shipping out. Mr. Kockenlocker, a veteran of World War I, knows enough to be suspicious of the boys. With two teenage daughters at home, he's also susceptible to a newspaper editorial asking, "Are Military Marriages a Menace?" occasioned by the editor's thinking about "the girls in the towns and the soldiers around the towns." When, later that evening, the constable refuses to let his older girl, Trudy (Betty Hutton), go to a farewell dance for the boys, her levelheaded but loyal fourteen-year-old sister Emmy (Diana Lynn) helps out by claiming, "People aren't as evil-minded as they were when you were a soldier, Papa." She's wrong, of course.

When Mr. Kockenlocker remains adamant about Trudy's staying away from the soldiers, she wishes that her mother were alive. Sturges zeroes in on the problem as Elbridge Gerry might have conceived it—what happens to a girl who doesn't have an upstanding mother to guide her—but he runs more current through it than you'd expect in a romantic comedy. Hutton's Trudy is like a downed power line whipping and crackling. When she's getting dolled up to go to the dance, she's got boogie-woogie music blasting from the radio, and she's already jitterbugging, even as she hooks her stockings. (A 1939 photo caption said Hutton was "called by many 'America's No. 1 Jitterbug.'") Trudy and her father form a perfect, unsettling pair—a symbol of vigilance (as constable, he's a symbol for the whole town) and a symbol of heedlessness. Sturges has matched a brusque, tough man, who handles his daughters like a drill sergeant and even takes swift kicks at his younger daughter (who scurries even more swiftly—Demarest, showing the vaudeville training that had got him to the Palace in its heyday, takes stunt falls on his keester), with an older daughter who's like something that pops out of a novelty peanut can. At one point, Trudy says to her sister, "You know me, I never get tired," and we're set to expect what can happen to girls who sneak out of the house and stay up all night.

Because of her gang date with the soldiers, Trudy doesn't accept an invitation to the movies from Norval Jones (Eddie Bracken), a plain-faced, orphaned bank clerk who's been in love with her since childhood, and who lives in miserable shame over not being accepted by the induction board because of high blood pressure that speckles his vision with spots when he gets especially nervous (he's never very far from collapse). But when her father refuses to let Trudy go to the soldiers' dance, she uses reliable Norval as a beard. Trudy gets Norval to sit out the triple feature he'd invited her to and to hand over his car keys by making a speech about how disappointed the soldiers will be not having anyone to say good-bye to them, especially the orphans. She's suckering the parentless Norval, turning on the waterworks when he initially refuses, but she's also suckering herself, recklessly insisting, "Why should I get caught? Anyway, I'm not doing anything wrong."

Norval gives in, and Trudy goes out dancing and drinking with the soldiers as if it were impossible that she could be left holding the bag. She returns at 8:00 A.M. with Norval's car banged up and covered with confetti and is unable to remember where she's been and unaware that the car is trailing a "Just Married" sign. Back home she and Emmy retrace her steps—one of the soldiers cried out, "Let's all get married," and Trudy went along. She also remembers that someone said, "Don't give your right name," so it turns out she doesn't know whom she's married to and can't recall enough facts to trace the transaction. In the next scene, she's at the doctor's office with the positive results of the fact that, as one character says, "The marriage was celebrated, I presume, they usually are." Thirty minutes into the movie and our heroine is crying for real.

Trudy, the irresistible id clashing with her father as the immovable superego, fills a strange sexual role for a Hollywood comedy because she *is* a nice girl. Even after she's pregnant, Emmy defends her as "a very nice girl" and adds, "It just happened, that's all." Girls with such unrestrained sex drive are rarely comic heroines. In comedy it's the part of the she-moose sidekick; in heroines it's a recipe for melodrama. Any number of weepers start with a wayward "nice" girl; at the higher end of the scale, sexual willfulness, even to the point of murderous depredation, serves as the basis for some of Bette Davis's strongest roles—*Of Human Bondage* (1934), *Jezebel* (1938), *The Letter* (1940). In *Morgan's Creek,* as in *The Lady Eve,* Sturges goes beyond the forgivable what-I-did-for-love unscrupulousness of female comedy leads. He distinctively combines unacceptable and acceptable behavior, in effect mixing black and white without producing gray.

I'm not claiming that Hutton is in a league with Bette Davis, but the role of Trudy doesn't make the coy compromises that are standard for the genre. In *The Lady Eve* Jean says, "You don't know very much about girls, Hopsie: the best ones aren't as good as you probably think they are . . . and the bad ones aren't as bad . . . not nearly as bad." In *Morgan's Creek* the strict moral distinction between good and bad itself starts to waver but not dissolve; when a character later tries to protect Trudy from an "abductor," the term sounds plenty archaic, but the issue of a girl's reputation isn't, really. Trudy is "good," but the first thing we know of her is that a girl on the street recommends her to five soldiers looking for a date for the party—her datability is common knowledge. And then we're introduced to her in the music shop where she works entertaining soldiers by lip-synching to a solo by a basso profundo. It's a funny low routine, with Hutton retracting her jaw while sinking to her knees as if the deepest notes were occasioned by a trebling of the force of gravity. Understandably the soldiers think she's a wow, but the mismatch of her blonde good looks and the recorded voice is jarring. It implies what was a genuine question for ordinary people: do high spirits imply a girl isn't what she should be? (I can remember high school girls as late as the seventies being admonished not to laugh too much or too loud.)

Almost all of Sturges's scripts up to this point took place largely in big cities or among sophisticates, if not both. But from early script outlines, Sturges conceived of Morgan's Creek as a "village," and even on the page, Trudy is a hoyden: she thanks Norval for rescuing her from her father, since she was "all dressed up like a horse and everything." Trudy would have to be a gawk with Hutton in the role. When B. G. DeSylva, Hutton's mentor and Sturges's nemesis at Paramount, produced *The Stork Club* in 1945, an uncredited remake of *Easy Living* with Hutton as the working girl mysteriously set up in a penthouse and outfitted with mink, the makers were aware of how much more incongruous she was than Jean Arthur in the top-scale setting. So they made her a hat-check girl in the famous nightclub instead of a magazine writer and gave her the song "I'm a Square in the Social Circle." As Hutton said in a 1944 interview, "When I was a child, riches to me meant a white fox coat, something gaudy and showy. . . . I read the movie magazines and wanted the things the stars wore in pictures." Hutton brings the hungry edginess of the lower-class audience to her performing, and as much as her flat Michigan accent, it's perfect for the role of Trudy because we can interpret it as the sort of desperation for experience that a girl will find difficult to satisfy in the kind of micropolis that Hollywood traditionally represented as the garden of authentic values.

Betty Hutton is also ideal for the role because like Jim Carrey today, her looks are almost fantastically variable: in the same movie, she can be a scrunch-faced zany and a soft-skinned sweetheart. So, in *The Perils of Pauline*, the 1947 fictional biopic of Pearl White, Hutton's throwing herself into a raucous number like "Rumble" doesn't preclude her later singing a melting ballad like "I Wish I Didn't Love You So." (In *The Stork Club* she is said to "hit" the first kind of song and "caress" the other.) Hutton has untrammeled energy, a manner when speaking to groups of leading a beer-barrel sing-along (she gained her earliest experience as an entertainer at age five with her older sister Marion "singing and dancing in a series of beer joints their mother operated"), and is great at exaggerated double takes (jutting her head forward as if she'd been hit from behind with a two-by-four) and a kind of splay-limbed galumphing that just suits the big-band music of the period. At the same time, she's pretty enough that Paramount cast her as a *sexy* galoot. Near the opening of the 1943 *Happy Go Lucky*, in which she arrives on a Caribbean island wearing a fur coat, when a man asks her if she's anemic, she drops the coat to reveal a bathing suit with a cutout midriff and brags, "Whadda *you* think?" Hutton is so visibly healthy she radiates comic vibes, and she combines some of the most potent female comedy types of her era: the man chaser, the swing singer, the bombshell. This last is what enables her to play leads, unlike Martha Raye, whose emphatic style is similar.

Sturges didn't create the uncontainable Hutton character; he picked it up from the earlier Paramount pictures that had teamed Hutton and Bracken. In the 1942 patriotic revue *Star Spangled Rhythm*, set largely on the Paramount lot, and in which Sturges appears briefly as himself with the couple, Bracken plays a sailor who has courted Hutton by letter and who comes to meet her for the first time at Paramount, where she's a switchboard operator. He brings five buddies, warning them, "And no cracks in front of my girl. She's kind of bashful and she might be a little embarrassed meeting me for the first time." But when she sees him, she shrieks, leaps over her desk, and gloms onto him; one of the sailors comments archly, "The mother type." A little later Hutton sings "I'm Doing It for Defense" while on the back of a bouncing jeep with Bracken and friends, in which she claims to be making love to sailors not for love itself but to sustain morale, which is Trudy's motivation, or at least her justification, in *Morgan's Creek*. However, in

Star Spangled Rhythm it's treated not as something that could upend her life but as a rowdy boast (though in the story it isn't true).

Star Spangled Rhythm also features Hutton in an extended slapstick routine with Walter Dare Wahl & Co., a Mutt-and-Jeff pair of acrobats, in which she tries to get a boost from them over the studio wall. She appears in ladylike dress and heels that only make her look more ungainly as she throws herself at the bricks and tries to scrabble up them, clutching at a vine and falling on her rump. When she does get a foothold on the bent-over backs of her cohorts, she soon loses it and somersaults forward between them and the wall, landing on her butt again. In addition, the trio can't let go of each other's hands and while trying to disentangle them keep tying themselves into Möbius strips. There's no reason for the stuck hands (no molasses, glue, pine resin); it's just pure slapstick that, like Laurel and Hardy's, takes place in the maddening silence of a daymare. It's a classic in the limited realm of female slapstick because Hutton isn't just a bystander. She motivates the assault on the wall and takes the punishment with her backside: what more can you ask of a slapstick clown?

However, Hutton isn't glamorous when she's doing slapstick. She *is* considered marriageable, but by Eddie Bracken, a not very virile hero. (In *Happy Go Lucky* Hutton shows a hotel doorman a photo of Bracken and asks, "Have you ever seen this jerk?" The doorman, a Caribbean islander unfamiliar with our slang, says, "Jerk? What's that?" and Hutton, pointing to the photo, replies, "Why, it's a *man,* sort of.") In any case, in *Star Spangled Rhythm,* Bracken is called off to combat before they can actually tie the knot, leaving Hutton a bit stranded, though not in the soup as in *Morgan's Creek.* In *Happy Go Lucky* he was sick on their wedding day, and when she sued him for standing her up, he took off for the islands; she has to use a voodoo love potion to get him to the altar. Sturges, like his colleagues at Paramount, understands why men would be drawn to a Roman candle like Hutton and also why they'd want to keep their distance. There's something in Hutton's eyes in *Morgan's Creek,* as there was again in *Annie Get Your Gun*—an anxious sparkle—that connects the character's hungry recklessness with what we now know of the star's chaotic life story. Eligible young beauties in movies usually don't have this depth of desperation, and getting into Trudy's story is a bit frightening, like trying to rescue a drowning girl who keeps clutching at you and pulling you down—essentially the plot of *Morgan's Creek,* seen as it should be from Norval's point of view.

What's distinctive about *The Miracle of Morgan's Creek* is that

Sturges plays this ambivalence out in terms of slapstick. When Trudy is sliding down the slope in the first part, we see her lip-synching for the boys; cutting the rug while dressing; jitterbugging with a series of soldiers, one of whom, in a scene added to please the censors, lifts her up and conks her head against a mirrored dance hall ceiling fixture, thus explaining her errant behavior; and arriving home drunk, where she catches her coat on the front gate and falls backward, landing with her dress up over her head (a reenactment of the highlight of her evening, in a sense). After Trudy gets into trouble, about a third of the way into the picture, Norval starts competing with her in terms of physical comedy.

Hutton is such an artist of mania that she can accent it according to the requirements of the scene. She's probably most inspired when Trudy, without telling Norval she's already married and pregnant, deviously gets him to propose to her. She's been in the habit of discouraging Norval so plainly that she now has to hint quite largely; he properly perceives it as *her* proposing to *him,* but he's so glad he doesn't care. Hutton almost visibly swells with the suspense of whether her wiles are working, and Bracken keeps getting more and more nervously excited, until he falls off the porch railing, pulling a vine and the roof gutter down on top of himself. It's an exaggeration of the kind of unhealthy excitement that a culture of innuendo and euphemism can build up in susceptible boys and girls. More important, it's a transition—Norval and Trudy starting to fill the social roles of suitor and maid. Trudy is asking for it, in a sense, but technically she's waiting to be asked. And though she's manipulating Norval outrageously, when he starts telling her about how long he's loved her, she breaks. She can't snag him underhandedly because his devotion finally makes her love him back.

In retrospect this scene portends that Trudy will never be the focus of the slapstick again as she had been in the early scenes. When she's a sexually independent and morally questionable young woman, she can be at the center of the rumpus. But look at how her image progresses: first she mimes to a basso profundo voice before going out drinking and dancing and having sex as if there could be no consequences; then she becomes a tearful miss reliant on a man to rescue her and ends up a legendarily prolific mother. Sturges plays Trudy's character like a slingshot—he pulls it way back into typically male assertiveness and then lets it fly into the ultramaternal. As soon as she begins settling into her role as expectant mother and loving girlfriend, she takes a backseat to Norval as knockabout clown. Thus the opening gambit of the movie, Trudy's escapade, marks the extent of Sturges's identification with Trudy—and its limits. In his memoirs, Sturges reiterated his intention that *Morgan's Creek* serve as a "sermon" to "young girls who disregard their parents' advice and who confuse patriotism with promiscuity." (He wrote this line into an actual sermon to be delivered in church in the movie but cut the scene.) When I first saw *Morgan's Creek* as a teenager, I assumed that Sturges identified with Betty Hutton in her jam. After all, Trudy is never more enjoyable than in the opening sections when she carries on with Hutton's own floor show flair. But though the movie is basically sympathetic, in a sense that's only because she has to be a nice girl for the hero's sake.

Sturges identifies more with Bracken as Norval—you know because Norval manages to take pratfalls when he's already seated. Slapstick is not only traditionally a male form of entertainment for the audience but a male form of identification for entertainers as well. As Mack Sennett said, people don't find slapstick that involves pretty girls funny. By contrast, it doesn't matter if the man is a sleek matinee idol like Cary Grant or the young Henry Fonda, solidly handsome like Joel McCrea, or admittedly homely like Eddie Bracken; he falls all over himself for the girl he loves. In romantic comedy, slapstick becomes an expressionistic form of clowning for men: it makes visible how it feels to have the success of a romantic suit depend on the persuasiveness of your personality. Courtship makes men feel vulnerable, since they have to take the initiative but don't have the final say. Norval is miserably uncertain even in the scene on the porch in which Trudy flagrantly primes his pump until he spurts a proposal.

The Miracle of Morgan's Creek plays off the expectations of propagandists like Elbridge Gerry that girls be pure and boys be valiant, expectations that were often jacked up in patriotic wartime melodramas. Thus in the script Sturges specified the last shot of the third feature Norval sits through while Trudy is out with the soldiers: "A young military hero receives not only the girl, but the congressional medal of honor and also a million dollars in cash. As it fades out CUT BACK TO NORVAL. He watches the screen dismally." So when Norval can't get into the army because of the high blood pressure that stipples his vision, he feels like a washout as a man, hopeless. Sturges doesn't intensify cultural expectations of the hero, but rather the hero's unfitness to meet them, which is a shrewd comic choice because it sets the hero's quadrupled wackiness within the kind of generally realistic setting moviegoers are used to identifying with. In all of Sturges there's nothing at once as strange and as understandable as Norval's stuttering and whinnying when Officer Kockenlocker, while cleaning his gun, bluffly

advises him to boss Trudy into marrying him. When the gun accidentally fires, Norval tries to walk into the house to get away but is so
nerve-shot he can't open the screen door and so walks *through* it.

Sturges doesn't pull back from identification with his characters,
ambiguities and all, at times without regard to their sex, but he does
retreat from Trudy as the movie progresses. For example, after the
change in Trudy's attitude toward Norval, the story is pushed forward
by *Norval's* initiative: he concocts a scheme whereby he'll marry Trudy
in the guise of the vanished soldier-husband, but he's such a mess that
he signs his own name and is arrested for abduction, among other
things. Constable Kockenlocker, having found out what Norval was
trying to do for his daughter, lets Norval escape from jail to find
Trudy's missing soldier-husband. When Norval, having failed, comes
back to Morgan's Creek on Christmas Day, he's arrested again. Trudy
is about to tell the town leaders the truth to clear Norval's name when
she goes into labor and produces not one but six boys. Thus, by the
end, Trudy has made her own childbed and has to *lie* in it—lie still, in
fact, flat on her back and spent. Norval's taking the lead signals the
state Sturges would consider a happy resolution. We don't get stability
in the picture, ever, but Trudy *is* brought back into line, and Norval *is*
more physically dominant, even as a jittery mess.

In fact, during production Sturges was always building Norval's
role up. For instance, his fall off the porch railing after proposing to
Trudy isn't in the script but appears to have been arrived at during
shooting, in the best silent method of improvisation, which was predi-
cated on the stumbler being the star of the show. (Bracken, a veteran of
Hal Roach's Our Gang series, must have had some relevant experience.) Sturges also scratched a scene outside the quick marriage motel
in which Trudy wraps Norval's puttee to the car fender, and they both
fall over in a heap. Hutton had to keep her veteran performer's eye
open for any opportunity: it was, according to Bracken, Hutton's idea
to have Trudy start stuttering like Norval does when they're riding to
their secret marriage ceremony. Sturges may have allowed it because it
fits perfectly with the terms of Norval's romantic comedy—it's another
way in which Trudy, now deeply stirred by Norval, is identifying with
her beloved.

For Sturges, slapstick is so much a male sport that we can say he
identifies in some ways nearly as much with Trudy's antagonistic father, who shares Sturges's first name, Edmund, and who repeatedly
falls on his prat, as with his heroine herself. Thus if we take the sermon to young girls as the motive behind the picture, then Officer

Kockenlocker, whose suspicions were, after all, dead-on, is the motive spirit of the movie. But Trudy can't obey her father any more than she can be like sensible Emmy—or no picture—and so as moviegoers we can't help finding the lawless girl appealing. But Officer Kockenlocker's idea of orderly sexual conduct is where the movie ends up, not Emmy's "It just happened, that's all."

The "miraculous" birth brings about both Trudy's and Norval's redemption, with Norval in uniform and Trudy a respectable mother of six boys, all that Officer Kockenlocker could wish and more than he expected. This ending reshapes the couple to fit Elbridge Gerry's typecasting of men and women—the international headlines announce a "platoon" born in the Midwest—but only by the most credulity-stretching, farcical of miracles. We understand at the end that Trudy and Norval will have to live up to their parts from this point on. At the end of comedies, everyone has to promise, whether implicitly or explicitly, to behave. But at the same time, Officer Kockenlocker's cynicism about family life (one of his refrains is, "Daughters! Phooey!") also persists. For instance, Norval, who's spent his life pining for Trudy, starts running by instinct when he finds out about the birth of "his" six sons. This allows Sturges to resolve the comedy and yet keep the movie raucous right through the last second.

In Sturges's next picture, *Hail the Conquering Hero* (also a 1944 release, his last made at Paramount), Norval's story from *Morgan's Creek* doesn't have to compete against the girl's story. This time Bracken plays Woodrow Lafayette Pershing Truesmith, who feels he was born to be a marine like his father, a World War I hero who died in Belleau Wood on the day Woodrow was born. Woodrow's opportunity for glory arrived with World War II; he signed right up but was discharged after a month for hay fever. For a year he's been working in a shipyard and sending letters home to his mother via pals going overseas so she won't know that her son isn't the kind of hero her husband was. We meet Woodrow despondent in a bar when he treats six broke marines and then tells them his story. One of the marines, called Bugsy (Freddie Steele), is a mother-fixated orphan, and in the middle of Woodrow's story, he borrows change to call Mrs. Truesmith and tell her that her son is coming home a wounded hero. The marines are on leave, so they muscle the resistant Woodrow onto a train and drag him home, where the alerted town goes crazy feting him—the preacher burns his mother's mortgage, which has been paid off by subscription, from the pulpit of the church; the citizens commission a heroic father-son monument in granite; the reform party nominates him for mayor. Furthermore, because he didn't want her to share his shame as a combat reject, Woodrow had written to his girl, Libby (Ella Raines), that he doesn't love her anymore. But though *Hail the Conquering Hero* ends happily for Libby and Woodrow, it's a structurally ironic romantic comedy with the young hero trying to give his girl away. *Morgan's Creek* is more traditional, with Norval getting the girl he wants despite the obstacles. Since Trudy is herself the major obstacle, her story is more important than the devoted Libby's. *Hail the Conquering Hero* is a boy's story.

However, pointing out the irony of the romantic comedy doesn't begin to suggest the difficulty in describing the movie's genre. Sturges claimed to have come up with the story by reversing the terms of a melodrama. As he wrote in a 1944 letter:

> I thought for a month or so along the lines of what I call Monsieur Beaucaire in modern clothes. By that I mean a hero who is believed by all to be a villain but who in the end is introduced as a man of great honor with a long list of decorations. I had some difficulty in finding a valid reason for the hero to pretend he was not a hero and while searching around for a reason it suddenly occurred to me that it would be very easy to find a reason for a man who was NOT a hero to pretend that he WAS a hero.

Monsieur Beaucaire is a textbook example of a melodrama in which the virtuous hero is unjustly reviled and a usurper is undeservedly ascendant, right until the climactic public declaration of who is truly virtuous and who truly evil. (It's the most symmetrically schematic kind of melodrama—revealing the truth merely involves switching the reputations of hero and villain.) As an inversion of *Monsieur Beaucaire,* *Hail the Conquering Hero* actually puts Woodrow in the position of the undeserving usurper who is publicly exposed, but his resistance to the charade and his voluntary confession to the townspeople at the movie's climax indicate how virtuous he is despite his inability to serve his country as a marine.

Furthermore, Sturges wrote the script for *Hero* after Warner Brothers refused to relinquish the rights to *A Connecticut Yankee in King Arthur's Court* to Paramount for him. (It's probably just as well, since he'd already used one of Twain's major plot devices—Hank Morgan and King Arthur going in disguise among the lowly to see what their life is like and ending up slaves on a chain gang—for *Sullivan's Travels.*) Twain's sometimes jocular, sometimes bitter disgust over chivalric codes doesn't really find a way into *Hero.* That is, Sturges may make the town overexcitable, the marines crude and hardheaded fabulists, and Woodrow sickly, self-pitying, and too pliable, but he doesn't debunk the idea of heroism. Woodrow isn't a coward, like the character Bob Hope always played, for instance. However, the plot device of Sir Launcelot allowing Sir Kay to claim Launcelot's victories as his own does become Sergeant Heffelfinger attributing his own battle experiences to Woodrow. In fact, when it is announced in Twain that the prisoners were captured by Sir Kay rather than Launcelot, Guenever says, "Sir *Kay*, forsooth! Oh, call me pet names, dearest, call me a marine! In twice a thousand years shall the unholy invention of man labor at odds to beget the fellow to this majestic lie!" If Sturges worked at all by association of ideas, the plot of *Hail the Conquering Hero,* originally titled *The Little Marine,* lies in the queen's response to this deception.

In addition, *Hail the Conquering Hero* had a contemporary precursor in *Star Spangled Rhythm* (screenplay by Harry Tugend and the uncredited Arthur Phillips), in which the former vaudevillian Victor Moore plays a washed-up cowboy star, now working as a Paramount gate man, who has written to Bracken as his son in the navy that he's an executive at the studio. (This is the picture in which Sturges appears on-screen as himself with Bracken and Hutton.) When Bracken visits Hollywood on leave, Hutton helps Moore pull off the masquerade. And in both *The Miracle of Morgan's Creek* and *Hail the Conquering Hero,* Sturges makes use of two of the basic characters of service comedy, pitting Eddie Bracken as the sad-sack (would-be) enlistee against William Demarest as a tough but sentimental marine sergeant.

However, in *Hail the Conquering Hero* Woodrow isn't as clear-cut a protagonist as this suggests because the story developed as a variation on yet another formula, further complicating things, so that it's impossible for all lines of development to conclude satisfactorily. This last formula also operates in *Monsieur Beaucaire:* the hero is what is called in Greek comedy an *eiron* (the root word for "irony"), or self-deprecator, and his rival is an *alazon,* or impostor. They were originally "the man who pretends to less knowledge or power than he has" in order to outwit and triumph over "the man who pretends to more," respectively. But in our popular comedies, the opposition is between a modest, decent guy and a rival who attempts to lord his superiority of class, wealth, strength, or accomplishment over him. Thus the format will be more familiar than the Greek terms because it's still in use.

George Cukor and Garson Kanin's *It Should Happen to You* (1954) gets at the essence of the American version of this contest by making the unassuming hero a documentary filmmaker, a professional truth teller, and the rival an English-accented soap company heir who involves the girl in an advertising campaign for his product while trying to seduce her. In the clearest recent example, *The Wedding Singer* (1998), Adam Sandler is the self-deprecating small-town boy who doesn't pretend to have anything to brag about but whom the girl enjoys being with because he genuinely likes her. His opponent is Matthew Glave's big-city stockbroker, who publicly embarrasses Sandler for being a nobody but who is cheating on the girl he's actually indifferent to. In addition, Glave has got rich selling junk bonds—he's the embodiment of inflated worth. The self-deprecator's humility and decency are the qualities by which we recognize him as the hero, and for us there's no contest, as there is for the girl until the resolution of the plot. For some reason, the fact that Monsieur Beaucaire turns out to be a prince of the blood enables the formula to operate in its pure form, but the story has to be removed in time for the democratic audience. Plus, Tarkington has the prince reject one highborn beauty because she's a snob about rank. Still, the prince can prove himself objectively worthy as Woodrow cannot, which adds to the headline immediacy of Woodrow's story a quaver that lingers despite the upbeat ending.

What Sturges has done, however, is to make Woodrow both *eiron* and *alazon*—both a decent guy who's hiding in order to spare his mother and girl pain and a guy who's pretending to be a soldier returning from battle in glory. It's true that both *eiron* and *alazon* may be slippery; for example, the hero may resort to subterfuge, especially to expose the rival to the girl. And as Chaplin's early career shows, a slapstick hero can be a swaggering impostor and win the *audience,* if not the girl. In addition, the fact that the six marines *force* Woodrow into the imposture would make it all work neatly if Sturges hadn't provided an opposite figure for Woodrow in both his roles. Thus Woodrow comes home to find that Libby is now engaged to the mayor's son, Forrest Noble (Bill Edwards), a rich-but-modest, plain-dealing, and better-looking young man than Woodrow (even Heffelfinger says to Woodrow of his father, "He was a fine lookin' fellow . . . he didn't look anything like you at all"). Sturges cools down the rivalry by putting Forrest in a situation very similar to Woodrow's: he too lives in the shadow of his father (who unfortunately in his case is alive) and has likewise been kept from serving in the war because of hay fever. But Forrest never lied about it and even suffers having Libby throw it in his face that Woodrow never let hay fever hold *him* back. This makes

Forrest the boy who plays down his own virtues in contrast to Woodrow as the phony town hero.

At the same time, Woodrow, in his guise as reform candidate drafted to run against Forrest's father, is the man who keeps denying the false claims made on his behalf by the marines until he really does seem like someone you could vote for in place of the supremely pompous Mayor Noble (Raymond Walburn), who practices his flabbily grandiloquent public comments in private while Al Bridge as his political planner blandly quacks, "Save your voice, Evvie." Comedy, as pop entertainment for an unassuming populace in a democratic society, by its nature makes us root for the young hero who doesn't make exaggerated claims. So we readily root for Woodrow to be elected mayor but feel stranger about rooting against Forrest's hopes with Libby. Moviemakers have successfully fiddled with this formula, but Sturges is not removed enough from—and is thus more up in the air about—what he's doing in *Hail the Conquering Hero* to produce a consistent variation. It's this up-close confusion that needs explaining.

Sturges had no enthusiasm for World War II, even *after*ward, from which I infer that his serious sentimentality about it in *Hail the Conquering Hero* has some other source of significance for him. In this light, a line early in the script stopped my attention: when the six marines are dressing Woodrow in a uniform on the train to his hometown, they keep adding medals, and one of them overrides his strenuous balking by saying, "You can't come back from the Solomons without nothing." Earlier Bugsy had said they're just back from Guadalcanal. This isn't a glitch: Guadalcanal is the largest island in the Solomons group (site of the decisive American victory in 1942 and 1943). However, this way of restating the location of the battle reminded me that Solomon was the name of Sturges's stepfather, of whom Sturges said, when reminiscing about being reunited with him at age eight, "I adored this big man . . . this ex-football player, this ex-bicycle champion of Illinois. . . . I loved . . . the perfume of my father, a mixture of maleness and the best Havana cigars." This outpouring was occasioned by Sturges's retelling of the traumatic night in 1907 when his parents had decided to separate; asked to choose between them, little Preston said without hesitation, "I want to stay here with Father," to which his mother's second husband replied, "I am not your father."

Solomon Sturges later played a likewise vexing part in his stepson's unsatisfactory military adventure in World War I. Determined to fight, Preston enlisted in the Canadian Signal Corps; when Solomon heard of it, he notified officials that Preston was underage. The son's response:

"Shocked, furious, impotent, and feeling completely dishonored, I was stopped in my tracks." Mary Desti then used her connections to get him into the U.S. Signal Corps, which had earlier rejected him for "an enlarged blind spot" (reminiscent of the spots Norval sees when he tries to sign up—like Trudy's illegitimate babies, Norval's problem comes in multiples). But he never saw action: "My friends and I were getting along pretty well with our flying instruction when a terrible disaster overtook us all: on the eleventh of November, 1918, the war ended." It was Preston himself who was kept from being a war hero in Belleau Wood or anywhere else, in part by the father who lingered as the very image of a man.

Sturges's handling of the boy's moral-identity crisis brought on by the reality of never living up to his father is peculiar but much preferable to David O. Selznick's handling of a similar vignette in the home front propaganda soaper *Since You Went Away*, released the same year as *Hero*. In Selznick's picture (he both produced it and wrote the script), shy young Robert Walker has been rebuffed by his colonel grandfather (Monty Woolley) for failing out of West Point (not for cowardice but for lack of interest; he wants to be an engineer). But Walker's greater problem is that he lacks confidence; Jennifer Jones points out that he's the only boy she knows who asks permission to smoke. But her love itself starts to build his confidence, and he goes off to battle unambivalent about the way fate has given him an opportunity to prove himself to his grandfather. As we can see from the broad detailing of the performances, Woolley always loves the boy and is brought around to showing his affection, but too late—he misses the transport train that takes Walker to the battle in which he'll die a hero's death.

What makes it soapy is that the resolution is too on the nose. The boy doesn't want to be a soldier and disappoints his grandfather; but the boy becomes a soldier anyway, rising to historic demands, and the grandfather forgives him before his turnaround. So even though the grandfather learns from a houseful of females to bend his martial principles, Selznick doesn't challenge the audience's feelings about what boys should be like. Neither does Sturges, but Selznick gives it to us both ways: the grandfather learns to appreciate Walker's special sensitivity, and Walker becomes a warrior who announces, "I'm a Smollett, all right, and before this thing is over I'll, well, I'll make him proud of me yet," before he goes off to earn his glory shroud.

Sturges frames the dilemma better by having the patriarch dead. In *Star Spangled Rhythm* it was shameful for Bracken's father to have to admit that he's not what he's let on to be, but it's not as archetypally crushing as the story of a son's failure to live up to a legendary father enshrined at the height of his youthful glory. The son's failure seems to reverse the course of nature, as if it were diminishing with every renewal. And Woodrow's father not only can't forgive the boy, as in *Since You Went Away,* but his disposition can't be known in the first place. The boy's torment over disappointing his father is all projection, itself an aspect of the son's struggle to become a man.

Furthermore, Forrest's losing out despite his assets means that though Libby is as devoted to Woodrow as Norval is to Trudy in *Morgan's Creek,* the prize bride makes you a little uneasy as well. Forrest's own mother flutters around, prattling that she fully understands why Libby would throw her son over for Woodrow and why people would vote for the hero instead of her husband, which naturally only makes things worse. Libby isn't changeable by choice, yet Sturges seems to have developed her character out of a fear of sexual abandonment that he would put on paper in a less amusing form in a later, unhappier day in the late fifties when his fourth wife had gone to L.A. with their two sons and he, having remained in Paris, hadn't heard from her:

> *My sweetest, dearest, beloved, adorable little darling,*
> Listen you dirtie *[sic]* little bitch, it's lucky for you that you're not within hitting distance or I would take your antipays down and give you such a swatting it would be a long time before you would again plunge your husband in the condition I have been staggering around in for the past two weeks . . . unable to concentrate . . . unable to work . . . just plain unable.

In this light, it's strange that Sturges gives Libby faster and sharper verbal exchanges with Forrest than with Woodrow (just as the melodrama is less melodramatic because Sturges doesn't specify what corruption his detractors think Mayor Noble is guilty of). The benediction of verbal slapstick on Libby and Forrest indicates how divided Sturges is about his heroine. On the one hand, we like and trust her for her devotion to Woodrow despite his limited endowments (as one columnist wrote of Bracken, "He is nobody you would look at twice—aggressively so"). And yet we distrust her for the ease with which she breaks off with Forrest: before walking out on him in front of his parents, she plops her engagement ring in his drink. (Libby, the childhood sweetheart, might well prompt from us the Judge's response in *Strictly Dishonorable,* "Cruel woman.") This gesture doesn't appear in the script, which implies that on the set Sturges was just bulling his way through an irresoluble story.

This also means that Sturges couldn't work the picture out satisfactorily because he hadn't settled for character and plot outlines he'd used before. Thus though Woodrow is technically a reject, he isn't as deprived of heroic attributes as Norval was. Norval got nervous, stuttered, saw spots, and fell down whenever he had to go to the draft board or when he set out to marry Trudy—to be a man, by military or sexual conquest. Surprisingly for a boy in a comic movie who's constantly frustrated by the position he finds himself in but powerless to change it, Woodrow isn't a sputtering slapstick klutz. (We even see him use his fists capably.) Bracken thought of himself not as a clown but as the "serious guy" like Harold Lloyd "who is constantly involved in comic situations."

But *Hero* isn't developed in the manner of a Lloyd feature; it's always threatening to break into all-out physical slapstick but holds back. (The funniest physical gag occurs twice, when the townspeople surge up to Woodrow, who automatically assumes they've come to collar him as a fraud, and the marines take up improvised cudgels—in one case these include a rolling pin and a pestle—to protect him.) In *Morgan's Creek* Demarest's Constable Kockenlocker all but drives Bracken out of jail so that he can play the hero, whereas in *Hero* Sergeant Heffelfinger straitjackets him in the role, which has been reduced to nothing but appearance. Thus Heffelfinger stations the marines to guard Woodrow's bedroom door and window at night to keep him from running out on the hoax. So Woodrow doesn't have the physical freedom to take any tumbles; his only pratfalls occur when he discovers the surveillance blocking his escape. As a result, Bracken's role in *Morgan's Creek* is altogether looser and funnier than in *Hail the Conquering Hero*. The marines force Woodrow to live up to the impossible image of male prowess that precludes bumbling and setbacks and the threat of failure and thus keep him away from the nerve-racking sources of comedy in a Sturges movie. (Plus Woodrow encourages his girl to find another fellow, and so sex is less distressing for the hero, because he's more demoralized, than in most Sturges scripts. Hope is what hones a romantic plot's edge.)

The boy's story *is* similar in *The Miracle of Morgan's Creek* and *Hail the Conquering Hero*—his social and emotional chances are ruined by the military's rejection. However, the plots come at the same crisis from two directions: Bracken's getting into uniform is the resolution of *Morgan's Creek* and the problem in *Hail the Conquering Hero*. But even though Norval's story is painful—he's a romantic comedy hero who apologizes to his girl for being ugly—Sturges did develop *Morgan's Creek* in nearly the classic silent method employed by Lloyd. In the script, he specifies which components of Norval's World War I uniform should be too small and which too big—just like Chaplin's outfit, and Lloyd's as Lonesome Luke, and Harry Langdon's. And at the end, he returns Norval to mumming: when completely unaware of what's happened, Norval enters Trudy's hospital room, Emmy signals to him, What's with the uniform? and he answers with a shrug that says, Beats me. Then he asks Emmy if the baby was a boy or a girl, and she crooks her finger to say, Follow me. Sturges places the camera in the nursery looking out at Norval and Emmy on the other side of the glass. Thus the buildup and frantic payoff to Norval's inevitable question "Which one of the six is mine?" are pulled off in pantomime. The emphasis on slapstick makes sense to Sturges because of the greater emphasis on sex in *Morgan's Creek*. In a discarded draft of the disastrous fake marriage, Sturges wrote, "Norval is being held by the MPs, the Sheriff, the State Police and the FBI men, not to mention Trudy who is trying to pull him away from them. He is in imminent danger of being dismembered." Romantic slapstick comedy is a form of Dionysian calamity that enables men to laugh at the way in which their attraction to the slaughterhouse employee endangers their sweetbreads.

Still, *Hail the Conquering Hero* is funnier than a spectrogram of its vibes makes it sound, mainly because of the verbal volatility of the town's celebration and of the marine's freestyle debates with Woodrow. (In 1947 Sturges could justifiably write to Darryl F. Zanuck, "Fortunately, I spritz dialogue like seltzer water. My trouble has never been in inventing it but rather in throwing three-quarters of it away.") In the talkies, the Marx Brothers combined visual and verbal slapstick but divided the duties between the talkers Groucho and Chico and the silent Harpo with his stunt props. Sturges's pictures make the division between the sexes: mixed groups break out in volleys of verbal slapstick, but though the heroines may say clever things, it's the men who take the pratfalls. *Morgan's Creek* is the exception with respect to the sexual divide in Sturges, in that the pretty girl begins as a physical clown, but that's the point of the story, that's her flaw. In *Hail the Conquering Hero* Sturges started with a character, and an actor, he thought of as a slapstick hero, but in the process of telling of the boy's struggle to match his father's overwhelming legacy of physical heroism, the impulse to physical slapstick was shivered out of him.

Thus *Hero* climaxes not with mayhem as in *Morgan's Creek* but with Woodrow's earnest avowal before the town meeting of the fact that he isn't the hero they think him. This is a type of scene you get in comedies when there is a split between the good and bad male figures, as at the end of *The Great Dictator* or the 1953 Martin and Lewis picture *The Stooge;* or when a good character perpetrates a hoax and is thus himself the bad character as in Lewis's solo picture *The Nutty Professor,* or *Star Spangled Rhythm,* in which Victor Moore makes his humbling confession. All these pictures climax with moralizing speeches that indicate the moviemakers feel they've gone beyond the formulas of comedy and have to guide us in sorting out our feelings about the protagonists. In terms of the genre, Sturges opts for the *eiron* as Woodrow's true self, our guy, which we do know all along because his temptation to fake a big reputation was always externalized in the six marines. And the play between irony and melodrama helps him out of the mess by having the madly resourceful Sergeant Heffelfinger, who's largely responsible for putting the hoax over on the townspeople, bark at them after Woodrow's confession, "I seen a lot of brave men in my life . . . that's my business . . . but what that kid just done . . . took *real* courage."

The ending of *Morgan's Creek,* where the imposture is made official and must be worn like a costume, is as demented as the beginning that it resolves. By contrast, the ending of *Hero,* a movie that begins with imposture, resolves the boy's conflict in terms of sustainable small-town male heroism that doesn't cloy. Woodrow, we find, does speak to some sense of heroism valued by his townspeople, who may be gullible but aren't the malicious spies and backbiters that they are in the script of *Morgan's Creek,* where Emmy says of them that "nobody believes good unless they have to if they've got a chance to believe something bad." *Hail the Conquering Hero,* in both crisis and resolution, operates on the opposite principle. And in both these pictures, Bracken's forlornness, unlike Danny Kaye's, doesn't feel like the product of the usual Hollywood calculation whereby a comic hero is only as irresistible as he is innocuous. Sturges's mistakes in *Hail the Conquering Hero* are all his own, all impulsive.

Sturges clearly made *The Miracle of Morgan's Creek* and *Hail the Conquering Hero* as companion pieces, which allowed him to bring out more sides to the failed soldier's story by playing it in, and then pointedly out of, a slapstick mode. Taking them together, you can see how he plays for comedy his anxiety over the cultural understanding that Elbridge Gerry voiced, according to which if girls are what they should be, there's no story to tell about them, while if boys are what they should be, they are the valiant heroes of history and epics. (Even unsentimental Emmy sits at home playing Wagner's "Wedding March" on the piano, and when her father asks her gruffly if she's got marriage on her mind, she replies, "Generally yes I think about marriage . . . what else do you think I think about?") However, there are pitfalls even for the successful: conventional heroines tend to be insipid, and conventional heroes stolid. We want movie stars to live up to cultural ideals, but if they do, we may get bored and even derisive. Hollywood comedies were often freer than melodramatic pictures in disrupting these conventions (it was Mae West pictures that brought on the Code in 1934), and Sturges was among the freest disrupters of all. Even when following (or mangling) generic formulas, Sturges's comedies get at their conflicts more resoundingly than most contemporary melo-dramas did. Thus André Bazin wrote that "comedy was in reality the most serious genre in Hollywood—in the sense that it reflected . . . the deepest moral and social beliefs of American life," and for this reason, he felt, "we must consider Preston Sturges as a moralist." Still, I dis-agree that Sturges satirizes our *expectations* of plot and character, or of our ideals more generally. Rather, he tickles them right up to the edge of torment.

Because Sturges was the most writerly slapstick artist our movies ever produced (as opposed to the great silent gagmen of whom Buster Keaton claimed, "I don't think any of them ever had his name on a book, a short story, or even an article in a fan magazine. . . . They were not word guys, at all"), it's tempting to figure out his intentions in terms of literary themes, as if greatness must lie there. His scripts *are* more adult and complicated than those of the silent slapstick greats, and no matter how insane his stories get, he never throws the plots away as part of the joke, as the Marx brothers do. (Sturges wouldn't even throw dialogue away to give the slapstick more impact, which is why Harold Lloyd was so unhappy during the shooting of the second half of *Harold Diddlebock*.) Nonetheless the intensity in Sturges comes not from literary development but from the free play he gives his im-pulses, which is very much in the classic silent slapstick line. (The rewriting while shooting of *Morgan's Creek* indicates how late he was still composing.)

Sturges lost momentum fast on Broadway after his initial success in 1929 because he wanted to write more serious comedies, but he lacked the skill to get at themes head-on, and his movies aren't essentially re-flective or discursive. Even when they're about boys and girls in jams as humiliating as he could contrive, we laugh almost from beginning to end (Norval's speech about his love for Trudy and Woodrow's confession are the major exceptions in these two pictures). These home-front traumas make his pictures more honest portrayals of life during wartime than was usual in the forties. And Sturges, who as a teenager had witnessed the red-eyed male mourners, gathered in a brasserie after the funeral of Isadora Duncan's children, burst into uncontrollable laughter, knew that laughter can be a nervous and even nearly hysterical response to touchy issues. But Sturges opens up these issues intuitively rather than intellectually—which helps explain why the genre of *Hail the Conquering Hero* turned out so muttly. He wants you to experience the turmoil as comedy, which to him is an explosion of meaningfully nervous agitation about the aspects of life you can only hope to govern.

CHAPTER SEVEN

Jerry Lewis: The Once and Future King of Comedy

Take it from me, if you need to convince your friends that Jerry Lewis deserves a chapter to himself, show them the 1953 release *The Stooge*, in which Martin and Lewis play a vaudeville team whose act is based on the nightclub act that had made them big stars in the late forties. Cue the tape to the end to catch Dean Martin singing the team's signature song in the movie, "Who's Your Little Whosits?"—one of the many times when they peculiarly sing a love song as if to each other— and Lewis, a half step upstage from Martin, miming to the audience that Martin wears dentures and has had a nose job. Lewis's pantomime is broad, with simultaneous mouthing of what he's trying to convey, but it also gets brilliantly exact when he parodies what Martin thinks cosmetic upgrading has made of him: an ascot-wearing Mr. Suave, as English as his stage name makes him sound. And there's another component that makes it wildly funny, the paradoxically sneaky blatantness of it. Lewis steps behind Martin to expose and mock him—for the camera and hence mass distribution. The movie is full of showbiz gush about how much the partners need each other, but it's memorable because Lewis's peculiar intensity about these emotions is backed by malice toward his partner, which in this moment he is able to turn into entertainment equally appalling and funny.

Lewis's best bits, which, like this one, are very good, some fantastically so, aren't bunched together in time: there's the way he leans forward with naively undisguised curiosity and asks a psychiatrist who has just mentioned a dominating father who committed suicide, "Do you know of any similar cases?" in *That's My Boy* (1951); the sandwich-stealing routine in the train dining car in *Jumping Jacks* (1952); his lunch counter two-act with Donald MacBride, whose slow burn is expertly prolonged, and his rendition of "Louise" in which he sounds like Chevalier only when he sets his straw boater on his head, in *The Stooge*; the pep talk he gets from his own reflection in *Scared Stiff* (1953); his frenetic jitterbug with Sheree North and his impersonation of the three foreign doctors in *Living It Up* (1954); his trek up and down the stairs to answer the phone for Martin who's in the bathtub in *Artists and Models* (1955); his walk across the vast, empty auditorium that he has to fill with folding chairs, and his appearance as his high-muck-a-muck self trailed by a huge pack of overeager toadies as he tries to check in to the hotel in *The Bellboy* (1960); a packed elevator routine in *The Errand Boy* (1961); the jumpy-town opening and later his destruction of Buddy Lester's hat in *The Ladies Man* (1961); his wincing at his own failed attempts at humor in his job interview with Ray Walston and secretary, and then the silent air typewriter solo, his most Chaplinesque bit, in the better sense of the word, in *Who's Minding the Store* (1963); and a brief moment when Lewis as a retirement village Jewish mama comes on to a postman also played by Lewis in *Hardly Working* (1981). And then, of course, there's *The Nutty Professor* (1963), by far his most accomplished movie in every way.

What works best in Lewis's movies is as often verbal as physical. In fact, some of his biggest physical comedy set pieces, the TV antenna disaster in *Rock-a-Bye Baby* (1958) and the black hole vacuum cleaner demonstration in *Who's Minding the Store,* for example, make you strain with unrecompensed goodwill. Even when he has conceived a sequence with some sophistication—for instance, the sea captain's flashback in *The Family Jewels* (1965) in which his present-day narration doesn't match what we see occurring in the past, something like the technique of Sacha Guitry and of *Kind Hearts and Coronets*—the physical slapstick is hopeless. Lewis has to disarm a torpedo using the contents of a toolbox, but the hammer and the drill don't suggest different gags to him. He ineffectually bangs both on the metal shell, acting out his incompetence as a sailor. We, however, perceive it as his incompetence as a slapstick performer—he lacks the necessary discipline of mind (Stan Laurel's reservation about Lewis's work). Even a first-rate sight gag—Martin and Lewis sipping champagne together through the stems of a stethoscope in *Living It Up*—isn't presented crisply enough for full impact.

Still, Lewis's great popularity wasn't a fluke although the movies he appeared in, with and without Dean Martin, as people remember all too well, are pretty lame. Breakout bits like those listed above have to work without much enhancement from the surrounding movies, in terms of either storytelling or style. Lewis is a genius—*the* genius of Martin and Lewis—but Hollywood so quickly and thoroughly deviled and tinned him that when he took over producing his own movies, he didn't alter or abandon the industrial method and rationale. Hal B. Wallis, the producer who brought the team to Hollywood, never made a comedy on a par with *The Nutty Professor,* but Lewis himself couldn't sustain that level; unlike the silent greats and the Marx Brothers, W. C. Fields, and Preston Sturges, he never had a streak. The strange result is that although Lewis has a distinct public image (even apart from his high profile as the host of the Muscular Dystrophy Association's Labor Day telethon), almost no one recalls any of Lewis's routines with that combination of affection and obsession with which people recall Chaplin and Marx Brothers routines, even if they can't remember which movies they're from.

Lewis got his training as the national circuit of live theater was gasping its last, and he came up with a new concept of skill, which was in large part amplification. At the end of *The Stooge,* during the instrumental break in Dean Martin's song, Lewis steals the spot with some demented, spastic dancing. The point is that he can't really do the kind of routine he's sort of parodying (as we see when he and Martin do a big, straight soft-shoe number together in *Living It Up*). Lewis isn't an all-round entertainer, and unlike that versatile thistledown hoofer Donald O'Connor, who is physically brilliant when Paramount's misbegotten 1957 *Buster Keaton Story* permits him to be, Lewis could not have been a silent slapstick star. What Lewis has that O'Connor lacks is the ability to take over any kind of number by a determination so undeflectable it transforms incompetence into a new kind of slapstick.

Lewis's physical mayhem thus differs from that of the silent clowns whose "awkward" tumbles revealed their acrobatic training. No slapstick loser had ever been so genuinely underequipped and yet so forceful. Lewis was not one of those dynamos like Al Jolson who, according to Gilbert Seldes, made raising the roof seem effortless. Lewis's *will* to be funny is glaring, and so his playing the jerk contrasts with the energy he puts into stealing the picture from that "weak" position (and, when you read about his life, with his tyranny at home and on the set). This means, however, that you *can* see Lewis as an answer to Seldes's plea, when praising Jolson, "for violence *per se* in the American theatre, because everything tends to prettify and restrain, and the energy of the theatre is dying out." The violence of Lewis's determination to entertain us explains why he became the most influential slapstick comedian in the sound era. He made obvious the eclipse of an acrobatic tradition and simultaneously extended its life in a new guise.

At the same time, Lewis tied his performing to the earlier tradition: least by his skill at stunts, a bit more by the conception of them, but most of all by sentiment. The Marx Brothers maintained their unruly stage act in the movies by openly parodying their own story lines.

Lewis never had that touch, in part because he *did* want his simple stories to move us, in the later Chaplin manner. But Chaplin had a certain talent for Victorian melodrama; sentimentality mixed badly with Lewis's act as he had developed it with Martin in the free, adult atmosphere of nightclubs.

It's telling that Martin and Lewis's act originated informally, in the Manhattan nightspot the Havana-Madrid in March 1946. The singer and comedian alternated vaudeville-style on a bill with other acts throughout the night but would josh "each other when one was offstage and the other was performing. . . . At the end of each night's closing show, these sorties grew into a wild, riffing jam session. [Orchestra leader Pupi] Campo would stick around and try to play for Dean while Jerry ad-libbed interruptions." A *Billboard* reviewer caught this impromptu mayhem and thought it had the makings of a solid act, as it did.

Four months later, Lewis, still a single, was working at the 500 Club in Atlantic City when the management needed to hire a replacement singer. Martin was sold with the promise that he and Lewis got into sensationally funny interplay. Martin arrived, and for the first time, Lewis had to formulate an act for them as a team, in a matter of hours. As he recalled:

> After writing down the title, which I called "Sex and Slapstick," I laboriously typed out these words: *Since the time immemorium, there has never been a two-act in show business that weren't two milkmen, two food operators, two electricians, two plumbers, and for the first time here we have a handsome man and a monkey.*

The nearest model for their goofing around was Hope and Crosby, but Martin and Lewis were more unbridled, not only before they made their partnership an official deal but afterward as well, and even when they appeared together on TV. In a very early appearance on NBC's *Welcome Aboard* on 10 October 1948, orchestra leader Russ Morgan introduces Martin and Lewis—announcing that they're about to leave for Hollywood to make a movie for Wallis—and they go into their nightclub clowning in a freer form than moviegoers would recognize. Martin's singing has a less unctuous swing phrasing, and he flashes a sexy grin as he polishes the tip of his tongue with a finger before starting "Rock-a-Bye Your Baby with a Dixie Melody." The basic joke is that Martin wants to get Lewis offstage so that Martin can sing alone; in response, Lewis's gears turn madly: how to stay onstage, how to get his share of attention. It's a pointy-elbow contest, but the pair are having fun because everything is throwaway. You can see right away why it was hip at the time. Americans in the twentieth century have perennially gone for manic nonchalance, from the Marx Brothers to Hope and Crosby to Martin and Lewis to *Animal House;* we love to see the old routines reupholstered with the latest in humor, music, sex, and topical targets. But since in nightclubs and on TV there's not even the fragile story line of a *Road* series picture, the early Martin and Lewis just play grab bag.

After "Rock-a-Bye Your Baby" they start the jokes by clinching nose to nose as Rhett (Martin) and Scarlett (Lewis). Martin's Gable is not bad; Lewis breaks the bit up by responding with a Yiddish accent. Afterward Lewis does a Cagney imitation that Martin introduces with, "This is really very bad," and interrupts with, "This is James Cagney? Sounds like Menosha Skolnick." The problem, Martin tells him, is that Cagney is manlier and more robust. To prove that he can be manly, Lewis says in a "swish" voice, "Listen, Harry," at which Martin claps his hand over Lewis's mouth and really laughs. This is the "nance stuff" that trade reviewers told them to keep away from, even in nightclubs, but Lewis is very funny at it, not least because he knows he's being wicked, and for no reason. His motive is the great showbiz ethic, which he yowls to Martin, "Well they *laughed*—what'd ya stop me for?" Martin then does his own very bad impression of Cary Grant; when Lewis joins in, loud, Martin recurs to his basic complaint, "C'mon, it's the only one I can do—let me do it alone." A little later Lewis does Bette Davis in *The Letter,* and he and Martin turn nose to nose again; this time Lewis darts a lizard tongue flick at Martin's nose.

Their byplay primarily follows Lewis's fixation on horning in on Martin's act, which they both assume is the kind of performance an audience would really want to see. (Lewis's original solo act, which he advertised as "laffsational . . . pantomimicry," featured him lip-synching parodistically to popular records; the team's act in part uses Martin as a living record player for Lewis to overwhelm with clowning.) Their exchanges are sharp: Lewis makes whiny demands, and Martin pushes back while attractively keeping his showman's cool no matter what.

Underneath the Hope and Crosby formula, Martin, confident and detached, and Lewis, infantile, needy, and innocuous but a magnet for trouble, work a variation on the Laurel and Hardy formula. The logic of Laurel and Hardy's partnership was to split the slapstick hero into his two aspects—his inability to maneuver in the physical world without mishap and his frustration at this inability, respectively. (What Jerry Lewis called the *shlemiel* and the *shlimazel:* "the guy who spilled

the drinks . . . and the guy who had the drinks spilled on him.")
Though Lewis felt enough affinity with Laurel and Hardy to seek Stan
Laurel out at the end of his life and offer him a consulting job, Martin
and Lewis don't make as archetypal a pair because they don't have as
close a complementary bond in slapstick terms. Jerry screws up, but
the ceiling doesn't consistently fall in on Dean as it did on Ollie. And
Dean's specialized manner is too imperturbable to register the needed
depth of frustration. Still, they do have *some*thing together: Lewis's biographer Shawn Levy gets the irony of their partnership just right
when he writes that "Martin and Lewis were presented as complete
opposites, two guys you'd never figure to know each other at all if not
for their being partners." Lewis's awe of Martin, whom he first saw as
a teenager, seems like a boy's crush on a handsome, athletic camp counselor. As Lewis said of his first meeting with Martin, "When we shook
hands in farewell, I thought it would be the last I'd ever see of Dean.
Such an Adonis. And look at me, weighing 115 pounds—still fighting
acne."

Though Lewis plays a variation on mishap-prone Stan and Martin
on apoplectic Ollie, their partnership isn't structurally comic in an impersonal way, as Laurel and Hardy's was, because the motive for it is
ardently personal: Lewis's feeling like less of a loser, less unattractive
by association with Martin. That's why the stray impulses are madly
funny in their knockabout nightclub set, because underneath they
aren't really stray. In the 1948 TV appearance, for instance, Lewis's interruptions of Martin's smooth act, and his whining about whether
Martin really likes him like a pal when he treats him so bad, are funny
because the pair seem peripherally aware of the buried implications.
However randomly the pair slips in and out of roles, we still recognize
that the momentary impulse to "be" homosexual does resonate with
something about their interplay. They have a more intense personal relationship than the Marx Brothers did.

However, Lewis's impulses, such as moving in to kiss Martin, were
more opaquely unsettling in the movies—where they're central yet un-
acknowledged—than they had been in nightclubs. The plot in picture
after picture draws on the dynamic of Jerry's unrequited love for Dean
or Jerry's misplaced faith in Dean. The rub was that Martin didn't
think of their partnership personally, and yet Lewis admitted no alter-
native. At the same time, the affection between Martin and Lewis
seems pure showbiz schmaltz, *especially* when you see that Lewis is
sincere about it. (He is at times unwatchably ingenuous.) Calling Martin and himself a handsome man and a monkey represents Lewis's per-

spective: Martin sexy, Lewis not. Martin's view of Lewis was a nice kid but a thin-skinned pest, which Lewis co-opted on-screen, playing it for pathos and further widening the gap between them off-screen.

To Martin, Lewis also took himself too seriously as an artist and, worse, always fished for Martin to return his affection, publicly insisting that their mutual love was what held them together as a team. Martin responded to Lewis's view of their partnership by telling a UPI reporter, when rumors of their splitting up hit the press in 1955, "To me, this isn't a love affair. . . . This is a big business. I think it's ridiculous for the boy to brush aside such beautiful contracts." After their breakup, Lewis complained to the press that Martin "never was as warm and outgoing as I hoped he'd be"; their partnership may not have been a love affair, but to close observers, its dissolution was "as painful as a divorce."

The nightclub success of Martin's casualness and Lewis's anxiously continual assaults on it led to the movie producers' bidding war won by Hal Wallis, a man who as head of production for Warner Brothers had overseen the production of two of old Hollywood's finest temperamental dramas, the Bette Davis vehicles *Jezebel* (1938) and *The Letter* (1940), both directed with discretion and potency by William Wyler, and its greatest detective story, John Huston's *Maltese Falcon* (1941). But Wallis never specialized in comedy (intentional comedy, that is, so *The Story of Louis Pasteur* doesn't count). And when as an independent producer releasing through Paramount, he signed Martin and Lewis, he processed the teams' nightclub shtick as cheaply as possible: his Martin and Lewis productions outgrossed Abbott and Costello's without outspending them. Wallis scrimped on scripts and production, and it shows, painfully, especially in the first seven of the eleven pictures he had them crank out in their eight years as a movie team. (Hal B. Wallis, Hal-be-quick.) Though at first Lewis "was overwhelmed with respect and admiration" for Wallis, he grew "increasingly antagonistic" toward him, in part because it became clear, as Lewis later said, that "Wallis didn't know how to make fucking comedy. He was a butcher. . . . If the film got released, I was in complete shock. Even in my beginning, when I didn't understand what film was." However, although Lewis, unlike Wallis, had a passion for comedy, and despite the care and money he would lavish on them, his solo productions in the sixties aren't consistently funnier than his Wallis pictures.

It's revealing to contrast Lewis's apprenticeship in moviemaking with Buster Keaton's. Under Arbuckle's tutelage, Keaton learned to apply his mechanical ingenuity to the movie camera, leading him to come up with the stunts and in-camera tricks that are undoubtedly the funniest demonstrations of the mechanical model of physics. And Keaton's silent work, over which he had artistic control, has a special grace because he didn't care at all about money. (He was one of the all-time worst businessmen-stars, a kid gamboling around the high altar.) Like Keaton, Lewis would become a "total film-maker" (Lewis's term), but he went about it by straying around the Paramount lot to the various studio departments, learning from the in-house by-the-book pros. Wallis unimaginatively saw Lewis's curiosity about filmmaking as a sign of egomania. So it's peculiar that Lewis overrode his disgust at Wallis's lack of comic sense and his cynicism about the shady accounting methods of studios and learned his craft as Paramount taught it. As a result, his 1971 book *The Total Film-Maker* and his 1982 autobiography prove frustrating for fans because he talks about his movies in the most grindingly industrial terms of cutting the deal and then stacking the cash. And though you can appreciate the technical know-how visible on the screen—his love for the gigantic set, covering two soundstages, in *The Ladies Man* is manifest throughout the movie—he doesn't distinguish between the importance of knowing what size lens to use and getting product endorsements. In the 1960s Lewis was still at Paramount making movies that were often indistinguishable from the Martin and Lewis vehicles, and measuring his success like a studio head, by money, not even popularity, which would have been his right.

All the same, no one can deny that Lewis left his imprint on the dreck he made in the Wallis years, more than Martin or their directors did (including Frank Tashlin), and certainly more than Wallis did. Even people who hate Martin and Lewis movies hate them because of Lewis, not anyone else. Lewis was becoming more popular than Martin in their nightclub act by 1947, and a review of their first movie, *My Friend Irma,* in 1949 reduced Martin to Lewis's "collar-ad partner." (The opposite prevailed among coworkers, as one of the nightclub owners remembered: "Between the two, everybody liked Dean and practically no one liked Jerry.") Lewis became so clearly the star of the team that the movies were written for his dominant personality long before he started getting screen credit for his collaboration on the scripts.

Lewis has said that he worked out the act and "looked after all the business details while Dean played golf" (just like Laurel and Hardy, respectively). Martin happily left things to Lewis, who recalled, "My hero was my partner. . . . And his best friend in the world was this kid that was helping him make a fortune." But even though Martin trusted

Lewis's business dealings, the team couldn't hold together once Martin realized how irresistible Lewis found the temptation to build up his own material at his partner's expense. Martin worked very unassumingly but did have a definite star persona, a certain nothing that no one else could bring to a picture in quite the same way. Yet his coasting-as-a-calling left him vulnerable in the partnership. Lewis worked with the screenwriters with Martin's blessing, but everyone from Hal Wallis to composer Walter Scharf noticed that Lewis's time with them had the effect of "push[ing] Dino into the background."

Lewis has always been careful to insist that he and Martin were "*two* comics, not a comic and a straight man," but the comedy in the movies is unmistakably canted toward Lewis's antics. It's a double cross for Martin, but not necessarily a bad thing for us. Martin is appealingly decadent because unlike Lewis he could see that their movies were just product and not something to feel particularly invested in. But as a result, he can often register as little more than a leer pasted on the screen. As cheap and bland as their movies could be overall, they still allow Lewis to cut up like all three Marx Brothers while Martin plays a seedy Zeppo. (He's actually like Chico cast as Zeppo.) Our expectation of fun arises almost entirely in response to Lewis's shtick. You can always hope for a classic moment with Lewis on-screen; with Martin you come to fear a song.

Lewis had a crush on Martin, but the way the movies favor Lewis isn't coincidental. Soon after Martin and Lewis became a successful nightclub act, Lewis, who idolized Martin and "studied [his] charm, looks, appeal to women, and general demeanor," started imitating Martin's after-hours lounge rake vices, hanging out with "tough guys" and cheating on his wife. But Lewis could never replicate Martin's offhand image, not by screwing around, or by taking up golf in addition to covering the business end, any more than he could break through to Martin and get him to return his affection. So it seems plausible that Martin's "best friend in the world" would have worked out his resentments against his impassive partner who played partner but wouldn't *feel* the role. That's certainly the vibe we pick up on in *The Stooge,* and people noticed the toll it took on Lewis at the time. For instance, Norman Lear, who worked as a TV scriptwriter for the team, remembered that "Jerry's involvement was intense, that he strove for control, while Dean remained distant, almost disinterested in the process of developing material and putting together the shows." Lear also recalled that Lewis "couldn't stand it if Dean got any laughs. . . . Any morning that Dean would come in and start being funny with the lines or do funny things, Jerry would wind up in a corner on the floor someplace with a bellyache. . . . This was always true. Whenever Dean was very funny, strange physical things happened to Jerry."

Yet if Lewis's passive-aggressiveness queered the partnership, it powered him as a performer, and its covertness adds a subtext to his manic cavorting. In *Living It Up,* a remake of William Wellman's *Nothing Sacred* from Ben Hecht's original script, via a Broadway musical adaptation called *Hazel Flagg,* Lewis takes the Carole Lombard role of a small towner who exploits a false diagnosis of radiation poisoning to get a free farewell trip to New York from a newspaper that thinks it's exploiting *him* for publicity. The paper plants Lewis's Homer Flagg in a penthouse where he orders shrimp cocktails from room service for the three thousand well-wishers gathered on the street below his room. Thus the movie, which has him hollering to the crowd, "Hello, New York! Hello—I love you!" implies that his exuberance is inherently generous. But in an earlier publicity newsreel from July 1951 of Martin and Lewis hanging out of their dressing room windows at the Paramount Theater in New York and waving down to a throng of fans blocking the intersection of Broadway and Forty-fourth, the routine plays somewhat differently. Lewis yells, "I tell ya what—ya wanna come up for cawfee?" and then, after pausing for response, bellows moronically, "We ain't got any!" Thus the original joke has a more ambiguous kicker—You want to come up but you can't because I'm a big star and you're just the anonymous masses—that was nipped for *Living It Up* to keep Lewis a nice boy. But I think that Lewis's performing style and his immense popularity derive from the fact that the impulse behind even the reconstructed joke is aggressive. The aggression registers as lack of restraint, and this is the case even when he goes in for "Chaplin shit," to use Martin's jaundiced term for his partner's posterity-conscious pathos. In other words, if Lewis isn't turning it on Martin or the other characters, he's turning it on us. No star had demanded such unwavering attention or clamped a more lethal grip on our hearts.

Innocence makes sense to us as an attribute of the small-statured silent stars—Chaplin, Lloyd, Keaton, Langdon, Laurel, Larry Semon, Lupino Lane—whose slight builds can be taken to represent how even large people can feel in the face of overwhelming forces. But though Lewis was nine years younger than Martin, and just twenty when they teamed up, and though Martin called him "the Kid" and "the Boy" and gave him the juvenile buzz cut he wore in their early pictures, Lewis wasn't literally the little one. He exaggerated his relative youth by having "fractions of an inch shaved off the soles of his shoes and fractions added to the soles of Dean's" and "would intensify it by performing in a crouch and peering up at Dean like a little kid." He had to fiddle with their shoe heels because they both measured just over six feet (giving Lewis about seven inches on Chaplin and Keaton). If anything, Lewis is more physically assertive than Martin. At first you take Lewis for a wimp, but he gets more threatening the more you see and think about him.

The Stooge shows how much more interesting their movies can get when Lewis's aggression has a focus. Wallis postponed the film's release for nineteen months, checked by an uncharacteristic non-income-generating fastidiousness because there "was something about it, that faint undertow of reality, that he did not like." It's the most fascinating Martin and Lewis picture because something in it survived the studio processing, as if you bought a block of Velveeta and every fifth bite had the pungency of Camembert. *The Stooge* doesn't hang together as a story as well as *Living It Up* because *Living It Up* derives from a screenplay by a master and features a somewhat more intricate blend of tones (Lewis isn't always so innocent). But *The Stooge,* a multilevel sneak attack against Martin from beginning to end, does feel like an original artifact that wouldn't get to you if they'd put it together any other way. That is to say, it lingers, in a way that *Living It Up,* which *resembles* a competent movie, does not.

The Stooge stars Martin as Bill Miller, a thirties vaudevillian who keeps trying to succeed as a solo comic singer rather than as a singing straight man to a comic partner, only to fail miserably. (Remember that Martin's desire to work by himself was the premise of their act on *Welcome Aboard* in 1948.) The solo act he's given certainly reeks—telling Precambrian one-liners with an accordion hung around his neck like an albatross. He tanks (starting in Newark, Lewis's hometown), and his agent has to bring him down: "You got yourself in a spot because you got a swell head. Some fairy godmother must have whispered to you and told you that you don't need nobody. Well, you'd better stop listening to pixies and listen to your agent. You're not a single and you never will be."

Miller's agent sets him up with Lewis's Ted Rogers, a scrawny clod of a song plugger, who will be his stooge-partner: Miller will introduce Rogers to the audience as the writer of his new pop songs whereupon Rogers will bow from the front balcony and engage in a little patter. But Ted balls up his scripted role, which he doesn't fully understand, and the act accidentally becomes a rollicking comedy routine with

Ted interrupting Bill's song with slapstick and challenging banter. Predictably, the audience goes crazy for it as if it had been intended. (Miller and Rogers click by turning into Martin and Lewis—but innocently, not as an "act.") Bill scores only when working with Ted, but he never thinks of Ted as anything more than an appendage. However, when Bill passes out drunk, Ted goes on alone and is a big hit. The script repeatedly reveals Martin as undertalented or selfish and then delivers a rebuke or a comeuppance; it plays as if Wallis and Paramount were worried that half of their golden team was restive and so concocted a barely cloaked allegory to pound into his head the futility of going out on his own. But there's an added message that could only have originated with Lewis: Martin will be a bad person if he doesn't cherish his connection to "the Kid." Rejecting him would be like Chaplin throwing the infant Kid down the storm grate instead of raising him.

Of course, the script hands Lewis his usual punishment as well, beginning with the emasculated unattractiveness of his character. Ted is almost nauseatingly infantile. He whines and squawks in a strangled yet unmodulated kind of Jew-boy baby talk, purses his lips up against his nose in a cross pout, toddles when he has to move in tight spaces, and hits with his hands bent back at the wrist. Ted's music store boss sells him to Bill to get rid of a useless employee. When his secretary tells the boss that the crash he heard was Ted dropping a stack of records, the boss asks hopefully, "Is he bleeding?" Ted openly needs love and protection in such a world; as Bill's stooge, he tails Bill so loyally he doesn't even realize Bill is taking advantage of him—paying him $40 out of the $1,250 weekly pay the act receives, and giving him no billing at all, even when they reach the Palace. The movie features scene after scene of Bill humiliating Ted.

But Ted is more than a trouper, always defending Bill and saying of Bill's having picked him for the act, "I never did nothing before. I'm never gonna do nothing again." Ted is the classic put-upon mate remaining without complaint at the disposal of the selfish heel, mending his clothes, yet. Ted, solicitous even when the drunken Bill abuses him and then passes out, asks the theater manager, "You won't tell anybody that he was 'sick' will you?" This is where the picture most noticeably deviates from the source material, Sid Silvers's anecdotes about working in vaudeville in the twenties as accordionist Phil Baker's stooge. Silvers was put-upon—unbilled, underpaid—at the same time that he was often perceived as *making* the act. The scenes of producers whispering to Ted that he should dump Bill are historical, but Ted's nobility is not. In interviews, Silvers had the kind of backstage comic cynicism about the experience you'd expect, quipping that a stooge is "a comedian that gets all the laughs during the week but doesn't get paid on Saturday." Lewis's Ted doesn't even have the awareness of injustice to protect him.

Lewis sacrifices his self-respect and manhood so that we can feel virtuous for appreciating him as Martin cannot. But nobody's quite this stupefyingly nerdy. Lewis, helplessly displaying Ted's extreme social and sexual maladjustment, and mawkishly pushing his bravery and loyalty forward, squirms on-screen for us as if crucified on the canvas. (The extremity comes at the end of 3 Ring Circus when, having failed to make a crippled orphan girl smile with clowning and pleading, he lowers his head and cries, at which she not only laughs but stands up—a schlock miracle.) There's something queasy about the equation of Ted's weakness and goodness; it's a Jewish actor's fantasy about being a nice, normal person, too decent and trusting, if anything. (Remember Sophie Portnoy: "You know what my biggest fault is, Rose? I hate to say it about myself, but I'm too good." Her son calls this "transparent, self-serving, insane horseshit that even a pre-school-age child can see through.") Ted, unlike Lewis himself, could never be the kind of table banger who takes care of dates and contracts and money and all those heartless details that only the Bill Millers of the world care about.

The showbiz trick to this resides in the fact that being the martyr somehow enhances Lewis's position as star of the show at his partner's expense. Lewis uses his ambiguous weakness as a character deviously; Ted's defenselessness makes it impossible for us to object when Lewis shamelessly shows his partner up. For instance, seated in a cab between Martin and Polly Bergen as Bill's wife Mary, Lewis steals the scene—not much of one, just expositional dialogue of Mary chiding Bill for ignoring her while furthering his career—by mugging as if he were part of the conversation. Ted's harmlessness serves as Lewis's cover for scene stealing.

The difference between the nightclub act, in which Martin and Lewis interrupted each other, and their movies stands out here: the requirements of realism (however minimal) pinion Martin while Lewis gets to be as wacky as he likes, whether it adds anything specific to the story or his character. As early as 1947, they accused each other of upstaging, a bizarrely grumpy charge, since that was the essence of the act. All the same, it shows that Martin was sensitive to this potential for discord. But the script of The Stooge clearly assumes that Lewis is more entertaining than Martin, that he saves scenes by stealing them, and in fact that he justifies the movie's being made at all. This must have emerged as a sickening development for Martin, who had been able to hold his own in nightclubs because his specialty was natural for the venue.

The Stooge culminates with Bill's astounding apology to the audience when he tries to go solo for the second time. By this point in the movie, Ted has begun to speak almost normally, and it's then, as he approaches a human character, that Bill tells him off. Earlier, Mary had said of Bill when he missed her birthday party, "I know this is just ambition but down deep inside there's a wonderful sweet guy," but then his treatment of Ted becomes so shabby she decides to leave him for Europe (to resume the singing career that he asked her to end when they married). Bill's treatment of Ted so disgusts even his agent that the agent tears up their contract (arguably the phoniest behind-the-scenes showbiz moment in movies until Jerry Maguire's "fewer clients, less money" conversion). So it doesn't come out of the blue when Bill stops his act in the middle of its death throes and says, in a confession worthy of the Moscow Trials, "I can play an accordion and sing a song. But I need that spark, that something, chemistry that makes two men a successful team. I've bored you and I've imposed upon you. I've done an injustice to an audience and this is the biggest sin in show business—to be a ham. I humbly apologize." (Of course, devoted Ted waits in the balcony to rescue him.) Bill's apology at the end—not just for being a crumb but for being a bad performer as well—practically makes *The Stooge* into a snuff film for Martin as a romantic actor in light comedy. In this scene it becomes Martin's turn to squirm, and not in character.

The hostility toward Martin isn't even buried, really, as we see when Lewis mimes to the audience about Martin's dentures and nose job. This wasn't a revelation inasmuch as Martin's cosmetic surgery was immediately public knowledge in the forties when he was still a nightclub singer. But Martin had always been sensitive about his Italian-immigrant nose—obviously, hence the surgery. Martin might well have felt surrounded by Lewis as he upstaged him to dig at his vanity. Lewis teases and stings him, all the while warning him that the price of ending the partnership will be oblivion.

Lewis's to-and-fro between enamored awe and spite in his relationship with Martin suggests what Lewis might have done to his partner, perhaps without realizing it, while claiming to love him and to have his best interests at heart. He must have got something out of watching Martin being forced to kneel in *The Stooge*—he positively glows when he gets to come onstage and cut up during Martin's numbers. Early on there's a brief gag that symbolizes the whole enterprise: in a Pullman sleeper, Ted crawls into Bill's lower berth with him and pulls the blanket up—it comes up comfortably to his own chin but covers Bill's head. No wonder Lewis preferred *The Stooge* to all the other Martin and Lewis pictures.

Lewis could act publicly on his ambivalence because he was acknowledged to have the greater public appeal in their movies. What may have been most maddening to Martin is that Lewis was never funnier than when he tells us about Martin's dentures and nose job—that must be why it became a staple of their act in the first place. And you have to admit it: everything that should turn you off—the neediness, the grabbiness, even the back stabbing—makes his good moments better. For instance, on a 1953 episode of their Colgate TV show, when Martin ad-libs a line to cover for a bum sight gag and gets a laugh, Lewis veers from the script for a full minute to top him; his motivation can't purely be to entertain us, though that's the result. Lewis has not just the talent, skill, and energy but also the insistence and even malice to drive you crazy, to put you on edge in a way that knocks laughs loose. *The Stooge* terrorizes Martin into a public apology for his inadequacy, and then his genius partner terrorizes him at close range. When the terrorist is as talented as Lewis, the audience can find itself rooting for terror.

Of course, it isn't only in his almost malignant comic offensives that Lewis is at his funniest. He has an amazing range of wackiness: he tends to conceive of his character as an innocent kid involved with more corrupt adults (like Harry Langdon in *Long Pants*), but then he's an *obnoxious* kid—louder, more demanding, more useless. The twisted sneak shows up relatively rarely in his output, perhaps because it draws on his adult personality as he lived it much more than the braying adolescent—the Idiot, as he often referred to him, using his own nickname as a schoolkid—who derives from his unhappy youth, and his fears and his fantasies about himself, that he's unsightly and yet morally superior. *The Stooge* typically sanitizes experience: the actors' wives complained about their working too much in part because they knew their husbands, both drill sergeants inordinately given to dishonorable discharge, weren't faithful. That's why you're drawn to Lewis's obnoxiousness and even ill will, because they poke like thorns of reality through the layers of sentimental phoniness. This undermining of piety is one of the most sensational of slapstick effects, even when it's not the scripted intention.

There's one aspect of Martin and Lewis's relationship that does seem almost inevitable—the pairing of an Italian and a Jew in the era when those two European ethnic immigrant groups assimilated into the American middle class. Martin and Lewis, the Anglicized stage names of Dino Crocetti and Jerome Levitch, thought of each other as an Italian and a Jew, though in the midcentury it was often considered bad taste to stress your ethnic identity publicly. In their pictures, Martin played Italian only once, in *The Caddy*, and Lewis never played a Jew. Actually, Lewis's Jewishness is both suppressed and assumed: for instance, at one point in *The Stooge*, Lewis's Ted Rogers uses Yiddish phrasing—"You want I should . . . ?"—and when he disguises himself from Martin's Bill Miller by patting flour in his hair, Ted's mother (the otherwise seemingly gentile Frances Bavier, later Andy Griffith's Aunt Bee on TV) helps by referring to him as "my uncle Sholem." However, as Lewis remembered, Martin always called him "pallie, or Jew, or pardner" in private. And when Martin would deflect business discussions to Lewis, he would say, "Talk to the Jew." In Lewis's mind, the act's appeal interlocked along ethnic lines: "'Who were Dean's fans?' Men, women, the Italians. 'Who were Jerry's fans?' Women, Jews, kids."

Popular entertainment was a logical outlet for Italian and Jewish entertainers, as it was for blacks, because it allowed them to make a glamorous yet down-to-earth virtue of their exclusion from WASP respectability. Gilbert Seldes saw this early on, writing in 1924 of the Jewish performers Al Jolson and Fanny Brice: "America is a Protestant community and a business organization—and none of these units is peculiarly prolific in the creation of daemonic individuals. We can bring forth Roosevelts—dynamic creatures, to be sure; but the fury and the exultation of Jolson is a hundred times higher in voltage than that of Roosevelt." Seldes considered it noteworthy that Jolson and Brice "bring something to America which America lacks and loves . . . and that both are racially out of the dominant caste. Possibly this accounts for their fine carelessness about our superstitions of politeness and gentility" and for their going "farther . . . with more contempt for artificial notions of propriety, than anyone else."

That's onstage, and Seldes is talking about Jews. Offstage Jews and Italians may have got along because their personae weren't seen as overlapping. Abbey Greshler, the first man to manage Martin and Lewis as a team, had been an "asthmatic" kid with a "pasty complexion" growing up in

a mixed neighborhood . . . where Jewish kids were regularly beaten up
by their Italian and Irish neighbors. Abbey . . . [traded] homework for

protection so that he could hold on to the pennies he earned hawking Yiddish newspapers. Across the street lived the Fischetti family, cousins of Al Capone—the toughest kids on the block, and Abbey prudently befriended them.

To both Italian and Jewish men, the Italians seemed free to be real men, and Dean Martin represented ethnic arrival at its most relaxed. This is probably what the Italian American Patti Lewis is referring to when she cracks about her first meeting with Lewis, "I thought he was Italian. (At times, he did too!)"

Lewis also thought the difference between the male roles associated with their ethnic backgrounds explained their irreconcilable differences. As he said to the British press in 1953: "I'm Jewish with a theatrical background and I have to show my emotions. Dean is Italian from a tough steel town in Ohio where it's supposed to be sissy to show what you feel. So he covers it up and pretends never to be serious or nervous." Lewis's emotionality is intricately entwined with his memories of his maternal *bubbe* Sarah, with whom his parents often left him in Irvington, New Jersey, while they followed the burlesque circuit. In his autobiography, written forty-plus years after the events, his memories of sharing a hankie with her when his parents failed to show up for his bar mitzvah evidently still move him. His grandmother also wiped his bloody nose when he came home from a melee with an anti-Semitic boy at grade school, and she advised him, "Sonny, you can't fight the world."

On-screen Jerry Lewis plays the unmanly Jew, extremely impulsive but also extremely ineffectual, who would be most smitten with Martin's effortless masculinity—both his imperturbability, even impenetrability, and his sexual success—because he feels most distant from it. However, Lewis has been much less distant from it in life, as Leslie Bennetts's 1993 *Vanity Fair* article reported: "In the old days he used to haul off and hit people with a kind of vengeful glee. 'At the moment you do it, it's wonderful,' he recalls wistfully. 'Watching a guy go on his ass—particularly when it's "Why should a Jew get his car before anybody else?"—it's wonderful to see him hit the deck.'" And in TV interviews, he's still a scary man with eyes that look out at the rest of us as no more interesting or consequential than grubbers in an ant farm. Yet on-screen his character acts out Lewis's feelings of powerlessness in the world.

Which is not to say that Lewis is fey, as Jewish comics such as Eddie Cantor and Danny Kaye were. He's simply underdeveloped. With his

pout, his sissy slaps, and his adolescent honk, he seems stalled in boyhood, the opposite of precocious. This screen persona—the incompe-
tent *Errand Boy,* the disappointing son who runs the wrong way on
the football field in *That's My Boy*—dramatizes his unsuitability for
anything and everything, and at some level he insists on the psychological (and even psychiatric) reality of the role. Lewis's pictures make a
bid for him to be let into 1950s mainstream kitsch culture, but at the
same time he exaggerates his difference from the audience he's entertaining. He plays a "Jew" insofar as that means someone irrecuperably
different from the average male moviegoer—someone out of sync, pathetic. But lovable. That's the thing: he's so damaged he becomes a
mascot, and the manly and successfully assimilated Martin sets an example of how to love and accept him. However, the Jew can't live
peacefully with his feeling of bartered-away manliness, as we see in
Norman Mailer's storming, for instance.

Thus the team's interaction balances Martin's easy assertion of
manhood against Lewis's frantic negation of it, a split between the ethnic generalizations of the big, sexual Italian man and the little, sexless
Jewish boy that obtained both on- and off-screen. (Still operative as of
1999 in the pairing of Robert De Niro and Billy Crystal in *Analyze
This,* which, as if inevitably, culminates in the most Jerry Lewis–like
scene not starring Lewis himself, when Crystal poses as De Niro's con-
sigliere at the mafia powwow.) This resembles the split between the
Dictator and the Jewish Barber in Chaplin's *Great Dictator,* but with
even more spurious moral associations. Chaplin makes meekness a
sign of goodness; so does *The Stooge,* but it also associates Martin's
confident self-reliance with badness. But the split exists within Jerry
Lewis as well, between the lonely boy who feels monkey ugly and cries
when his parents miss his bar mitzvah and the mean, sleazy big shot,
the dichotomy in his personality he exploited to turn *Dr. Jekyll and Mr.
Hyde* into *The Nutty Professor.*

Chemistry professor Julius Kelp, physically humiliated in class one
day by a football player, concocts a formula that turns him into Buddy
Love, a two-fisted, heartless smoothie, able to woo a pert coed who's
simultaneously drawn to and repulsed by his abrupt, direct come-ons.
(Buddy is both smooth and unpolished.) Kelp keeps chugging his potion and going back and forth between his personae, but with less and
less control of the duration of a dosage. At the climax, as he transforms from Love back to Kelp onstage at the prom, he publicly apologizes for his deception. He finds that the coed loves Kelp as he is, but

we see that she's kept a couple bottles of the formula for purposes of her own.

In *his* humiliating curtain speech at the end of *The Stooge,* after he's had the nerve to go out as a solo act, Dean Martin defers to the "chemistry that makes two men a successful team." *The Nutty Professor* treats that cliché literally. Kelp the chemist has to create his other half to make a sort of partner who does in fact save the movie—because as his own "straight" man, an over-the-top hipster caveman, Lewis goes after laughs even more aggressively than when he plays the loser to get them. Lewis had the stylistic insight to go against Hollywood tradition by making his Hyde, Buddy Love, the *less* disfigured role. (Harry Ritz's Hyde in a routine in *Sing, Baby, Sing* looks like Jerry Lewis's Jekyll.) Julius Kelp has buckteeth and looks like he combs his hair with an eggbeater. Buddy Love is Lewis without special effects makeup, suited and slicked like a lounge singer. Lewis usually let his aggression as a comic gnaw through dense windings of pathos; Buddy Love, a figure who comes out mainly at night, is funnier for being nakedly aggressive. It's the difference between the invisible burn of ultraviolet rays and a blinding flash of moonlight.

The Nutty Professor is Lewis's best movie, and he deserves almost all the credit: he not only cowrote, produced, and directed it but starred in it as a team. In many ways, it owes more to *The Great Dictator,* released when Lewis was fourteen, than to Stevenson, which Lewis may not have read and probably knew only from movie adaptations (there had been two major Hollywood versions in his lifetime, in 1932 and 1941). By 1963 Lewis had become, like Chaplin, a bastard-mogul, and in *The Nutty Professor* he acts out the two poles of his personality, the same innocent-but-pesty character that had made him a star and a callous, successful persona that he'd hidden so well from his public that they assumed he was parodying his old partner. In making *The Nutty Professor,* Lewis was aware of Chaplin's example, but Chaplin had a body of brilliantly heartless shorts as the Tramp when he played Adenoid Hynkel. Lewis had played a son of a bitch on-screen only once in his career before *The Nutty Professor,* in that telling cameo appearance as himself in *The Bellboy. The Bellboy* was his first picture as director, and he couldn't resist undercutting the silent, sinless title character with a glimpse of the nature of the man playing him.

Those two halves showed up earlier in his life (along with the setting of *The Nutty Professor*) in Lewis's anecdote about how he got thrown out of high school: after an accident in chemistry lab, Lewis, his face blackened, was summoned to the principal's office, where the

German American Mr. Herder began, "Why is it that only the Jews—" at which Lewis slugged him in the mouth. There's another account of the slapstick mishap that landed him in the principal's office, but both versions feature Lewis doubling as screwup and hothead. Even the traits that supposedly clinch Buddy as a parody of Martin—that is, he's a sexy singer—are ambiguous because Lewis always wanted to be like Martin and do everything Martin could do. This cemented their partnership: Lewis worshiping the Italian singer, whose low-down *sprezzatura* was so mellow it oozed. But Lewis isn't parodying Martin's vocal *style,* or anyone's, when he wows the college crowd with "That Old Black Magic" in *The Nutty Professor*—he's diversifying his act. It's his Anschluss of the musical branch of entertainment.

Overall, *The Nutty Professor* is better written than *The Great Dictator* because it solves Chaplin's major script problem, that there's no connection between his two roles. The malevolent character doesn't represent the timid character's buried desire; hence, no click, no X ray. By contrast, in *The Nutty Professor* the repellent Buddy Love *does* reveal something about nice, harmless Julius Kelp. At last, Lewis's insistent sincerity in his movies seems backed by an honest urge to spatchcock himself. As a result, his sincerity comes across most vividly not in Kelp's maudlin confession speech in which he advises the crowd, "You might as well like yourself. Just think about all the time you're going to have to spend with yourself," but in Buddy Love at his most egregious.

What's surprising is that Lewis is funnier as Buddy Love combining the verbal slapstick of somewhat hostile, overripe bebop slang with limited physical aggression—for instance, pushing and talking the irascible dean of the university through a bad rendition of Hamlet's soliloquy—than he is as meek Julius Kelp with his more conventional incompetence. The physical slapstick involving Kelp is mostly mistimed, even when the conception is good; his funniest moment is the sequence of point-of-view shots in his classroom when he has his first hangover—aural rather than visual comedy.

Buddy Love represents what Jerry Lewis really developed out of Chaplin's Tramp, not "gracious humility" as he claimed but the opposite—the comedian's competitive itch to entertain us at a soul-devouring extreme. It's the slapstick of character drive: a man who acts on his impulses within a loose, progressing frame of identity. Generally, Lewis's actions are wildly physical, idiosyncratically maladapted if not acrobatic, but they're adjuncts to the character that is set mainly by his attitudes and his voice—that voice. This has been Lewis's real contribution to American slapstick, and though Buddy Love isn't at all spastic, it links Buddy as much as Julius Kelp to Lewis's usual boy idiot.

Buddy Love is as stylized as Chaplin's farthest-out creation, the Great Dictator, and even more *inappropriately* egomaniacal. He's also funnier because Lewis was more conscious of the sins on his own head. His long-suffering wife Patti has said that he used to tell her "that every person is really two people," and she commented, "He certainly was—the husband and father who was solicitous one day and vindictive the next." The element of Chaplin's performance as Hynkel that could be called self-flagellation was circumscribed, and anyway the licks he got in could be salved by his consciousness of the virtue in daring to affront Hitler. Lewis can't claim this extenuation; for a vain public figure, he's a mighty energetic flagellant. As he shouted at his biographer thirty years later:

> You wanna rip me? I'll give you shit that's real. That I'm guilty of. That'll make great reading. Why the fuck would you have to make up anything? Putz: ask me! I'll give you shit that you won't believe, that no one's ever written. As long as it's real, and it's true, it's okay with me. I don't care how I come off as long as it's the truth.

Lewis made *The Nutty Professor* in the spirit of this theatrically macho self-excoriation, yet he had never had surer control of comedy. He wasn't always on to himself. For instance, during the wearying transcontinental press junket for *The Nutty Professor*'s release in 1963, he started shouting at a member of his entourage, "I'm sick and tired of looking at your worthless face!" until he noticed that "he had an audience of journalists," at which "he hugged the man and patted his head, proclaiming, 'I love this guy. He's been with me for years, just like most of my staff. We're fantastically loyal to each other. They love me, and I love them.'" But if reading about a real-life scene like this impedes our belief in Julius Kelp's humility in his "moving" final speech, it only emphasizes that the concept of the warring personalities comes as undiluted out of the bottle as Lewis could pour it and still make it bubble.

The Nutty Professor resembles what *The Stooge* would be if Lewis played both roles and thought about what the aggression he directed at Dean Martin implied about himself. Which isn't unthinkable. We've grown used to the unmasking of big stars when we compare public statements with private reports, but Lewis presents a special case in that he has revealed both sides of himself for attribution. For instance, he wrote of JFK in his autobiography:

What a man! . . . Before I left he gave me a gift. A plaque. . . .

The plaque is a tangible reminder of his ideals. It reads: *There are three things which are real. God, Human Folly, and Laughter. Since the first two are beyond our comprehension, we must do what we can with the third.*

This didn't prevent Lewis from later boasting to an *Esquire* interviewer that Kennedy was "one of the great cunt men of all time. Except for me."

Lewis's frankness should have helped him make the transition from plastic fifties comedy to the woollier comedy of the seventies, but once the counterculture started to affect American movies in the mid-sixties, the game was up for Lewis as an important star. (Drug addiction didn't help his instincts any.) Time always poses a problem for pop icons, because of the relative youthfulness of the most enthusiastic segment of the audience. This usually limits older stars to a nostalgic and always diminishing older audience. However, as Shawn Levy wrote, Martin and Lewis had started out as "cutting-edge, hip, and sexy. Their night-club shows in New York and Los Angeles drew a tony crowd of celebrities, gangsters, and swingers. But in the two decades that followed, Jerry Lewis had become a family act, and then finally a kiddie act." Lewis expanded his range in *The Nutty Professor*, not only in Buddy Love's macho boorishness but also in Julius Kelp's quiet self-containment. Even Kelp's amusing himself with a little gawky toe-tapping at the prom, a Lewis specialty from *That's My Boy* that went atomic in *Living It Up*, is furtive. But the self-exposure of *The Nutty Professor* turned out to be a threshold Lewis backed away from, immediately reverting to the pitiable loser in *Who's Minding the Store?*, *The Patsy*, and *The Disorderly Orderly*. By 1970 even kiddies had better things to do than watch the bleary-eyed star in *Which Way to the Front?*

Jewish comedy of the post-Lewis era has taken us behind the scenes of the Jewish son's log-jamming need to be a good boy despite a flood of urges he can't contain. Lewis was in many ways a Portnoy—robbed of dignity by being the funny one, the child of demanding, insensitive parents, the Jew. His memories of the Catskills in the thirties and forties are prime Jewish shtick:

When it rained I usually stayed on the porch, bored silly listening to some of the adults as they rudely talked and laughed into each other's faces, or snored loudly in their chairs, or argued over cards, or exchanged family snapshots and bragged about this genius son and that

darling daughter while others shuffled from one spot to the next complaining about their rooms, the food, the service—everything.

And when Lewis, a guilty son whose success far outstripped his father's, collapsed in 1956 with coronary strain, he remembers the old
man's visit to the hospital: "His face pushed further into the [oxygen]
tent. 'Do you know what you're doing to your mother?'"

But Lewis seems to have taken the changes in moviemaking mores
in the late sixties and early seventies as a personal rejection, and to
have retreated behind an unproductive prissiness:

> The picture business was not doing what I believed they should be
> doing. . . . I got a whole moral code about that. I turned down discus-
> sions with [Richard] Zanuck at Fox about *Portnoy's Complaint*. I told
> him he's a fucking lecher. Ha! I said . . . I wouldn't know how to fucking
> make that movie, nor would I know how to appear in it.

Such language to vaunt your moral code! Lewis had everything for the
part of Portnoy except, finally, a broad enough self-awareness. Instead
he insisted that he was "the Jewish Holden Caulfield" and tried to get
Salinger to sell him the rights to *The Catcher in the Rye*.

Lewis wrote of this transitional period in Hollywood, "Everybody
crying out for happy entertainment [*Catcher*? *happy*?], while everything in sight was being tainted by the grime of 'realism' and magnified
on celluloid. . . . And that's what they were doing to our industry. It
was eroding under a heavy flood of X-rated films. So I backed off."
Lewis's pictures, with and without Martin, are sketchy, almost none of
them having plots of any significance. Even when Lewis remade a
script with a strong plot, Sturges's *Miracle of Morgan's Creek*, for instance, he wrecked it. But when a moviemaker combined Lewis's style
of sketch comedy with sexual naturalism, he could produce something
as engaging as *Annie Hall*, which has no plot at all, just an arc. Lewis
was in fact Woody Allen's first choice to direct both *Take the Money
and Run* and *Bananas*. Allen saw the continuity from comedy's past to
its future via Lewis, even if Lewis himself, unfortunately, could not.

Coda

Jerry Lewis has been the single most important performer of live-action slapstick in the talkie era, and despite his failure to see it, there is a vital link between him and contemporary slapstick comedy. Uncomfortable with the breakdown of censorship in the late sixties, he's still absurdly prudish about low comedy, saying of the fart jokes in the 1996 remake of *The Nutty Professor*, "Unnecessary. . . . When comics get in trouble, they go to the toilet." Nonetheless, the pop climacteric of the counter-culture helped make him a major influence on comedians young enough to be his sons. With an accelerating reversion to earthier, sexier material in comedy, going over the top has been at a premium, and only Lewis's personality has provided a model with enough stamina to keep up with the demands and stay broadly popular. By developing a style of delivery that united freakish physical and verbal assaults, Lewis modernized silent comedy while leaping past radio and musical-comedy stars. He was wilder and more powerful than anyone else—he is probably the most physically abandoned of clowns—and what he lacked in control, he made up for in detonation. You can even forgive him his mawkishness because although he *believed* in it, the naked aggression with which he seeks to make us laugh simultaneously undermines it. In this way, he updated something at the heart of what's alarming about so many slapstick clowns—they're both wistful and overbearing, as true of Jim Carrey in *The Mask* as it was of Chaplin in *A Dog's Life*.

Eddie Murphy was the first of Lewis's gale-force progeny whose stardom rivaled the master's. In the eighties, Murphy came out of the character comedy of *Saturday Night Live* and had an unstoppable career comparable to Lewis's in the fifties. Murphy, on both big and little screens, performed with the same kind of roll-'em-flat drive to take over every scene, but he didn't understand the significance of Martin to Lewis. Murphy flashed his edgy comic power *and* played it slick: Lewis's and Martin's strengths openly combined and openly appreciated by the star himself. Murphy was impersonally cocky, as if we could be entertained by seeing how easy it was for him.

I think this explains why his audience disappeared so fast once Mel Gibson commandeered the ballsy action comedy concession with the *Lethal Weapon* series. (Gibson's cop had aching eyes and was more believably reckless-daring.) But Murphy's recent long stretch of box office duds humanized him, and he came back better than he'd ever been in his 1996 remake of Lewis's *Nutty Professor,* the story of which forces the star to play both loser and winner, both Sherman Klump, the fat, lonely biochemistry professor, and Buddy Love, his thin, swaggering, loudmouthed alter ego generated in the lab. Klump, with a courtly manner and gentle southern baritone voice resonating out of his mammoth cave of a body, slows Murphy down. He's like a black Oliver Hardy but without ill temper, and Murphy pulls off making a man who's merely mild and pleasant actually funny, without milking us for "understanding." He can't avoid pathos in the role, but it works because Klump is never more miserable than when he's having dinner with his crass family, all except for a boy played by Murphy in an amazing round table of low-down impersonations.

Murphy's Buddy Love is as speeded up as Klump is slowed down, allowing the star to do some zippy, nasty stand-up at a nightclub where he goes with the grad student Klump had taken there on a date only to be humiliated by the house comedian's fat jokes. When Buddy Love gets revenge by literally beating the comedian on his own stage, it suggests that Murphy chose purposely to overdo the persona he strutted in *Raw,* in order to make himself into the image that hostile critics had of him—mechanically retailing bitter, crude jokes, which no one enjoys more than he does himself, while looking out at his audience with eyes so hard the seats might as well be empty. By the end of *The Nutty Professor,* when Klump makes his confession at a school function, it's really a confession for Murphy the star: "Buddy's who I thought the whole world wanted me to be. He's who I thought I wanted to be." Murphy is really asking why the audience tired of his shtick, though it remains an unanswerable question; audiences are fickle. But he does develop a new act here, as he himself noted: "I'd never played a woman before. I modeled Mama Klump on my own grandmother and Grandma Klump was sort of my take on Moms Mabley." And those are just the *women* in the big-assed family. It's a super act, but a hard one to follow: the movie succeeds because of the pleasure of watching Murphy play his disguises off each other, with a lot of help from director Tom Shadyac's syncopated timing.

Murphy has been aware of his need to reconnect with the audience at least since his 1992 black yuppie romantic comedy *Boomerang,* in which he tried to hand himself a comeuppance for his reputation as a pedigreed bird dog. It was as calculated as Katharine Hepburn's developing *The Philadelphia Story* to overcome her status with exhibitors as box office poison, but not as skillful. Still, *Boomerang* had one great scene, when Murphy and his friend played by David Alan Grier bonded in class embarrassment over Grier's parents' getting it on in the bathroom during a dinner party (to which they've brought an industrial-sized white plastic bucket of chitterlings). It was the forerunner of the even funnier scenes in *The Nutty Professor* in which Klump sits ashen in misery while Grandma natters about "having relations," Mama coos soothing inanities, brother Ernie comes on to Sherman's date, and Papa cuts whopping farts—all at once. These scenes make the pathos funny, which Lewis never pulled off, not to this extent. Murphy's expertise as a sketch comedian is fully orchestrated into a cacophony in which you can distinguish each discordant instrument. The two family blowouts show us the primordial family ooze Klump has crawled out of. The educated middle-class hero paralyzed by the excruciating vitality of his tacky parents is Philip Roth material, and Murphy is poised to become the black Portnoy, if he only knew it, and could find scripts good enough.

Jim Carrey is the second juggernaut star who shows the obvious influence of Jerry Lewis. Carrey has the freaky mutability without overworking the humanity of his characters. In fact, his fast changes of voice, expression, posture, and character are inhumanly mercurial. And he tones it *down* for the movies. For his comedy club impressions—Leonid Brezhnev, James Dean, and Clint Eastwood were all particularly remarkable—he seemed able to genetically recode his head; it's almost as creepy as it is hilarious. Carrey covers the screen the way Lewis did, and works *with* his partners far less than Lewis did (though Jeff Daniels was very funny in the same movie with him in *Dumb & Dumber*). Considering how voracious Lewis was, it's odd that his movies don't capitalize even more on the reason people went to them—to see Lewis act funny. But Lewis liked to fight for screen time against what he feared was his partner's inevitably greater pull. Carrey has no conflicts about dominating the movie (as his father quipped, "Jimmy's not a ham. . . . He's the whole pig"), and so you finally feel you're getting your money's worth from a Jerry Lewis movie. If Woody Allen improved on Bob Hope by adding realism, Carrey improves on Jerry Lewis by subtracting it. Carrey's pictures tend to be all inexhaustible Carrey—not the shambly, late-vaudeville, something-for-everybody entertainment that Lewis put on.

Lewis himself has called Carrey "the most brilliant physical come-dian to come along in decades," and Carrey acknowledges that when he was a kid, "Jerry Lewis was the king." But the succession isn't so di-rect. Carrey always wanted to play James Stewart, who he felt was like his father, "the good man who struggles with right and wrong and comes out on top," though "in real life, it doesn't always work out that way." His father, whom Carrey has called "a broken-hearted man," gave up playing the sax for a responsible career as an accountant, only to be fired after twenty-six years, leaving him with neither the musical career he loved nor the security he had given it up for.

At Christmas, Carrey's alcoholic grandparents would corner his fa-ther and "tell him what a loser he was" while the father turned "purple with anger," too nice to defend himself. Carrey, a Catholic boy who "wanted to be Jesus Christ" but "could never get the turn-the-other-cheek thing down," admits, "I'm not as nice as my dad." As soon as his grandparents left, he'd imitate them: "My father would be so relieved it was as if I pulled the pressure plug when I went into this routine." Carrey said of *The Mask,* "Every generation needs a Jekyll and Hyde story," and he described his Hyde personality as "someone who, when he walks into a room, is gonna fuck it till it bleeds." However, with the next breath, he says, "What was so great is that preview audiences they've shown it to really like sweet, nice Stanley as much or more than The Mask." That is to say, Carrey fucks the screen till it bleeds in de-fense of sweet, nice guys like his father who can't take care of them-selves. It's equally perfect that Carrey would have gone to a church ser-vice one Christmas to meet James Stewart, thinking "it would be like Jesus meets John the Baptist," and that far from receiving his hero's blessing, Carrey came on so strong Stewart retreated in embarrassment.

Lewis's movies leave a tang despite the smarmy coating because he was invested emotionally in them. However, though you can piece to-gether personal motivations from Carrey's interviews, his investment in his movies doesn't give them the anguished deliberateness of Lewis's—but then it doesn't moisten them either. Carrey comes across as pure phenomenon, and it's pleasurable because he doesn't ask for sympathy in character the way Lewis did. Stanley is a low-cholesterol loser, and so we don't feel pushed to choose between him and the Mask. The Mask has to be put aside so that Stanley can resume his own life, but we're left to enjoy the naughty outburst without a third-act apology. And inasmuch as the Mask defends a character Carrey as-sociates with his own father, Stanley is always free of *self*-pity. At his most arresting, Carrey is heartless and plastic in the best possible way, which is why the redemption of the yuppie dad in *Liar Liar* doesn't work (though an unscrupulous defense attorney is a perfect role for him). As Peter Weir, director of *The Truman Show*, said of Carrey in *Ace Ventura*, "He was daring and anarchic and lacked the 'please love me' attitude common to most comics you see on the Oscars" (though ironically you couldn't say it of Carrey in *The Truman Show* itself). Likewise, we can relax with him as Ace Ventura because he's equally artificial with friend and foe, and also because he gets laid. And when Carrey can't, as in *Dumb & Dumber*, his character doesn't take it personally, as he should. Carrey is usually impervious to pathos because a comic avenger can't let down his guard. Even as a loser-goon, he doesn't go soggy.

Carrey is alarmingly physical but incapable of the amazing stunt work that was the minimal requirement of silent clowns. In compensation *The Mask* marries live action with special effects animation to pull off the kind of hyper-slapstick we expect from cartoons. It's a technological solution to what was for decades the single biggest problem for slapstick, the fact that stunts work best as comedy when they're on a real scale shot live even if the star uses a double. Harold Lloyd was never in much danger working on *Safety Last!*, but the rooftop sets were so carefully constructed and the shots so expertly angled that when you see the street below him, it's the real street and you feel it in your knees. The kind of process photography projected behind the star dangling on wires that dominated in the midcentury is a great leveler: Harold Lloyd on a windowsill over a matte shot drop to the street in Preston Sturges's *The Sin of Harold Diddlebock* is no better than Jerry Lewis in the same situation in *Living It Up*. No American comic in the talkies ever consistently triumphed over this technology. (About the best you can do is to emphasize the fakeness, as Fields does in the mountain road chase that ends *The Bank Dick*.) The computer-generated special effects transformations in *The Mask* are thus a real jump; they have offered the best method so far for working around the lack of acrobatically trained comedians.

The makers modeled Carrey's howling at Cameron Diaz's song and dance on Tex Avery's wolf-in-the-nightclub cartoons, and it's as funny as the originals. This solution might have occurred to someone just from watching Carrey, who already seems like a special effect, for instance, when he does the incomparable instant replay in super slow motion and reverse in the first *Ace Ventura*. The animation simply completes his rubberiness, enabling him literally to bounce off the walls. The unpretentiousness of silent slapstick allows it to rest very lightly on its followers. It's perfectly acceptable if Preston Sturges shifts the emphasis from physical to verbal slapstick, or if the Warner Brothers cartoonists defy physical possibilities, as the slapstick clowns had stopped doing when they moved into features, and compact the same number of gags into half the footage, or if Jim Carrey lets computer animation do the acrobatics for him. Don't look a virtual gift horse in the mouth.

Nicolas Cage, for whom Jerry Lewis was "an idol for many years," is by far the suavest of current high-octane comedians. In *Raising Arizona* he has just the right lanky, prairie scavenger scamper for the slapstick, but though he claims to have modeled his performance on Woody Woodpecker, Cage also plays against the manic pace. He uses a forlorn, pacifying tone when he tries to reason with his tough, tense, childless wife as she badgers him into kidnapping a sextuplet, since the parents have more babies than they need. Both his criminality and a supremely impractical gallantry (a kind of trailer trash quixotry) push him forward into the classically deranged episodes. He's lucky to be working with the Coen brothers in their most accessible mode, using our awareness of the camera work and editing for a slapstick effect, like creatures stitched together from bits of Orson Welles and Tex Avery. (Also true of Sam Raimi in his berserkly alert gore cheapie *Evil Dead II*, with perhaps some James Whale sutured in for camp horror.) In *Raising Arizona* the stretch from the visit of Cage's foreman to the couple's home through the convenience store heist is a perfect two-reeler, ending as it should with a chase and the quick capper of Cage reaching out from a speeding car to grab a package of diapers off the asphalt.

Cage got much more manic in *Vampire's Kiss* as a yuppie editor who thinks he's turning into a vampire. This pretentious fool, who wills his life into the semblance of an urban gothic horror movie, is so frustrated at not growing fangs that he buys a plastic pair at a novelty shop. He tears into the bag feverishly and then feels ecstatically transformed when they're in his mouth. Cage keeps the character distinct in both the outbursts and the depressed lulls between them: seeing his absurd reflection in a public phone, he calls his shrink and, without removing the fangs, mumblingly reschedules his appointment for a day earlier. Immediately afterward he chases a pigeon to take home and eat raw before going to sleep in his "coffin"—a black leather couch turned turtle on top of him with a twittering alarm clock set within a pale arm's reach. The picture starts slow, but as the character's delusions and histrionics escalate, Cage takes over the picture by main comic force—he can get crazy laughs just by reciting the alphabet in sadistic exasperation. He becomes not quite a vampire but the weirdest rising star we've seen since the young Charles Laughton, and sexy into the bargain.

Vampire's Kiss proved a breakthrough for Cage into greater expressiveness. He went beyond his early performances by going through them, adapting his full-wing-spread goofiness to the more complex demands of *Leaving Las Vegas,* in which he plays Ben Sanderson, an alcoholic screenwriter who leaves Hollywood for Vegas to drink himself to death. Once Ben is fired by his production company (where he sits in his office pretending to be on a high-powered call, but holding the receiver upside down), his emotional life is all in the past—it's garbage to be burned or left at the curb. Standing in line at the bank, he tape-records a boozy pornographic fantasy about the blonde teller: the actor takes off, in character, and gets some of the most potent twisted laughs in American movies.

The comedy is really piercing because you can see that there's no other way through to Ben, who shields himself with one put-on after another. His comically flamboyant gestures make other people uncomfortable but are the only form of communication left to this skyrocket of a burnout. For the actor, they are a galvanizing way to express the perversity, self-pity, and remoteness under the forced gaiety and anomalous courtliness of a self-consciously florid, articulate drunk. In a way, Ben is a sad-clown role, but one breathtakingly free of pathos and, with his public displays of eccentricity, at times hilariously funny. Ben Sanderson, far more than Buddy Love, is a fan's platonic ideal of the real Dean Martin as played by Jerry Lewis. Cage's three-ring circus of a performance is more dramatic because it's so unexpectedly comic, and the comedy all makes sense for a writer who wears his literary sensibility (guessably influenced by Henry Miller and Charles Bukowski) like a corona of fumes.

In a 1996 *New Yorker* profile of Woody Allen, John Lahr wrote, "At the beginning of the century, Chaplin's kinetic tramp made a legend of dynamism; by its end, Allen's paralyzed Woody made a legend of defeat. . . . A climate of retreat had asserted its hegemony over hope. The shrug had replaced the pratfall." Especially in such early movies as *Bananas, Sleeper,* and *Love and Death,* Allen helped extend the expressive range of slapstick without replacing the basics. Now he has principally moved on to other kinds of comedy, for better and worse. In 1994 I liked Allen's *Bullets over Broadway,* but *Dumb & Dumber,* which I also liked, connected with a much larger audience; until the law of gravity is repealed, the pratfall will never be replaced. As

Ludwig Lewisohn was quoted in a 1907 editorial saying of the impersonal, eternal quality of the acrobat: "His is the oldest profession but one and quite the strangest. The ages change, he is changeless. Men babble with innumerable tongues; he is silent. He tumbles and does not break his neck, and he will tumble at the Crack of Doom."

Slapstick can't be replaced because it offers a fundamental affirmation in the face of the physical frustrations of existence in a form that no one in the audience has to reach for. But the silent tradition did die, fast. We have Jerry Lewis, perhaps the genius worst served by his success in Hollywood's history, to thank for the most forceful step forward in American slapstick performing since the talkies came in—because of Lewis, it is no longer accurate to typify a slapstick clown as silent—even though it was only a generation later that his style found more aesthetically satisfying forms. Constance Rourke quoted Vaughan Williams, who said that "the actual pioneers in a movement are most often inferior in expressive power, because they are plowing new ground with difficulty," herself adding that "the effect of ugliness may be the result of prepossessions, and a special pleasure may often be derived from fresh beginnings, from half-formed yet vigorous new directions." In this way, Lewis can legitimately claim credit for the subsequent successes of his unruly "sons." He was just the first monkey out of the barrel; his followers are still chattering and scampering in the banana trees.

Notes

Notes are keyed by page number. See "Works Cited" for full bibliographical information.

Preface

xi   Adam Sandler: Sandler interview.

xii   Codes of family entertainment: Gilbert, 113–14, 120–23, 204–5, 362–65; C. Stein, 24; Snyder, 133–34, 141.

1. Comedy Is a Man in Trouble

1   Henry Miller: *Capricorn,* 55.

1   "double paddles": White, 437.

1   Kenneth McLeish: He lists Chaplin, Keaton, Lloyd, Groucho Marx, and Jerry Lewis, among many others by name in his index.

1   "rough estimate": Lahue, xiii. Generally, comedy shorts ran one or two reels, features four to seven.

2   "visual comedy": Lloyd interview, 57.

2   "idea-men": "Harold Lloyd" (AFI seminar), 22–23, 25–26.

2   Arbuckle and Lloyd: Yallop, 86. Sneak previews: This process served as a logical replacement for men who had learned their craft in front of live audiences and believed in those audiences, which is what distinguishes their sneak previewing from the homogenization in search of a buck that results from the studios pretesting their product today.

2   Keaton was frank: Keaton, *Wonderful,* 112.

2   stealing the audience: As C. L. Barber said of Renaissance pageants, "In the written accounts of entertainments, the formal part [i.e., occasional verse] is obviously more adequately recorded than the impromptu or traditional humor" (34). This is one of the miracles of silent slapstick movies, the recording of the impromptu and traditional humor of the last full generation trained in the physical comedy of live popular theater.

3   M. Willson Disher: *Clowns,* 7.

5   Alva Johnston: pt. 1, p. 9.

6   Groucho himself: Arce, 136.

6   Sturges claimed: Johnston, pt. 2, p. 83.

6   title writers: Loos, 98–104.

7   James Agee: 4–5.

8   Mabel Normand: Sennett, *King,* 86–87.

9   Keatons' parody: Keaton, *Wonderful,* 53.

9   "What'll we do": Wilson, 317. *Merton* is one of the few books that can make you laugh out loud at written-out slapstick sequences. Gilbert Seldes pointed out that Ben Turpin's feature *A Small Town Idol* was released before *Merton* was published and that it "consummated a burlesque" of serious movies "with a vaster fun" (Seldes, *Seven,* 13). (Wilson almost certainly saw it because Turpin is the model for one of his key characters.) Though the dates of *A Small Town Idol* and *Merton of the Movies* are incontestable, the relative merits aren't; I think *Merton* is much funnier. Gertrude Stein would more than back me up. She claimed in 1937, "*Merton of the Movies* is the best book about twentieth century American youth that has yet been done" (250).

9   *Webster's: Third New International Dictionary of the English Language Unabridged,* 1971 ed.

10   Dilys Powell: 7.

10   Frank Capra: 52. The intransigence of inanimate objects is doubly relevant to slapstick movies, since Keaton remembered that the "props . . . never acted the same way twice when the camera's eye was on them" (Keaton, *Wonderful,* 137).

10   Johan Huizinga: 140.

10   Faulkner: *Light,* 70 (chap. 3).

11   Roscoe Arbuckle's: Edmonds, 49–50.

11–12   "train wreck": Blesh, 77.

12   Even the solicitous: The comedy producers realized the importance of maintaining the audience's belief that nobody got hurt: "Arbuckle was caught off-guard when several reporters printed stories about the violence and serious injuries that occurred 'on a daily basis' on the Arbuckle sets. Sprains, cuts, broken noses and arms during stunt attempts were considered part of the day's work by those in the movie business at that time. But film audiences experienced only the thrills and laughs of wild and perilous stunts, probably assuming that it was all make-believe. When reporters wrote in horror of the real-life injuries, Arbuckle was ordered to smooth things over. Triangle/Keystone was afraid that if audiences learned of the real danger in many stunts, they would not find them funny" (Edmonds, 87).

12   "An audience": Dardis, *Keaton,* 56.

12   Bert Williams: C. Stein, 241. Williams was the first black to break the color line in vaudeville and the musical theater and has left a record of his famous one-man poker game in the 1916 Biograph two reeler *A Natural Born Gambler* (Smith, 180).

12   Gene Fowler: 196.

13   "And while": Lloyd, *American,* 170.

13   St. Ambrose: Jacobus, 232.

13–14   Feast of Fools: Barber, 25.

15   William Dean Howells: C. Stein, 76.

15   ritual: Huizinga wrote, "Just as there is no formal difference between play and ritual, so the 'consecrated spot' cannot be formally distinguished from the playground. The arena, the card-table, the magic circle, the temple, the stage, the screen, the tennis court, the court of justice, etc., are all in form and function playgrounds" (10).

15   Harpo Marx: 27.

15–16   C. L. Barber: 213.

16   Jerry Lewis: Levy, 73.

16   Mack Sennett: *King*, 28–29.

16   When he worked: Ramsaye, 510.

16   Mack Sennett: *King*, 74–75.

17   Hugh Kenner: 60.

17   Iris Barry: 128.

17   "little guy": Sennett, *King*, 29.

18   Gilbert Seldes: *Seven*, 24.

18   Disher: *Clowns*, 33.

18   Jerry Lewis: *Film-Maker*, 197.

18–19   "The particular type": Seldes, *Hour*, 57.

19   "tragic appeal": Ibid., 69–71.

19   "We're too good": Thomas Burke reported this attitude of Chaplin's unashamed-
        ly: "He is an idealist. But an idealist whose ideals are not strong enough to stand
        up to the sight of human nature. That kind of idealism, on contact with life, al-
        most always freezes, and it has done so with him. It has become impatience and
        despair" (148).

19   Otis Ferguson's: 117.

19   Frederick Lewis Allen: 228.

19   James Agee: 10. This opinion persists: in the summer 1998 special edition of
        Newsweek, announcing the American Film Institute's "100 Best Movies," a
        sidebar in the section on comedy called "Our Favorites" praises *City Lights* as
        "Slapstick Chaplin that breaks your heart" (24).

19–20   Walter Kerr: 162.

20   silverware: Harold Lloyd used the flying silverware stunt as a running gag in his
        1930 feature *Feet First,* in a range of sizes from soda fountain spoons to trench-
        digging shovels.

20   C. L. Barber's: 220–21.

20   "began by": Seldes, *Seven*, 13.

20–21   "Our whole": Ibid.

21   "piety and wit": Ibid., 51.

21   "wisdom" and "loveliness": Ibid., 54.

21   Jerry Lewis: Levy, 164.

21   "the genteel": Seldes, *Seven*, 24.

21   Seldes claimed: *Hour*, 66.

21   Chaplin acknowledged: Young, 44, 174.

23   "Instinctively guarding": Tolstoy, 889–90 (book 10, chap. 32).

23   Joe Rock: Rosenberg and Silverstein, 54.

23   beyond his comprehension: Tolstoy, 859 (book 10, chap. 24).

23–24   leg is amputated: Tolstoy, 906–8 (book 10, chap. 37).

24   Disher: *Clowns*, xiii.

24   "For the best manures": Flaubert, 168 (part 2, chap. 8). The French propels the joke with a single word, "Fumiers," where the English almost hobbles its stride with the longer prepositional phrase (French ed., 202).

25   Baudelaire: vol. 2, p. 80.

26   "To endure": Tolstoy, 941 (book 11, chap. 6).

27   Keaton's source: Dardis, *Keaton,* 139.

27   Keaton felt: For example, gagman Clyde Bruckman favored ending *The Navigator* with Buster and Kathryn McGuire leaping into the sea, without showing them resurfacing atop the submarine. Keaton disagreed, saying that "it was in the books for us to die all right. But not in the jokebooks. We were making a comedy, remember?" (Blesh, 256).

27   Agee noted: 6–7.

27   Gilbert Seldes: *Seven,* 22.

27   "dependable barometer": Fowler, 94.

27   "Abraham Lincoln": Ibid., 195.

28   Regular Army Clowns: Hooker, 46.

28   "Hail to the Chief": Hooker originated it, 47–48.

28   Lord of Misrule: See Barber, 24–30.

2. Chaplin as Proteus, Low-Down and High Up

Biographical information in this chapter is drawn from Chaplin's autobiography and biographies by David Robinson, Joyce Milton, and Kenneth S. Lynn.

31   Mack Sennett: Sennett, *King,* 172.

33   Starting in 1916: Maland, 27–28.

33   Henry Miller: *Capricorn,* 53.

35   fight back: Joyce Milton accounts for the notable switcheroo later in the movie, when Hannah keeps the Jewish men from carrying out an assassination attempt, as Chaplin's accommodation of the flip-flop in the Communist line after the Hitler-Stalin pact.

36   Pauline Kael: "Comedians," 323.

36   Irving Howe: "Afterward," 820.

37   Thomas Burke: 129–30.

37   "At Keystone": Kerr, 74.

38   skill: Kevin Brownlow's description of Chaplin demonstrating both Brando's and Loren's roles to them while directing *A Countess from Hong Kong* in 1966 suggests that the skill, or at any rate the impulse, never left him (507).

38   "A one-reel film": Lloyd, *American,* 143.

38   Thomas Burke: 129, 135.

39   Gilbert Seldes: *Seven,* 194.

39   K. J. Dover: 41.

40   Mack Sennett: Sennett, *King,* 16, 19–20.

40   Jerry Lewis: *In Person,* 278.

40   Karno company: Fred Karno (1866–1941) was a British vaudeville showman whose troupe included Sydney and later Charlie Chaplin, and Stan Laurel.

41   Kerr thinks: 79.

42   his confession: Arce, 155.

42   Stan Laurel: Guiles, 29.

44   cop as symbol: See also Sennett, *King*, 53, 75. For kids who grew up poor in the big cities, however, cops weren't necessarily symbolic: "There was no such character as 'the kindly cop on the beat' in New York in those days. The cops were sworn enemies. By the same token we, the street kids, were the biggest source of trouble for the police. Individually and in gangs we accounted for most of the petty thievery and destruction of property on the upper East Side. And since we couldn't afford to pay off the cops in the proper, respectable Tammany manner, they hounded us, harassed us, chased us, and every chance they got, happily beat the hell out of us" (Harpo Marx, 36).

47   Henry Miller: Miller seems to have had a more conventional preference: "Have just left the cinema after seeing *City Lights* with the profound conviction that Chaplin is great. For years I have been railing against him, but now, after those last two minutes of the film, I believe in him. He will give us something powerful in the years to come. This picture marks a turning point" (April 1932; *Letters*, 37).

48   Constance Collier: 242–43.

48   stealing food: See also Eddie Cantor's memories of pushcart pilfering (21); Groucho Marx, 41, 72–73; Harpo Marx, 41, 46, 78; Hook, 9. Predictably, this is an immemorial source of comedy; see Agorakritos the sausage seller's boyhood tricks in Aristophanes' *Knights*, p. 84, lines 417–20.

48   Napoleon project: David Robinson has shown that in a draft of a script Chaplin wrote with John Strachey, a speech devised for Napoleon includes material very similar to the Barber's speech at the end of *The Great Dictator*.

49   Jim Tully: Maland, 109.

50   don't match: Chaplin was defiant about such technical slovenliness.

55   crushed by life: Kenneth Lynn has convincingly demonstrated that Chaplin's stories of his mother's losing her voice onstage while he, still a child, watched from the wings and then came on to sing in her place are fabrications, though as stories they do interestingly connect his theatrical avocation with his mother's undeniable psychological decline.

56   messy jokes: Chaplin changed in the face of charges of vulgarity during his first few years in the movies (Maland, 15–18).

56   villains: This makes more sense coming from Chaplin than from Harold Lloyd, who said the same thing (Lloyd interview, 11).

57   Thomas Burke: 168.

3. Junior

Biographical information in this chapter is drawn from Harold Lloyd's three-part autobiography published in *Photoplay Magazine*, his book-length autobiography *An American Comedy*, and Tom Dardis's biography of Lloyd; Buster Keaton's autobiography and biographies of Keaton by Rudi Blesh, Tom Dardis, and Marion Meade.

59   "ordinary" restaurant: Moore, 106–8, 114; Kirkpatrick, 59.

59   These three: For instance, they were grouped in a 1925 *Photoplay* article induct-
        ing Sennett's latest discovery into their ranks: "Like Harold Lloyd's horn-
        rimmed glasses, Charlie Chaplin's derby hat, bushy hair protruding, and swish-
        ing stick; Buster Keaton's frozen face and flat little hat, [Harry] Langdon also has
        his 'trade mark'" (North, 127). And James Agee set them securely at the top,
        with Langdon just below, in "Comedy's Greatest Era."

60   Keaton's fatalism: Walter Kerr's chapter "The Keaton Curve: A Study in Coopera-
        tion" is the best writing about this.

61   horn-rimmed: Lloyd interview, 25.

61–62   "Once we": Keaton, Franklin interview, 15.

62   Agee: 16.

62   tight: Lloyd interview, 18.

63   "They must like": Lloyd interview, 72.

63   "In our early": Keaton, Franklin interview, 26.

64   same numbers: On the other hand, his MGM talkies were very profitable.

64   Luis Buñuel: Aranda, 272.

64   "strictly male": This was Myra Keaton's view.

64   Agee: 16.

65   Henri Bergson: 149 (French ed., 152). "Crystallise" is "se solidifier" in the origi-
        nal, not a literal translation but a good one; Harold Lloyd used the same meta-
        phoric verb when describing the process by which he arrived at his glasses charac-
        ter (Lloyd, *American*, 101).

66   "what is essentially": Bergson, 146 (French ed., 149).

66   "Any individual": Bergson, 134 (French ed., 137).

66   unjust society: Charles J. Maland, Joyce Milton, and Kenneth Lynn have probed
        the influence of radical politics on Chaplin during the making of *Modern Times*
        and *The Great Dictator*. See Maland, 127–94; Milton, 346–50, 363–64,
        371–72, 378–82; Lynn, 345–423.

68   rather than shorts: Even though 67 of his 72 Lonesome Luke shorts are lost, 64 of
        his 166 one-, two-, and three-reelers made from 1915 through 1921 are known to
        exist, compared to the 33 much better known shorts made by Buster Keaton from
        1917 through 1923.

69   the Lynds: 266.

71   "Though he is": Gill, "Speedy," 29. When Lloyd: Gill, *New York,* 280.

71–72   Hal Roach: Rosenberg and Silverstein, 27–28.

73   "I wanted": "Harold Lloyd" (AFI seminar), 28.

79   tornado: The original script featured a flood at the end but had to be changed at
        the last minute owing to expense and the fear of bad publicity because of recent
        floods in the South. The tornado was Keaton's idea for a substitute.

79   died of alcoholism: Chaplin Sr. dies on page 36 of David Robinson's 632-page
        biography.

80   Joe Schenck: Rudi Blesh is very good on Buster's father figures named Joe—both
        Schenck and his mountainous adversary in his short films and early features, Joe
        Roberts.

80   "Daddy": Gabler, 113; Beauchamp, 136. The connotation of Talmadge's pet name for her husband was slightly different from, yet related to, Keaton's reliance on him—Schenck promised to provide for everyone.

81   "baseball mustache": A touchy topic for young men. For instance, after failing to see action as an aviator in World War I, Preston Sturges returned from Camp Dick to his stepfather's house in Chicago. "Things began rather badly when Father asked me at the station why I had shaved off the mustache I had written to him about before showing it to him. As I *hadn't* shaved it off and had trimmed it only that morning, this hurt my feelings a little" (Sturges, *Preston,* 174).

83   Northrop Frye: 164.

84   Dreiser: 338.

84   Faulkner: *Absalom,* 222 (chap. 7).

84   Mack Sennett's father: Fowler, 28.

85   Lorca's: 282.

85   Pauline Kael: "Dream City," 17.

87   "clean" pictures: Yallop, 63; Edmonds, 257.

88   despite warnings: Keaton would later grow skeptical of his deal with Joe Schenck.

89   adult stoicism: Keaton's outlook in his personal and professional lives as well— he never bad-mouthed the immovably bitter mother of his sons, and he never wept over his professional or personal fate.

89   late starter: This is always tricky material. Langdon was the best at it: in the 1925 two-reeler *Boobs in the Woods,* Langdon plays a tiny, inept lumberjack; when the frisky girl tries to kiss him, he raises his ax over his head to fend her off. The ridiculously hyperbolic threat of violence blows the powdered sugar off the scene.

90   Hal Roach: Rosenberg and Silverstein, 27. Lloyd had made all his silent classics by the age of thirty-five.

90   "young man": Agee, 8.

4. Girl Heroes

Biographical information in this chapter is drawn from Betty Harper Fussell's biography of Mabel Normand, the autobiographies of Gloria Swanson, Colleen Moore, and Beatrice Lillie, Marion Davies's posthumously published memoir, Katharine Hepburn's autobiography, and Barbara Leaming's biography of Hepburn.

92   "One of the things": Sennett interview, 186, 188.

94   her reputation: Such moralism must have amused O'Neil and Haines, who, among the guests at Hearst's San Simeon "ranch," were both members of an informal group dubbed the "Younger Degenerates." These also included Louise Brooks and Charles Lederer (L. Brooks, 41).

95–96   Mildred and the navy: Lloyd, "Autobiography," pt. 3, p. 115.

96   "big French doll": Ibid., 56.

97   Daniels's roles: Even knowing of Daniels's high-spirited escapades—"stealing a couple of bicycles from Western Union" with Adela Rogers St. Johns "and riding them home" (Yallop, 79), or turning a ten-day sentence for speeding into a circus by having her cell "furnished by the best decorator in town" and her meals "served by a waiter in full dress," and then capitalizing on it afterward in a picture

called *The Speed Girl* (Daniels and Lyon interview; Yallop, 98–100)—can only make you want even more to see the movies that no longer exist, but it doesn't help you theorize about what they must have been like. We may not be missing much if the moviemakers didn't use her any better than Lloyd does in the glasses comedies, even when the material is promising, for instance, when she plays a ritzy spirit medium who outsmarts a couple of thieves in the 1918 one-reeler *Are Crooks Dishonest?* or when she does a *danse apache* with Lloyd in the 1919 one-reeler *Young Mr. Jazz.*

97   criteria: Meade, 98; Blesh, 147.

97   "There were usually": Keaton, *Wonderful,* 130.

98   Marion Mack: Meade, 163–66; see also the interview with Mack in "Comedy—a Serious Business."

99   flump: This fall is actually performed in part by dummies, and the seamless matching probably owes something to having Elgin Lessley, who had earlier coshot Keaton's *Sherlock Jr.,* behind one of the cameras.

99   Gloria Swanson: Swanson felt so dwarfed that she recalled Astor as six feet tall.

99   played trombone: McBride, *Variety* article.

99   caption: Astor file.

99   "delicate": Jacobs, 191.

99   "almost timid": Curtis, 122.

99   her virginity: Slide, 70.

99   Bonner thought: Ibid., 73.

100   get to play: Lillian Roth as the singing ingenue in *Animal Crackers* is the exceptional young female who's as appealing as the bad gals, an ingenue with the pertness of a soubrette. In Max Fleischer's 1932 half-cartoon, half-live-action singalong "Ain't She Sweet?" Roth, with her almost butch swagger, is more animated than the animation. Thus *Animal Crackers* gives us Dumont, Irving, and Roth, three lively, contrasting ladies in one picture, almost unheard of in slapstick.

100   In 1926: Higham, 106–7.

101   Miriam Cooper: 181.

101   Sennett referred: Edmonds, 62.

101   last jobs: Sennett, *King,* 19–20; Rosenberg and Silverstein, 14–15.

101   One interviewer: Guiles, 19.

101   Harold Lloyd: *American,* 105.

101–2   Groucho Marx: Arce 402–3, 222. C. A. Lejeune wrote in 1931, "It was the women, I think, who killed slapstick comedy, just as it is the women who have killed the music-hall. They wanted romance and pathos, heroism and gallantry in their entertainments, and slapstick denies all these things" (191).

102   Gilbert Seldes: *Seven,* 12.

102   model: Young, 37; Giroux, 182.

103   "But permit me": Ramsaye, 257–58, 270–71.

104   prowling: St. Johns, *Honeycomb,* 92–93.

104   boy-and-girl team: They costarred in thirty-six movies for Sennett between 1913 and 1916. Arbuckle directed eighteen of these shorts as well as one in which Normand starred without him.

104 Arbuckle "did not like": Young, 33. The Marx Brothers offer another example of men with a surprisingly prissy double standard. All four had whored around extensively, "but if a woman said a four-letter word, they'd get *so* upset" (Arce, 80–81, 411).

104 Normand fumed: Marion, 88.

107 hated slapstick: She considered Chaplin's rejection of her as a costar after her audition at the Chicago Essanay studios "a real compliment"; see also Chaplin, 166.

108 experience at Keystone: The director shot a scene in which Tessie dressed as Chaplin's Tramp for a party, but the scene was cut before release.

108 Allan Dwan: Bogdanovich, 71.

108 Louis B. Mayer: Gabler, 106.

109 Diana Trilling: 53.

109 Pat Nixon: Eisenhower, 48.

109 Gimbels: Dwan says it was Macy's, and, like the subway ride, his idea (Bogdanovich, 70–75).

110 "again and again": Young, 32.

110 unchaperoned: St. Johns, *Honeycomb*, 93–94.

111 narcotics: Cooper, 181; Giroux, 199–217. Giroux points out that the stillbirth of her illegitimate child by Goldwyn may also have been drug related (197–98, 201).

112 Frederick Lewis Allen: 108.

112 moralizing endings: Ibid., 101–2.

112 "*Live Stories*": Lynd, 241.

112 ninety percent: St. Johns, *Honeycomb*, 103.

112 Iris Barry: 59.

112–13 "I didn't have": Harry Leon Wilson makes the faking of such spreads a running motif in *Merton of the Movies*.

113 Cinderella: Terry Ramsaye wrote in 1926, "[Athanasius] Kircher chose the Devil for his star [in a 1640 magic lantern projection] quite as naturally as the motion picture maker of to-day reaches for Cinderella in some guise, purveying the positive appeals of hope and sex instead of the negative emotion fear" (6). Cinderella, transported out of her endless daily toil, acted out the aptest fantasy for working- and middle-class women in the audience, who would go to the movies for the same kind of transport, which means in a sense that it wasn't entirely vicarious. Ethan Mordden has also written that Cinderella plots were "the rage" of twenties musicals (*Make Believe*, 10). At the same time, all these crashing-the-movies stories probably derive from *Merton of the Movies*.

113 young heroine's high spirits: This gambit is most enjoyable in the first half of Mary Pickford's *Daddy-Long-Legs* (1919), which takes place in an orphanage where the spunky family comedy is surprisingly irreverent. For instance, the grim headmistress banishes Mary and a young boy to the yard with no dinner. Mary prays, "Please, Mr. God, we want food," just at the moment that a burglar on the other side of the enclosing wall inspects his take—a box of sandwiches and a jug of applejack—and, disgusted with them, throws them over the wall, hitting famished, pious Mary on the head. The two kids gorge on the sandwiches and get drunk on the applejack, and the slapstick jokes just keep coming. It's truly funny—a tilted version of Jane Eyre at Lowood—and the Manhattan audience I saw it with in 1997 roared.

113   Mervyn LeRoy: 68–69.

115   Neal Gabler: 66.

115–16 prominent social figure: St. Johns, *Born Great*, 11–12.

116   dollhouse: On permanent display at the Chicago Museum of Science and Industry.

117   both styles: Lillie would incorporate physical comedy even into the dialogue-driven camp comedy of manners *On Approval* in 1944 when, for instance, she throws Clive Brook's hat out the train window with such lightning timing that the gesture seems to precede the thought.

118   director doesn't tell her: An inspiration based on Buster Keaton's advice to director King Vidor, "Above all other things, don't anticipate. You can't anticipate getting hit with the pie. You have to turn into it unexpectedly" (Vidor interview, 89). Arbuckle had taught Keaton this on Keaton's *second* day of film work (Meade, 64).

118   William Randolph Hearst: Vidor, *Tree*, 165–71; Vidor interview, 88–89.

118   fake count: The pointiest jab at Gloria Swanson; Vidor had the source play rewritten on the basis of Swanson's career, which, unlike Davies's, had begun in comedy shorts (Vidor, *Tree*, 165–66).

118   "old-fashioned": Kael, "Raising Kane," 69. However, Bebe Daniels thought that Davies wasn't frustrated by, but rather shared, Hearst's judgment of material (Daniels and Lyon interview).

120   *male* fashions: de Frece, 125–26.

120   Vesta Tilley: Disher, *Winkles*, 76–79.

120   Charlot note: "Charlot for 1926."

120   impeccable: Lillie replicates great-lady stage manners—in part caricaturing her own mother, whom Lillie called "the *original* mezzanine soprano."

121   Ruth St. Denis: Paris, 37.

122   Camille Paglia: x–xii.

123   *Variety* reviewer: "Audiences won't like that ending" (*Variety Film Reviews*, vol. 3, 10 November 1926).

124   "The plot structure": Frye, 163.

124   "The obstacles": Ibid., 164.

124   "entrusted": Ibid., 173.

124   "the solution": Chaplin, 210.

126   Hepburn's background: Dr. Hepburn met his wife through her sister who was his fencing partner.

126   doctrinally: Hepburn was involved from childhood in women's rights crusades.

126   grammar school: As Hepburn put it: "I was freckled—wore my hair like a boy's. In fact, with one brother Tom older and my two younger, Dick and Bob, being a girl was a torment. I'd always wanted to be a boy. Jimmy was my name, if you want to know."

127   pictures with Tracy: See Pauline Kael on the difference between the Hepburn-Grant and the Hepburn-Tracy movies ("Dream City," 28).

128   "blocking character": Frye, 168.

129   Henry Miller: *Capricorn*, 189.

129–30 Mack Sennett: Fowler, 157.

130   "tug-of-war": St. Johns, *Honeycomb*, 102.

130   successful actresses: Beatrice Lillie wrote about the dissolution of her own marriage to Robert Peel, who by the time he died had inherited the title Sir Robert
Peel: "I literally *had* to make a living, and a good one, because careless spending
by the Peels, together with death duties, had drastically eroded Old 'Parsley's' fortune. Big Bobby's problem essentially was that he couldn't make people believe
that he desperately needed to work, the more so because I was kept so busy and
won so much recognition. It is a familiar tale, with an added twist; personal
achievement *vs.* marriage compounded by the nobility."

130–31 Philip Barry: 194 (act 3).

131   "mother is what makes": St. Johns, *Honeycomb,* 104–5.

5. The Marx Brothers

Biographical information in this chapter is drawn from Groucho and Harpo's autobiographies, Hector Arce's biography of Groucho, and the TV documentary *The Unknown
Marx Brothers.*

132   Dryden: 178.

132   "A satirist": Barber, 76.

132   "under leaders": Ibid., 18.

132   "the vitality": Ibid., 7.

132   "festive abuse": Ibid., 30, 36–57.

136   classically adaptable: for an explanation of this character type in Aristophanes,
see McLeish, 55.

137   *Strange Interlude:* For O'Neill's sources and intentions, see Sheaffer, 239.

137   moldiness: According to Douglas Gilbert, puns "were as prevalent in vaudeville
as parodies" (301).

139   Tom and Huck: Budd Schulberg categorically claimed that poor Jewish boys
from New York, survivors of what he termed "unchildhood," could not be Tom
Sawyers (Schulberg, 230–31).

143   Buñuel and Dalí: There are extremely close matches to these surrealist fantasies
in less consciously artistic movies; for instance, the joke in King Vidor's 1928
silent *Show People* in which William Haines in costume as a slapstick clown,
paying mockingly gallant deference to a stuck-up Marion Davies, kisses her
hand and his mustache comes off on the back of it.

143   trustworthily common: In *Love Happy,* Harpo currycombs his wig while looking
in a two-sided hand mirror; he then rotates the mirror in his hand to see the back
of his head. By 1950 the Marx Brothers were aware of surrealism—in the late
thirties Dalí had given Harpo a harp strung with barbed wire, wrapped in cello-
phane, and with knives, forks, and spoons glued to the frame. But the Marxes'
surrealism is happier, perhaps because their sources were more homely than intellectual; for instance, Harpo removing the hands from the one-dollar Ingersoll
watch Minnie had given him for his bar mitzvah to prevent Chico from pawning
it again. Not caring about its uselessness, Harpo wrote, "I wound it faithfully
each morning and carried it with me at all times. When I wanted to know what
time it was I looked at the Ehret Brewery clock and held my watch to my ear."

143   "Where else": Snyder, 46

145   "Chico was quick": See also Howe, *World,* 561: "Growing up in an immigrant
neighborhood made one familiar with a fine variety of accents, so that the young

entertainers coming out of the East Side or its equivalents were prepared for the kinds of ethnic humor popular in American vaudeville during the early years of the century." The Irish American James Cagney, for instance, surprised Sylvia Sidney on the set one day by his ability to speak Yiddish (Cagney, 116).

145   the streetiest: Chico ran with a gang, but these were all boys who carried black-jacks.

147   *Humorisk:* Harpo also appeared in the 1925 Richard Dix silent *Too Many Kisses*, recently rediscovered.

147   David Robinson: 551.

148   order of age: For the sake of reference: Chico (Leonard, 1887–1961), Harpo (Adolph, later Arthur, 1888–1964), Groucho (Julius, 1890–1977), Gummo (Milton, 1892–1977), Zeppo (Herbert, 1901–1979).

148   spontaneous: By sarcastically attributing the dialogue to the Marx Brothers' ad-libbing, Herman J. Mankiewicz's 1925 *New Yorker* review of *The Cocoanuts* reminds readers that George S. Kaufman actually wrote the play.

151   vaudeville program: For a summary of typical big-time vaudeville bills see Spitzer, "Business," 130, 133.

151–52   "I remember": This is similar to Chaplin's saying in a 1915 interview: "I'm going to make better pictures than I did last [year]. I am doing my own scenarios and my own directing. We're to have a little bit more legitimate plots. I like a little story, with maybe an idea in it, not too much, not to teach anything, but some effect, like in *The Bank* for instance. . . . One must consider the kiddies, not to go over their heads, and remember the grown-ups too" (Robinson, 164). If *The Bank,* in which Chaplin introduced the pathos of a janitor yearning for a girl who loves a more acceptable rival, is any indication, then Chaplin's idea of a "legitimate plot" wasn't too far from Thalberg's.

152   MGM: For a good two-page version of the Marx Brothers at MGM, see Ethan Mordden's enjoyable and clarifying archival history *The Hollywood Studios* (112–14).

152   "No truck driver": Keaton, *Wonderful,* 207.

154   *Il Trovatore:* This climax was probably inspired by René Clair's *Le Million.* But there's also an earlier source: around 1911 Groucho caught Chaplin in a Winnipeg vaudeville theater, probably in "A Night in a London Club" (Robinson, 88–90). As Groucho described the act, "while a big, buxom soprano was singing one of Schubert's lieder, he was alternately spitting a fountain of dry cracker crumbs in the air and beaning her with overripe oranges. By the end of the act the stage was a shambles."

154   "In past shows": Churchill.

155   Budd Schulberg: 98.

155   department store: Flamini, 16.

156   Thalberg was their Jewish American Prince: Gabler, 226.

156   German Jews: The most amusing testament to the relative status of German and Eastern European Jews in New York comes in Diana Trilling's description of her husband's early story "Chapter for a Fashionable Jewish Novel" published in the *Menorah Journal* in the 1920s. Lionel Trilling was of Russian-Polish descent and raised in middle-class comfort. But "among his high-school friends [he] numbered several wealthy German-Jewish boys who went to Yale—Lionel had hoped to go with them. 'Chapter for a Fashionable Jewish Novel' is about the world of these

well-fixed young people: German Jews had to suffice as Lionel's Guermantes" (Trilling, 89).

156 Eddie Cantor: This is true to such an extent that identical stories are told about Cantor and Harpo as sausage delivery boys. In Cantor's words: "I used to start out with an empty stomach and a full basket and wind up *vice-versa*" (Cantor, 21). If Groucho's version about his brother isn't historically true, it at least indicates that he thought of his brother's childhood as being generically interchangeable with Cantor's.

156 Mankiewicz understood: As an example of how in tune Groucho's and Mankiewicz's comedy was, here's Groucho in *Monkey Business,* produced by Mankiewicz: "I wish to announce that a buffet supper will be served in the next room in five minutes. In order to get you in that room quickly, Mrs. Schmalhausen will sing a soprano solo in this room." And here's a Mankiewicz anecdote: "When movie attendance briefly plunged in the thirties, Herman attended anxious gatherings of exhibitors, directors, writers, executives. 'I'll tell you what to do,' he told one meeting. 'Show the movies in the streets, and drive the people back into the theaters'" (Meryman, 162).

156 signed a photo: Meryman, 220.

156 "You're a middle-aged Jew": Ibid., 148.

157 Irving Howe: *World,* 182.

158 Meyer Schapiro: 217.

158 without anger: Harpo could claim that "poverty never made any of us depressed or angry"; "We just worked a little harder and schemed a little harder." You hear this too often in the autobiographies of poor New York boys of that era to discount it as guff. See, for instance, Hook, 11; or Cagney, 6, 11.

159 "festivity signals": Barber, 99.

159 "release": Ibid., 10.

6. Preston Sturges

Biographical information in this chapter is drawn from Preston Sturges's posthumously published autobiography and biographies of him by James Curtis and Diane Jacobs.

161 Elbridge T. Gerry: "Children of the Stage" (C. Stein, 139).

161 "do-gooders": Keaton, *Wonderful,* 32.

161 in the army: Meade, 79; Keaton, *Wonderful,* 97.

161 unaware of politics: Keaton, *Wonderful,* 270; Meade, 112–13.

163 Billy Minsky: Minsky, 18.

163 James Agee: 116–17.

164 *Strictly Dishonorable*: Sturges, *Dishonorable,* 174–75.

164 "Cruel woman": Ibid., 80.

166 wrote and directed: Sturges directed his own scripts from *The Great McGinty* in 1940 until the end of his career, with two exceptions when he worked on scripts without credit.

167 embellishing: The spouse who proves her nobility by making no demands is a singularly feminine fantasy Sturges had been floating at least since *Child of Manhattan,* the play he wrote in 1931 as he and Hutton were splitting up.

167   male confusion: Fonda's character is like a Harold Lloyd sap; specifically, his Egyptologist in the 1938 *Professor Beware,* who is afraid to let himself fall for the girl because of a curse he's deciphered on an ancient tablet. Hopsie's rejection of Jean isn't so quirky; it lies much nearer to the core of male hesitations about sex.

168   purely to help: Sturges had developed this most optimistic reading of women's sexual radiance more than a decade before in his unproduced 1931 play *A Cup of Coffee,* in which the sweet but not ingenuous Tulip says, "I guess a girl always tries to help the man she falls for" (35).

169   at the turnstile: Adapted from a stunt of Mary Desti's when Sturges was a child.

170   photo caption: *New York World-Telegram,* Hutton clipping file.

170   the Palace: Spitzer, *Palace,* 59.

172   "village": Henderson, 533.

172   "all dressed up": Sturges, *Four,* 614.

172   1944 interview: Arvad.

172   "lower-class": Betty Hutton was no relation to Sturges's second wife, heiress Eleanor Hutton.

173   age five: Johnson, 10.

174   chaotic life story: For details see Bob Johnson's *TV Guide* article the week Hutton's variety show debuted in 1959. And that just covers her early years, not the booze and pill trail that led to her bottoming out by the early seventies.

175   scene added: Henderson, 561.

176   cut the scene: Sturges, *Four,* 632; Henderson, 543.

176   last shot: Sturges, *Four,* 619. Since the Vietnam War it's hard to remember that young men could feel *excluded* from World War II, which most people saw as a justifiable war. Jerry Lewis failed induction, for a perforated eardrum and a heart murmur, and said years later: "It was a horrible kick in the behind to see myself rejected from military duty, to end up with a 4–F card hidden deep in my wallet. I guess that shamed me most of all, just knowing it was there" (J. Lewis, *In Person,* 102; see also Levy, 45).

177   his fall: Henderson, 567, 641.

177   Trudy wraps: Sturges, *Four,* 684–85.

179   melodrama: The first four chapters of Peter Brooks's wonderful work of genre history *The Melodramatic Imagination* influenced my ideas about melodrama.

180   "Sir *Kay*": Twain, 20.

180   *eiron* and *alazon*: Frye, 39–40, 172–75; McLeish, 53–54; Whitman, 26–27.

180   "man who pretends": Whitman, 26.

180   still in use: It's the central romantic competition for the slapstick hero in *Girl Shy* (1924), *Sherlock Jr.* (1924), and *Show People* (1928); in romantic comedies with female stars, such as *The Philadelphia Story* (1940) and *Born Yesterday* (1950), and male stars, such as *Honeymoon in Vegas* (1992) and *Tin Cup* (1996), alike; in musical comedies, such as *Cover Girl* (1944), *Funny Face* (1957), and *Bye Bye Birdie* (1963); and in comedies that attempt to be more hard-edged or naturalistic, such as *The Apartment* (1960) and *Breaking Away* (1979). It is also open to variations, in which the hero is the *alazon* and gets the girl, as in *Love at First Bite* (1979); the hero is more of an impostor than the *alazon* and doesn't get the girl, as

in *Mrs. Doubtfire* (1993); and the hero gets and loses both the girl and the *alazon*, as in *Cabaret* (1972).

182   "Solomons": Sturges, *Five*, 726.

184   "He is nobody": Rosenfield, 1.

185   "serious guy": Thirer.

186   In the script: Sturges, *Four*, 683.

186   "Norval is being held": Henderson, 574.

187   "nobody believes": Sturges, *Four*, 636.

188   André Bazin: 35, 41.

188   "I don't think": Keaton, 130–31.

188   throw dialogue away: Lloyd interview, 71.

7. Jerry Lewis

Biographical information in this chapter is drawn from Jerry and Patti Lewis's auto-biographies, Shawn Levy's biography of Lewis, and Nick Tosches's biography of Martin.

190   malice: The malice isn't lessened by the fact that the bit had been a staple of their nightclub act: it actually originated before they were partners, with Lewis amusing the crowd backstage by making fun of Martin while he sang.

191   Laurel's reservation: Guiles, 223.

192   effortless: Seldes, *Seven*, 192.

192   "violence *per se*": Seldes, *Seven*, 193.

193   500 Club: Versions vary widely; I tried to say only what all would agree on.

193   *Welcome Aboard*: For show data see Brooks and Marsh, 672.

194   "laffsational . . . pantomimicry,": From a photo of Lewis's record act promo card.

194   overwhelm with clowning: This reflects Patti Lewis's description of his record act.

194–95 *shlemiel*: Jerry Lewis, *Film-Maker*, 198.

196   "painful as a divorce": They couldn't keep this out of their later movies; in *Artists and Models* Martin, who wants to move out of their shared apartment, explains to Lewis, "Look, Junior, a divorce is the only way out. We've been together too long."

196   Wallis scrimped: To be fair to Wallis, the additional five pictures the team made for their independent company York Productions are indistinguishable in quality from the Wallises.

197   egomania: Wallis, 142.

197   gigantic set: Jerry Lewis, *Film-Maker*, 84.

197   measuring his success: And he's no different speaking to film school students: *Film-Maker*, 33.

198   "push[ing] Dino": See also Wallis, 142.

202   quipping: Creelman; see also Smith, 55–57.

202   Sophie Portnoy: Roth, 123.

203   singing career: This was the story of Patti Lewis, not Dean Martin's wives.

204   the Idiot: Jerry Lewis, *Film-Maker*, 58, 68, 179, 185, 193. schoolkid: Bennetts, 98.

205   suppressed: Henry Popkin wrote about the disappearance of Jewish characters as the century progressed for *Commentary* in 1952.

205   "Protestant community": Seldes, *Seven,* 191.

205   "bring something to America": Ibid., 200.

206   Leslie Bennetts's: 86.

208   *The Bellboy*: Shawn Levy's thinking runs along the same lines as mine here.

211   "cunt men": Angeli, 104.

212   "Jewish Holden Caulfield": Jerry Lewis, *Film-Maker,* 47.

Coda

213   prudish: Kaplan, 60.

214   "never played a woman": Wolf, 3.

215   Carrey's father: Lidz, 33.

216   Lewis himself: Buchalter, 4.

216   At Christmas: Ibid.

216   Catholic boy: Rebello, 51.

216   "I'm not as nice": Buchalter, 4–5.

216   "Every generation": Rebello, 51.

216   James Stewart: Sherrill, 103.

217   Peter Weir: Lidz, 2.

218   "an idol": Pall, 23.

218   Woody Woodpecker: Grobel, 84.

219   John Lahr: 72.

220   Ludwig Lewisohn: C. Stein, 113.

220   Constance Rourke: 50–51.

Works Cited

Adamson, Joe. *Tex Avery: King of Cartoons.* 1975. Reprint, New York: Da Capo, 1985.

Agee, James. *Agee on Film.* New York: McDowell, Obolensky, 1958.

Allen, Frederick Lewis. *Only Yesterday: An Informal History of the Nineteen-Twenties.* New York: Blue Ribbon Books, 1931.

Angeli, Michael. "God's Biggest Goof." *Esquire,* February 1991, 98–107.

Aranda, Francisco. *Luis Buñuel: A Critical Biography.* Trans. and ed. David Robinson. New York: Da Capo Press, 1976.

Arce, Hector. *Groucho.* New York: G. P. Putnam's Sons, 1979.

Aristophanes. *Knights.* In *Aristophanes, Plays: One,* trans. Kenneth McLeish. London: Methuen Drama, 1993.

Arvad, Inga. "Betty Hutton Has Energy, Talent—and Frankness." *Sun,* 16 January 1944.

Astor, Gertrude. Clipping file in the New York Public Library for the Performing Arts.

Barber, C. L. *Shakespeare's Festive Comedy: A Study of Dramatic Form and Its Relation to Social Custom.* Princeton: Princeton University Press, 1959.

Barry, Iris. *Let's Go to the Movies.* New York: Payson and Clarke, 1926.

Barry, Philip. *The Philadelphia Story.* New York: Coward-McCann, 1939.

Baudelaire, Charles. *Oeuvres complètes.* 2 vols. Paris: Gallimard, 1975.

Bazin, André. *The Cinema of Cruelty from Buñuel to Hitchcock.* Trans. Sabine d'Estrée, with Tiffany Fliss. 1975. Reprint, New York: Seaver Books, 1982.

Beauchamp, Cari. *Without Lying Down: Frances Marion and the Powerful Women of Early Hollywood.* New York: Scribner, 1997.

Bennetts, Leslie. "Jerry vs. the Kids." *Vanity Fair,* September 1993, 82–98.

Bergson, Henri. *Laughter: An Essay on the Meaning of the Comic.* Trans. Cloudesley Brereton and Fred Rothwell. 1900. Reprint, New York: Macmillan, 1911.

———. *Le rire: Essai sur la signification du comique.* Paris: Librairies Félix Alcan et Guillaumin Réunies, 1911.

Blesh, Rudi. *Keaton*. 1966. New York: Collier Books, 1971.

Blum, John Morton. *V Was for Victory: Politics and American Culture during World War II*. New York and London: Harvest/HBJ, 1977.

Bogdanovich, Peter. *Allan Dwan: The Last Pioneer*. New York: Praeger, 1971.

Brooks, Louise. *Lulu in Hollywood*. New York: Alfred A. Knopf, 1982.

Brooks, Peter. *The Melodramatic Imagination: Balzac, Henry James, Melodrama, and the Mode of Excess*. New Haven: Yale University Press, 1976.

Brooks, Tim, and Earle Marsh. *The Complete Directory to Prime Time Network TV Shows, 1946–Present*. New York: Ballantine Books, 1979.

Brownlow, Kevin. *The Parade's Gone By . . .* Berkeley: University of California Press, 1968.

Buchalter, Gail. "If You Give Up Your Dreams, What's Left?" *New York Newsday*, 15 January 1995, *Parade Magazine*, 4–6.

Burke, Thomas. *City of Encounters: A London Divertissement*. Boston: Little, Brown, 1932.

Cagney, James. *Cagney by Cagney*. Garden City, N.Y.: Doubleday, 1976.

Cantor, Eddie, as told to David Freedman. *My Life Is in Your Hands*. New York and London: Harper and Brothers, 1928.

Capra, Frank. *The Name above the Title: An Autobiography*. New York: Macmillan, 1971.

Chaplin, Charles. *My Autobiography*. New York: Simon and Schuster, 1964.

"Charlot for 1926." Review of *The Charlot Revue of 1926* (starring Beatrice Lillie). *New York Times*, 11 November 1925, 27.

Churchill, Douglas W. "The Marxes as Guinea Pigs for a Stage-Screen Experiment." *New York Times*, 20 October 1935, sec. 10, p. 5.

Collier, Constance. *Harlequinade: The Story of My Life*. London: John Lane, 1929.

"Comedy—a Serious Business." Episode 8 of *Hollywood*. Written, directed, and produced by Kevin Brownlow and David Gill. Thames Television. 1979.

Cooper, Miriam, with Bonnie Herndon. *Dark Lady of the Silents: My Life in Early Hollywood*. Indianapolis: Bobbs-Merrill, 1973.

Creelman, Eileen. "Sid Silvers Explains What Is a Stooge and Why, with Comments on His Career." *New York Sun*, 24 March 1934, 11.

Curtis, James. *Between Flops: A Biography of Preston Sturges*. New York: Limelight Editions, 1984.

Daniels, Bebe, and Ben Lyon. Interview by Anthony Slide. *Silent Picture* (spring 1971): n.p.

Dardis, Tom. *Harold Lloyd: The Man on the Clock*. New York: Viking Press, 1983.

————. *Keaton: The Man Who Wouldn't Lie Down.* Harmondsworth: Penguin, 1980.

Davies, Marion. *The Times We Had: Life with William Randolph Hearst.* Ed. Pamela Pfau and Kenneth S. Marx. Indianapolis: Bobbs-Merrill, 1975.

de Frece, Lady. *Recollections of Vesta Tilley.* London: Hutchinson, 1934.

Disher, M. Willson. *Clowns and Pantomimes.* London: Constable, 1925.

————. *Winkles and Champagne: Comedies and Tragedies of the Music Hall.* 1938. Reprint, Bath: Cedric Chivers, 1974.

Dover, K. J. *Aristophanic Comedy.* Berkeley: University of California Press, 1972.

Dreiser, Theodore. *Sister Carrie.* Philadelphia: University of Pennsylvania Press, 1981.

Dryden, John. "Absalom and Achitophel" (1681). In *John Dryden,* ed. Keith Walker. New York: Oxford University Press, 1987.

Edmonds, Andy. *Frame-Up! The Untold Story of Roscoe "Fatty" Arbuckle.* New York: William Morrow, 1991.

Eisenhower, Julie Nixon. *Pat Nixon: The Untold Story.* New York: Zebra Books, 1986.

Faulkner, William. *Absalom, Absalom!* 1936. Reprint, New York: Vintage, 1990.

————. *Light in August.* 1932. Reprint, New York: Random House, 1959.

Ferguson, Otis. *The Film Criticism of Otis Ferguson.* Ed. Robert Wilson. Philadelphia: Temple University Press, 1971.

Flamini, Roland. *Thalberg: The Last Tycoon and the World of M-G-M.* New York: Crown Publishers, 1994.

Flaubert, Gustave. *Madame Bovary.* Trans. Francis Steegmuller. 1856. Reprint, New York: Random House, 1957.

————. *Madame Bovary: Moeurs de province.* Paris: Gallimard, 1972.

Fowler, Gene. *Father Goose: The Story of Mack Sennett.* New York: Covici, Friede, 1934.

Frye, Northrop. *Anatomy of Criticism: Four Essays.* 1957. Reprint, Princeton: Princeton University Press, 1973.

Funke, Lewis. "Betty Hutton Headlines Variety Bill at the Palace Theatre—on Stage 50 Minutes." *New York Times,* 14 April 1952.

Fussell, Betty Harper. *Mabel.* New Haven and New York: Ticknor and Fields, 1982.

Gabler, Neal. *An Empire of Their Own: How the Jews Invented Hollywood.* New York: Crown Publishers, 1988.

Gilbert, Douglas. *American Vaudeville: Its Life and Times.* New York: Whittlesey House, 1940.

Gill, Brendan. *A New York Life: Of Friends and Others.* New York: Poseidon Press, 1990.

———. "Speedy." *New Yorker,* 26 May 1962, 29–30.

Giroux, Robert. *A Deed of Death: The Story behind the Unsolved Murder of Hollywood Director William Desmond Taylor.* New York: Alfred A. Knopf, 1990.

Grobel, Lawrence. "The Good Times of Nicolas Cage." *Movieline,* June 1998, 44–86.

Guiles, Fred Lawrence. *Stan: The Life of Stan Laurel.* New York: Stein and Day, 1980.

"Harold Lloyd: An American Film Institute Seminar on His Work." 23 September 1969. *New York Times Oral History Program: The American Film Institute Seminars.* Part 1, no. 113. Glen Rock, N.J.: Microfilming Corporation of America, 1977.

Harold Lloyd: The Third Genius. By David Gill and Kevin Brownlow. 2 episodes. Thames Television. 1989.

Henderson, Brian. Introduction to *The Miracle of Morgan's Creek.* In *Four More Screenplays by Preston Sturges,* by Preston Sturges. Berkeley: University of California Press, 1995.

Hepburn, Katharine. *Me: Stories of My Life.* New York: Alfred A. Knopf, 1991.

Higham, Charles. *Merchant of Dreams: Louis B. Mayer, M.G.M., and the Secret Hollywood.* New York: Donald I. Fine, 1993.

Hook, Sidney. *Out of Step: An Unquiet Life in the 20th Century.* New York: Carroll and Graf, 1988.

Hooker, Richard. *MASH.* 1968. New York: Pocket Books, 1971.

Howe, Irving. Afterword to *An American Tragedy,* by Theodore Dreiser. 1925. Reprint, New York: Signet Classic, 1964.

Howe, Irving, with the assistance of Kenneth Libo. *World of Our Fathers.* New York: Harcourt Brace Jovanovich, 1976.

Huizinga, Johan. *Homo Ludens: A Study of the Play Element in Culture.* 1938. Reprint, Boston: Beacon Press, 1972.

Jacobs, Diane. *Christmas in July: The Life and Art of Preston Sturges.* Berkeley: University of California Press, 1992.

Jacobus de Voragine. *The Golden Legend: Readings on the Saints.* Trans. William Granger Ryan. Vol. 1. Ca. 1260. Reprint, Princeton: Princeton University Press, 1993.

Johnson, Bob. "She Rules the Roost." *TV Guide,* 21 November 1959, 8–11.

Johnston, Alva. "How to Become a Playwright." *Saturday Evening Post,* 8 March 1941, 9–104; 15 March 1941, 25–93.

Kael, Pauline. "Comedians." 5 April 1982. Review of *Richard Pryor Live on the Sunset Strip,* directed by Joe Layton. In *Taking It All In.* New York: Holt, Rinehart and Winston, 1984.

———. "The Man from Dream City." 14 July 1975. In *When the Lights Go Down.* New York: Holt, Rinehart and Winston, 1980.

———. "Raising Kane." 1971. *The "Citizen Kane" Book.* New York: Limelight Editions, 1984.

Kaplan, James. "The Laughing Game." *New Yorker,* 7 February 2000, 52–63.

Keaton, Buster. Interview by Joan Franklin and Robert Franklin. November 1958. Transcript in the Oral History Collection of Columbia University.

———. Interview by Arthur B. Friedman. *Film Quarterly* (summer 1966): 2–5.

Keaton, Buster, with Charles Samuels. *My Wonderful World of Slapstick.* 1960. Reprint, London: George Allen and Unwin, 1967.

Kenner, Hugh. Review of *Keaton,* by Rudi Blesh. *Film Quarterly* (fall 1966): 60–61.

Kerr, Walter. *The Silent Clowns.* 1975. Reprint, New York: Da Capo Press, 1980.

Kirkpatrick, Sidney D. *A Cast of Killers.* New York: Penguin, 1987.

Lahr, John. "The Imperfectionist." (Profile of Woody Allen.) *New Yorker,* 9 December 1996, 68–83.

Lahue, Kalton C. *World of Laughter: The Motion Picture Comedy Short, 1910–1930.* Norman: University of Oklahoma Press, 1966.

Leaming, Barbara. *Katharine Hepburn.* New York: Avon Books, 1996.

Lejeune, C. A. *Cinema.* London: Alexander Maclehose, 1931.

LeRoy, Mervyn, as told to Dick Kleiner. *Mervyn LeRoy: Take One.* New York: Hawthorn Books, 1974.

Levy, Shawn. *King of Comedy: The Life and Art of Jerry Lewis.* New York: St. Martin's Press, 1996.

Lewis, Jerry. *The Total Film-Maker.* New York: Random House, 1971.

Lewis, Jerry, with Herb Gluck. *Jerry Lewis in Person.* New York: Atheneum, 1982.

Lewis, Patti, with Sarah Anne Coleman. *I Laffed Till I Cried: Thirty-six Years of Marriage to Jerry Lewis.* Waco, Tex.: WRS Publishing, 1993.

Lidz, Franz. "Relentlessly Nurturing the Odd Child Within." *New York Times,* 3 May 1998, sec. 2A, pp. 2, 33.

Lillie, Beatrice, aided and abetted by John Philip, written with James Brough. *Every Other Inch a Lady.* Garden City, N.Y.: Doubleday, 1972.

Lloyd, Harold. "The Autobiography of Harold Lloyd." *Photoplay Magazine,* May 1924, 32–119; June 1924, 42–111; July 1924, 56–116.

———. Interview by Joan and Robert Franklin. January 1959. Transcript in the Oral History Collection of Columbia University.

Lloyd, Harold, with Wesley W. Stout. *An American Comedy.* New York: Longmans, Green, 1928.

Loos, Anita. *A Girl Like I.* New York: Viking Press, 1966.

Lorca, Federico García. "Buster Keaton Takes a Walk" (El Paseo de Buster Keaton). Trans. A. L. Lloyd. Reprinted in Dardis, *Keaton,* 281–83.

Lynd, Robert S., and Helen Merrell Lynd. *Middletown: A Study in Contemporary American Culture.* New York: Harcourt, Brace, 1929.

Lynn, Kenneth S. *Charlie Chaplin and His Times.* New York: Simon and Schuster, 1997.

Maland, Charles J. *Chaplin and American Culture: The Evolution of a Star Image.* Princeton: Princeton University Press, 1989.

Mankiewicz, Herman J. Review of *The Cocoanuts,* by George S. Kaufman, starring the Marx Brothers. *New Yorker,* 19 December 1925, 17–18.

Marion, Frances. *Off with Their Heads! A Serio-Comic Tale of Hollywood.* New York: Macmillan, 1972.

Marx, Groucho. *Groucho and Me.* New York: Bernard Geis Associates, 1959.

Marx, Harpo, with Rowland Barber. *Harpo Speaks!* 1961. Reprint, New York: Limelight Editions, 1991.

McBride, Joseph. *Hawks on Hawks.* Berkeley: University of California Press, 1982.

———. Untitled article on Gertrude Astor. *Variety,* 15 October 1975.

McLeish, Kenneth. *The Theatre of Aristophanes.* N.p.: Thames and Hudson, 1980.

Meade, Marion. *Buster Keaton: Cut to the Chase, a Biography.* New York: HarperCollins, 1995.

Meryman, Richard. *Mank: The Wit, World, and Life of Herman Mankiewicz.* New York: William Morrow, 1978.

Miller, Henry. *Letters to Anaïs Nin.* Ed. Gunther Stuhlmann. New York: G. P. Putnam's Sons, 1965.

———. *Tropic of Capricorn.* 1939. Reprint, New York: Grove Press, 1965.

Milton, Joyce. *Tramp: The Life of Charlie Chaplin.* New York: HarperCollins, 1996.

Minsky, Morton. *Minsky's Burlesque.* New York: Arbor House, 1986.

Moore, Colleen. *Silent Star.* Garden City, N.Y.: Doubleday, 1968.

Mordden, Ethan. *The Hollywood Studios: House Style in the Golden Age of the Movies.* New York: Alfred A. Knopf, 1988.

———. *Make Believe: The Broadway Musical in the 1920s.* New York: Oxford University Press, 1997.

New York World-Telegram, 16 January 1939. Betty Hutton clipping file in the New York Public Library for the Performing Arts.

North, Jean. "It's No Joke to Be Funny." *Photoplay Magazine,* June 1925, 86, 126–27.

O'Neill, Eugene. *Long Day's Journey into Night.* New Haven: Yale University Press, 1956.

Paglia, Camille. *Vamps and Tramps: New Essays.* New York: Vintage Books, 1994.

Pall, Ellen. "Nicolas Cage, the Sunshine Man." *New York Times,* 24 July 1994, sec. 2, pp. 1, 22–23.

Paris, Barry. *Louise Brooks.* New York: Alfred A. Knopf, 1989.

Popkin, Henry. "The Vanishing Jew of Our Popular Culture." *Commentary,* July 1952, 46–55.

Powell, Dilys. Introduction to *My Wonderful World of Slapstick,* by Buster Keaton, with Charles Samuels. 1960. Reprint, London: George Allen and Unwin, 1967.

Ramsaye, Terry. *A Million and One Nights: A History of the Motion Picture.* 2 vols. New York: Simon and Schuster, 1926.

Rebello, Stephen. "Carrey'd Away." *Movieline,* July 1994, 45–83.

Robinson, David. *Chaplin: His Life and Art.* 1985. New York: Da Capo Press, 1994.

Rosenberg, Bernard, and Harry Silverstein. *The Real Tinsel.* New York: Macmillan, 1970.

Rosenfield, John. "Eddie Bracken Grows into Leading Comedian." *Dallas Morning News,* n.d., sec. 4, p. 1.

Roth, Philip. *Portnoy's Complaint.* 1969. Reprint, New York: Vintage International, 1994.

Rourke, Constance. *The Roots of American Culture and Other Essays.* Ed. Van Wyck Brooks. New York: Harcourt, Brace, 1942.

St. Johns, Adela Rogers. *The Honeycomb.* Garden City, N.Y.: Doubleday, 1969.

———. *Some Are Born Great.* Garden City, N.Y.: Doubleday, 1974.

Sandler, Adam. Interview. *Adam Sandler Movie Special.* Host/Writer Chris Connelly. MTV. 10 June 1999.

Schapiro, Meyer. "Mr. Berenson's Values" (1961). In *Theory and Philosophy of Art: Style, Artist, and Society, Selected Papers.* Vol. 4. New York: George Braziller, 1994.

Scherle, Victor, and William Turner Levy. *The Films of Frank Capra.* Secaucus, N.J.: Citadel Press, 1977.

Schulberg, Budd. *What Makes Sammy Run?* 1941. Reprint. New York: Modern Library, 1952.

Seldes, Gilbert. *An Hour with the Movies and the Talkies.* Philadelphia: J. B. Lippincott, 1929.

———. *The Seven Lively Arts*. New York and London: Harper and Brothers, 1924.

Sennett, Mack. "The Best Motion Picture Interview Ever Written." Interview by Theodore Dreiser (August 1928). *Spellbound in Darkness: A History of Silent Film,* ed. George C. Pratt. Greenwich, Conn.: New York Graphic Society, 1973.

Sennett, Mack, as told to Cameron Shipp. *King of Comedy.* Garden City, N.Y.: Doubleday, 1954.

Sheaffer, Louis. *O'Neill: Son and Artist.* Boston: Little, Brown, 1973.

Sherrill, Martha. "Renaissance Man." *Esquire,* December 1995, 99–106.

Slide, Anthony. *The Idols of Silence.* South Brunswick and New York: A. S. Barnes, 1976.

Smith, Eric Ledell. *Bert Williams: A Biography of the Pioneer Black Comedian.* Jefferson, N.C.: McFarland, 1992.

Smith, Frederick James. "The World's Most Unknown Comedian." *Liberty,* 21 November 1936, 55–57.

Snyder, Robert W. *The Voice of the City.* New York: Oxford University Press, 1989.

Spitzer, Marian. "The Business of Vaudeville." *Saturday Evening Post,* 24 May 1924, 18–133.

———. *The Palace.* New York: Atheneum, 1969.

Stein, Charles W., ed. *American Vaudeville As Seen by Its Contemporaries.* New York: Da Capo Press, 1985.

Stein, Gertrude. *Everybody's Autobiography.* 1937. Reprint, London: Virago Press, 1985.

Sturges, Preston. *A Cup of Coffee.* 1931. Reprint, New York: Samuel French, 1989.

———. *Five Screenplays by Preston Sturges.* Ed. Brian Henderson. Berkeley: University of California Press, 1986.

———. *Four More Screenplays by Preston Sturges.* Berkeley: University of California Press, 1995.

———. *Preston Sturges by Preston Sturges.* Adapted and edited by Sandy Sturges. New York: Simon and Schuster, 1990.

———. *Strictly Dishonorable.* New York: Horace Liveright, 1929.

Swanberg, W. A. *Citizen Hearst: A Biography of William Randolph Hearst.* 1961. Reprint, New York: Bantam Books, 1967.

Swanson, Gloria. *Swanson on Swanson.* New York: Random House, 1980.

Teichmann, Howard. *George S. Kaufman: An Intimate Portrait.* New York: Dell, 1973.

Thirer, Irene. "How to Prolong a Screen Career: Eddie Bracken Offers an

Optimistic Viewpoint." Unidentified source, in the Eddie Bracken clipping file of the New York Public Library for the Performing Arts. 1943.

Tolstoy, Leo. *War and Peace*. Trans. Louise Maude and Aylmer Maude. New
York: W. W. Norton, 1966.

Tosches, Nick. *Dino: Living High in the Dirty Business of Dreams*. New York:
Dell, 1993.

Trilling, Diana. *The Beginning of the Journey: The Marriage of Diana and
Lionel Trilling*. New York: Harcourt, Brace, 1993.

Twain, Mark. *A Connecticut Yankee in King Arthur's Court*. 1889. Reprint,
New York: W. W. Norton, 1982.

The Unknown Marx Brothers. By David Leaf and John Scheinfeld. 1993.
WNET. Rebroadcast 9 May 1998.

Variety Film Reviews, 1907–1980. 16 vols. New York and London: Garland
Publishing, 1983.

Vidor, King. Interview. *King Vidor*, by Nancy Dowd and David Shepard.
Metuchen, N.J.: Scarecrow Press, 1988.

———. *A Tree Is a Tree*. New York: Harcourt, Brace, 1953.

Wallis, Hal, with Charles Higham. *Starmaker: The Autobiography of Hal
Wallis*. New York: Macmillan, 1980.

White, Percy W. "Stage Terms." *American Speech* 1 (1926): 436–37.

Whitman, Cedric H. *Aristophanes and the Comic Hero*. Cambridge: Harvard
University Press, 1964.

Wilde, Hagar. "Bringing Up Baby." *Collier's*, 10 April 1937, 20–22, 70.

Wilson, Harry Leon. *Merton of the Movies*. Garden City, N.Y.: Doubleday,
Page, 1922.

Wolf, Jeanne. "The Heat Is On." *New York Daily News*, 9 June 1996,
Spotlight, p. 3.

Yallop, David A. *The Day the Laughter Stopped: The True Story of Fatty
Arbuckle*. New York: St. Martin's Press, 1976.

Young, Robert, Jr. *Roscoe "Fatty" Arbuckle: A Bio-Bibliography*. Westport,
Conn.: Greenwood Press, 1994.

Index

Abbott and Costello, 196

Absalom, Absalom! (novel), 84

Ace Ventura: Pet Detective (d: Tom Shadyac), 9, 217

Adventurer, The (d: Charles Chaplin), 52

Age d'or, L', (d: Luis Buñuel, Salvador Dalí), 22, 143

Agee, James: 226n; on the audience for silent slapstick, 27; on *City Lights*, 19; on Keaton, 62, 64; on Lloyd, 90; on slapstick, 7; on Sturges, 163

alazon (character type), 180–82, 234–35n

Alberni, Luis, 165

Allen, Frederick Lewis, 19, 112

Allen, Phyllis, 45, 95, 105

Allen, Woody, 137, 147, 212, 215, 219

All Jazzed Up (d: Lloyd "glasses" short), 21

All These Women (d: Ingmar Bergman), 23

Almodóvar, Pedro, 22

Altman, Robert, 28–29

Ambrose, St. (bishop of Milan), 13

American President, The (d: Rob Reiner), 35

Analyze This (d: Harold Ramis), 207

Animal Crackers (d: Victor

Heerman), 100, 134–35, 136–37, 141, 142, 143, 151, 158, 228n

Animal House (d: John Landis), 194

Annabel Takes a Tour (d: Lew Landers), 7

Annie Get Your Gun (d: George Sidney), 174

Annie Hall (d: Woody Allen), 212

anti-Semitism, 31, 34, 35, 50, 54, 206, 209

antisocial impulse behind comedy, 39–40

Apartment, The (d: Billy Wilder), 234n

Arbuckle, Roscoe ("Fatty"), 21, 30, 59, 65, 67, 80, 82; and black comedy, 23; and injuries on movie sets, 222n; Keaton, relationship to, 82, 196, 230n; mother figures in the work of, 92; and Normand, 104, 105, 110, 228n; persona of, 87–88; popularity of, 87; and preview test screenings, 2; and real-life mishaps, 11; and size of slapstick hero, 18, 87–88; theatrical experience of, 8, 102. Works: *Back Stage*, 67; *The Butcher Boy*, 82, 87; *Coney Island*, 64; *A Country Hero*, 82; *Fatty & Mabel Adrift*, 87; *Fatty's New Role*, 87; *Fatty's Plucky Pup*, 87, 92; *Fatty's*

247

Alan Dale worked at a Los Angeles talent agency before earning a Ph.D. in comparative literature from Princeton University. He has taught in the writing, American studies, and visual arts programs at Princeton. He lives in Hoboken, New Jersey.